Irrational Together

Irrational Together

The Social Forces That Invisibly Shape Our Economic Behavior

ADAM S. HAYES

The University of Chicago Press Chicago and London

The University of Chicago Press, Chicago 60637
The University of Chicago Press, Ltd., London

Published 2025
Printed in the United States of America

34 33 32 31 30 29 28 27 26 25 1 2 3 4 5

ISBN-13: 978-0-226-83929-5 (cloth)
ISBN-13: 978-0-226-83931-8 (paper)
ISBN-13: 978-0-226-83930-1 (e-book)
DOI: https://doi.org/10.7208/chicago/9780226839301.001.0001

Library of Congress Cataloging-in-Publication Data

Names: Hayes, Adam S., author.
Title: Irrational together : the social forces that invisibly shape our economic behavior / Adam S. Hayes.
Description: Chicago ; London : The University of Chicago Press, 2025. | Includes bibliographical references and index.
Identifiers: LCCN 2024042398 | ISBN 9780226839295 (cloth) | ISBN 9780226839318 (paperback) | ISBN 9780226839301 (ebook)
Subjects: LCSH: Economics—Sociological aspects. | Decision making—Social aspects. | Economics—Psychological aspects.
Classification: LCC HM548 .H39 2025 | DDC 306.3—dc23/eng/20241014
LC record available at https://lccn.loc.gov/2024042398

♾ This paper meets the requirements of ANSI/NISO Z39.48-1992 (Permanence of Paper).

To my beautifully irrational parents, for teaching me that the most important things in life are priceless.

CONTENTS

1 * A Feel for the Game: A Sociological Perspective on Economic Behavior

A few years ago, my mother revealed to me that she had run up some considerable credit card debt, mostly on account of unforeseen medical expenses. She was able to meet the monthly payments, but with a 20% interest rate, it would take many years and several thousand dollars in additional interest payments to close it out. Hearing this, I urged my mother to take out a home equity loan in the amount of the credit card balance and immediately pay it off, replacing it with a more affordable 5% mortgage—saving her thousands of dollars each year. I even suggested she take out some extra cash to remodel the bathrooms (something she had been wanting to do for a while already) and *still* end up paying much less every month than with the credit card. My mother did not take my good advice. Her face instead turned red as I explained the math of it, and she began to stammer and became quite incensed.

The house, she scolded, was nearly paid off! She would not, *could not*, take out another mortgage—even if it made financial sense. She saw the home as a symbol of stability, security, and the culmination of years of hard work. For her, taking on new debt against the house, even to replace high-interest credit card debt with a more favorable rate, felt like a violation of her personal values and the sacrifices she had made over the years. This, of course, is irrational. A 15% reduction in loan interest on a fairly sizable amount of money is objectively the right decision, regardless if one type of loan is swapped out for another (e.g., credit card debt for housing debt).[1] Plus, she could have saved even more with the mortgage interest tax deduction—it was a no-brainer, at least in my mind. Yet there was something about paying off the home and closing that chapter on the American Dream that stood firmly in the way of better judgment. Despite my sincere efforts to carefully explain the situation, jotting figures down literally on a napkin, and calling my father into the debate to take my side, it was all in vain. She simply could not reconcile my logic: "There are only two years left to pay off the house," she told me. "How stupid could you be?" My father later admitted to me that he saw I was right, and that they would have saved a ton if they'd listened (the credit card debt was ultimately repaid after several diligent years), but he quickly followed that for my mother, having the home fully paid off was far more important than the money, and so he had never broached the subject.

If we consider this story carefully, the forces playing upon my mother's rationality were *sociological*: her strong emotional reaction to the idea of extending the mortgage, even if it would result in significant savings, can be understood as a manifestation of deeply ingrained social norms and cultural values. These values place an emphasis on debt avoidance, the importance of home ownership as a symbol of financial stability and middle-class status, and a generational belief that one's home should be paid off and eventually owned free and clear. Moreover, the fact that my father recognized the benefits of my suggestion but chose not to raise the issue with my mother further highlights the role of social dynamics in economic decision-making. In this case, preserving harmony within the family unit and respecting my mother's preferences took precedence over pursuing the most financially advantageous course of action.

*

Consider another social situation that bears on economic judgment, this time a fictional one from the HBO series *Curb Your Enthusiasm*. Larry David (the creator of *Seinfeld*) is out to lunch with the actor Jason Alexander (who played George Costanza on *Seinfeld* and who is a good friend of Larry) to discuss a possible *Seinfeld* reunion. When it comes time to pay the bill, Larry wants to "coordinate" the tip and suggests, "What are you going to leave? We split the check, we both have the exact same bill. Why don't we leave the same thing so one of us doesn't look like an idiot?"

Larry announces that he will leave $12 and encourages Jason to do the same, who instead jots down an amount privately on his receipt, remaining tight-lipped even as Larry pleads to know what he left. The next day, Larry returns to the same restaurant and interrogates their waiter (paraphrased slightly for brevity):

LARRY: I have a question I want to ask you. Remember I was sitting right here yesterday?
WAITER: Yeah.
LARRY: Would you mind telling me how much of a tip the guy I was with left you?
WAITER: Oh, we don't share that information.
LARRY: I'm just curious, what did he leave?
WAITER: It was, uh, a healthy tip.
LARRY: Was mine a healthy tip?
WAITER: <*tepidly, trailing off*> Yeah.
LARRY: Was his healthier?
WAITER: <*stammers*>
LARRY: Was it over $12? Just scratch your face if it was over $12 . . . go ahead, just scratch it.
WAITER: I can really get in trouble for doing this . . . <*nervously scratches his face*>
LARRY: Oh, for God's sake! What an a**hole. . Let me ask you this question: <*exasperated*> was it over $15? Just tug on your tie up here if it was.
WAITER: This is making me really uncomfortable here . . . <*tugs quickly at his tie knot*>
LARRY: Oh my, <*expletive*>!
WAITER: Is that all . . . I can get you . . . ?
LARRY: <*pressing the waiter*> No, don't go yet, one second—I have one more question to ask you: did that son of a b**** give you a $20 tip?
WAITER: <*quietly while clearing a tea pot and cup from the table*> What if it was more . . . ?
LARRY: <*urgently*> How much did he give you? Huh? Was it over $30? If it was over $30 I want you to raise that cup up over that pot.
WAITER: Ok, I hope you enjoyed your meal, and come back soon. <*turns and raises the cup high in the air as he walks away*>[2]

The scene ends with Larry staring at the table, his mouth open in disbelief.

This moment provides some interesting insights. First, let's talk about tipping from the standpoint of traditional economics. Customers voluntarily pay extra beyond the listed menu prices, subsidizing owners by covering labor costs, while servers receive highly variable compensation unlinked to experience or even their hours worked. Robert Frank, a notable economist, labeled the act of tipping as "seemingly irrational," questioning why people tip their servers even when they could easily avoid doing so—especially if they don't plan to revisit the restaurant.[3] A pair of economists, Örn Bodvarsson and William Gibson, dug into this and discovered that people tip because they believe it's a social expectation and because it encourages a culture of good service that benefits them in the future.[4] In essence, they conclude that while the act of tipping may seem irrational if you disregard social norms, it suddenly becomes rational when you consider social conformity. This conclusion underscores the idea that tipping is more of a norm than an economic incentive. In the United States, it's standard to leave a 15% tip, or bump it up to 20% for exceptional service. Even unsatisfactory service usually gets a nominal tip, acting as a quiet critique. On the other hand, tourists from the United States may be caught off guard in places like France or Denmark, where tipping isn't the norm and there is no expectation to do so.

But there's another layer to our story: the unspoken rivalry between Larry and Jason over the amounts of their tips. Larry's indignation wasn't really about the quality of the meal or the service; it was about interpersonal dynamics. Larry feels slighted because Jason's larger tip overshadows his own, making him feel upstaged and damaging his self-image. The waiter's discretion about the amount only adds fuel to Larry's competitive fire. What we see here is a clash between the fairly straightforward economic gesture/social norm of tipping and the complex social codes governing friendships. This undercurrent is so strong it almost jeopardizes the prospect of a *Seinfeld* reunion (which, fortunately, does happen later in the series).

The quality of our interpersonal relationships and the effort we put into maintaining them often come into play even in contexts like tipping. For instance, you may tip well to make a good impression on a first date, or tip less to match what a good friend can afford if they're going through a rough patch financially. If you know the server, your tip could be more generous as a gesture of personal goodwill. The pattern of the decision-making might also change depending on which family member you're dining with. With your spouse, you may jointly decide on what to tip in close collaboration. Despite your mother's protests, you might decide to cover the entire tip; while with your brother, you might let him pay all of it without protest. Who you dine with can change the social dynamics at the table, and these different contexts can influence economic choices and behaviors, some of which may seem irrational from a purely economic perspective.

*

These two vignettes provide familiar glimpses into how social forces can impact our financial decisions. In the first case, my mother's strong desire to have the house fully paid off was so deeply rooted in cultural values and symbolic attachment that it overpowered any rational arguments for a financially smarter course of action. In the *Curb Your Enthusiasm* scene, we see how the desire for equality-matching, social status, and notions of fairness can influence even everyday transactions like tipping. Both instances show how our thinking is influenced by a mix of psychological *and* sociological factors, which often defy traditional economic reasoning. Moreover, these sociological factors extend beyond individual thoughts and cannot be explained by psychology alone. They are the web of invisible threads that tug on our purse strings and wallets, gently guiding us as we reach for our credit cards or having us hesitate before making a purchase. Woven from cultural expectations, social norms, and shared experiences, they pull us in directions we may not even consciously recognize.

Imagine, for a moment, that you could see these threads—where every transaction and financial decision leaves a lingering trace. You'd see connections linking each person to their family, friends, and coworkers. These threads would also stretch to the cashier at the local store, the customer service representative you spoke with last week, and the countless unknown individuals whose economic choices collectively influence the products, prices, and opportunities available to you. They connect us not just to our immediate social surroundings but to broader cultural narratives and societal expectations. If you zoomed out, you'd see the vast tapestry of economic life, woven from countless individual threads. Cultural patterns would emerge as distinct textures and motifs—the tight, intricate weave of close-knit communities, the subtle gradients of changing expectations and norms. Economic trends would appear as ripples across the surface, with some leaving lasting impressions and others fading quickly. This living, breathing fabric would pulse with the collective rhythm of human activity, each thread both influencing and being influenced by the grand design.

Some threads would bear the weight of generations—like the one tethering my mother to her home. Others might flicker rapidly with the back-and-forth of social comparison, like the ones connecting Larry David to his dining companion. In this tableau, you'd see that no decision stands alone. Each choice sends vibrations through the web, influencing countless others.

A slight tug urges you to leave a generous tip to impress a first date; a firm yank holds you back from splurging on a luxury item your spouse or partner would see as frivolous; a persistent pull incessantly draws you toward the same financial strategies your parents always used.

Sometimes, these threads work in harmony, weaving a sturdy financial fabric. Other times, they tangle and conflict, leaving us torn between competing influences: The young professional feeling the simultaneous pull of saving for the future and keeping up with their high-spending cohort. The immigrant entrepreneur balancing the American Dream against cultural obligations to support family back home. The retiree wrestling with the desire for a comfortable lifestyle and the ingrained habit of frugality born from leaner times. The social architecture of our economic lives is hiding in plain sight.

For sure, many of us intuitively understand that our economic decisions are influenced by a multitude of factors in addition to things like personal preferences and prices. Yet, surprisingly, much of the current understanding of economic behavior ignores these social complexities, simplifying our choices into either cold, hard numbers or else mistakes made in doing the required calculations. While simple and elegant models can be useful approximations, they miss much of what makes us human and forget that economic activity is inherently social. A buyer purchases from a seller, a borrower owes a lender, a tenant leases from a landlord, an employee works for an employer. In each interaction, the transaction is more than just an exchange of goods, services, or money—it's a human connection, fraught with the weight of social expectations, cultural norms, and interpersonal histories that shape the behavior and outcomes of the parties involved.

A tenant hands over rent to a landlord. Through our lens, we see the transaction clothed in social dynamics—the tenant's anxiety about making ends meet and ensuring the rent is paid on time is a social performance that speaks to a cultural mandate about one's reliability, responsibility, and standing; the landlord's struggle between compassion and the need to maintain their own livelihood reflects the unspoken negotiation of power between them. In a corner office, an employee accepts a job offer. Our lens reveals a range of motivations far beyond the salary figure—the employee's desire for status among peers, the employer's hope for loyalty and dedication, the shared excitement of building something together. This broader perspective invites us to see the economy not as a machine governed by cold logic and profits but as a living, breathing entity—an extension of our social selves. It challenges us to recognize that every dollar spent, every contract signed, every investment made, carries with it a piece of our identity, our relationships, and our place in the world.

But it's not just interpersonal economic relationships like these that are socially informed; even our own, personal financial decisions are deeply shaped by social and cultural contexts. Consider your approach to saving and investing. These decisions are not always about maximizing returns; they reflect who we are, where we come from, and how we relate to those around us. The ways we choose to save (money in the bank, cash under the mattress), the types of investments we make (stocks, real estate, socially responsible funds), and even our attitudes toward risk (conservative vs. aggressive strategies) are influenced by cultural background, social environment, and shared experiences. You might, for example, prioritize saving for future generations, while others focus instead on immediate enjoyment. Different financial strategies reveal much about our own social identities and relationships, communicating different priorities and aspirations not only to ourselves but also to others.

Take consumption and spending habits. The clothes you choose to wear, the foods you eat, and the brands you support all express something about your values, beliefs, and social affiliations. Choosing to buy organic products could reflect a commitment to both individual health and broader environmental sustainability; purchasing luxury goods could bring personal enjoyment while also signaling social status and wealth. Even our everyday purchases, from the grocery store to online shopping, contribute to a narrative about who we are and the world we aspire to live in. What we buy and sell carries social meaning in addition to economic value or individual usefulness.

The social dimension of purchasing behavior is perhaps most apparent when it comes to gift-giving practices. While economists might view gifts as an inefficient transfer of resources, sociologists and anthropologists understand that exchanging presents serves important social functions in maintaining relationships and communicating care.[5] The types of gifts we give, how much we spend, when we reciprocate, and the occasions we celebrate are all culturally dependent and signal our social ties. In fact, gift-giving can be seen as a form of social alchemy, transforming mundane objects into powerful symbols of connection, affection, and respect.

And it's not just how we use our money—it's also how we earn it. The job market, too, is a social arena. While you may think you've chosen your occupation based on your unique set of interests and skills, your career path is deeply bound up with the fabric of society. Aspects that feel deeply personal—a calling for a particular field, the professional ambitions we set for ourselves, the opportunities we perceive as viable—are shaped by the values we've absorbed from our culture, the educational opportunities available to us, and the social circles we move in. These elements collectively shape understandings of what is meaningful, accessible, and congruent with our sense of self—and at the same time subtly enforce barriers that deter or obstruct some individuals from accessing certain paths. Recruitment practices and incentives within organizations often reflect society's larger structures and biases, with hiring and promotion decisions mediated by having the right connections and apparent cultural fit rather than raw ability alone. The belief in a purely meritocratic job market is challenged by the reality that both occupational choices and opportunities are tied to sociological factors.

Society, it seems, is like another invisible hand guiding our economic behavior.[6] From the subtle to the overt, its influence permeates a range of decisions, behaviors, and priorities—our economic selves are not isolated from our social world; they are a reflection of it. Basic economic principles like supply and demand, or the pursuit of optimal choices, and newer psychological explanations still provide a foundational understanding of economic principles and incentives. However, they offer an incomplete picture when it comes to explaining what might be perceived as "irrational" behavior in the real world.

I put "irrational" in quotation marks to emphasize that the economic concept of rationality is just one lens through which we can understand human behavior and decision-making. When we broaden our perspective to include nonmonetary factors such as personal values, social relationships, and cultural norms, many behaviors that might seem irrational from a purely economic standpoint start to make a lot more sense.

Take, for instance, the decision to prioritize home ownership over other financial goals. While it might be more advantageous to pay off high-interest credit card debt before paying down a mortgage, for many people, the sense of accomplishment, security, and status that comes with owning a home outright is worth the potential financial trade-off. The pride of walking through your own front door, the satisfaction of making the space truly yours, and the comfort of knowing you have a place to call home can be incredibly fulfilling on an emotional level. It's a feeling of putting down roots, belonging to a community, and having a tangible representation of your hard work and success. But where do these feelings come from? They are deeply embedded in the social and cultural narratives that shape our understanding of success, stability, and the "American Dream." Owning a home is not just a financial investment but a symbol of having made it in our society.

This highlights the fact that incentives like status attainment are not just an individual preference or a driver of economic competition, as often portrayed in traditional economic models. Rather, status is a fundamentally social phenomenon—it's about one's relative position within social hierarchies. It's more about how others see us than how we see ourselves. Wanting status, then, is not simply a matter of personal ambition but a response to prevailing value systems for understanding what is desirable, respectable, and worthy of pursuit. For many, status is closely tied to wealth. Having financial resources can signify power, success, and respectability. A luxury car, a large house, or high-end fashion can serve as markers of this wealth, signaling to others a certain level of achievement. This association between wealth and status is so ingrained in parts of contemporary society that having money is often equated with other things like intelligence, moral virtue, and overall success in life.

This conflation of wealth and worth can have profound effects on economic behavior. It can drive some of us to pursue high-paying careers, even if they don't align with our passions or values. It can lead others to prioritize earning and spending over other important aspects of life, like relationships, health, or personal growth. And it can create immense pressure to "keep up with the Joneses," to maintain and display a certain level of consumption in order to maintain perceptions of standing, even if it's funded with debt.

For others, however, status derives from different sources. Educational achievements, for example, can be a significant status marker for certain individuals. Degrees from prestigious universities or advanced professional qualifications can elevate one's standing in the eyes of peers and society above and beyond the size of one's bank account. In some communities, status is more closely linked to charitable contributions or acts of service. Being known as a dedicated volunteer, a community leader, or someone who actively works to improve the lives of others can bring a different kind of respect and admiration. Religious devotion can similarly confer respect in certain circles. Being a recognized spiritual leader or a devout follower can elevate one's social standing especially within more traditional communities. These valuations are less about financial wealth and more about moral standing.

But these incentives can lead to behaviors that might be considered economically irrational. Someone might choose to pursue an advanced degree that puts them into significant debt, even if the job prospects in that field are limited. A person might donate a large sum to a charitable cause, even if it means sacrificing their own financial stability. A devout individual might choose to spend significant time and resources on religious contemplation, even if it results in detachment from economic life.

Many other sociological factors can influence our financial decisions aside from status seeking. Family obligations, for one, can be a powerful motivator. So can enduring cultural traditions, such as the expectation to host lavish celebrations for weddings or holidays, which may lead people to spend beyond their means. Collective identity, where individuals see their personal success or failure as linked to the prosperity of their group, can also lead to behaviors that prioritize group well-being over individual wealth accumulation. Norms, institutions, peer pressure, and the subtle cues from others around us—these all influence the way we deal with and think about money.

Economic behaviors, therefore, cannot be fully understood without considering the social world in which they occur. And it is this type of sociological analysis that this book aims to provide. The interplay between our financial decisions and the social world is all too often ignored, oversimplified, or misunderstood in conventional economics and behavioral frameworks: mainstream economic models still tend to fall back on outdated assumptions of rational actors making self-serving decisions isolated from society. And behavioral economics, while recognizing that individuals don't always act rationally, focuses primarily on cognitive and psychological defects, still viewing decision-making as centered on the individual. Each offers valuable insights, but both stop short of examining how our choices and behaviors are fundamentally enabled and constrained by the societies we live in.

To be fair, the notion that mainstream economics still views actual people as perfectly rational robots is somewhat exaggerated.

Many economists now recognize that real humans exhibit a range of biases and quirks that deviate from textbook logic, but their work nevertheless requires the assumption of rationality to make their models mathematically tractable and to derive clear predictions. Newer models attempt to incorporate these human realities by drawing on psychological experiments and considering emotional states, but they still struggle to account for how things like culture, identity, relationships, and meaning influence economic behavior in the messy real world. For instance, some economists will use "culture" as a catch-all to explain broad differences in preferences or outcomes across countries or between groups but without specifying the mechanisms or dimensions of culture that matter. Others adopt "identity" as a shorthand for social norms or expectations without considering the multiple and dynamic aspects of identity that influence behavior. Experimenters sometimes model "fairness" in simulated money games between anonymous strangers but overlook how fairness operates differently in relationships with friends or families, where sharing is a fundamental expectation.

To fully understand economic behavior, we must dive deeper into these social dimensions and allow for a more comprehensive and nuanced view of how people navigate the economic landscape as inherently social beings.

Another Book about Economic Behavior? Not Quite.

You're standing in a bookstore, perusing a shelf filled with titles promising to unravel the hidden mysteries that muddle your financial decisions. "Why do I spend so much money on things I don't need?" "How can I save more for retirement?" "What drives my irrational economic choices?" This type of book, oftentimes written by behavioral economists, promises to shed light on the myriad errors and biases that lead us astray when it comes to money.

While certainly insightful, these explanations often leave us wanting for more—there's a nagging feeling that something is still missing. It's like trying to complete a jigsaw puzzle with only half the pieces. Behavioral economics, to be sure, has revolutionized our understanding of economic decision-making. But with its roots firmly planted in cognitive psychology, it overlooks a crucial dimension: the social forces that invisibly guide our financial choices.[7]

Which is where this book comes in. Rather than rehashing the same old stories about how our brains process information poorly or how money clouds the mind with emotion, this volume takes a different approach. It recognizes that our economic behavior is not just a product of our individual psychology but deeply embedded in the social world around us. In doing so, it offers a fresh perspective, one that goes beyond the confines of the individual mind to explore the rich social and cultural dimensions of economic behavior. By peering into these often-overlooked corners, we can paint a more comprehensive and nuanced picture of how we navigate the economic landscape as inherently social beings.

Behavioral economists, among others, often use the metaphor of the brain functioning like a computer to explain how people make decisions. This analogy helps conceptualize the ways human beings process information, store memories, and ultimately act in the world. If we do something irrational, it's because of "faulty wiring," or a "bug" in our "central processing units." This, of course, greatly oversimplifies the complexity of human decision-making. But let's push the analogy further: if our brains are the hardware, then culture is the "operating system" (OS) that regulates how we interpret and interact with the world. This "cultural operating system" provides the fundamental framework through which each of us perceives value, understands economic transactions, and makes financial decisions.

Consider how iOS and Android users often have different approaches to customization, app availability, and user interface preferences. Similarly, individuals from different cultural backgrounds may have fundamentally different approaches to economic life.

A "Western capitalist" OS might prioritize individual wealth accumulation and consumer choice, while a "Confucian" OS could emphasize family obligation and long-term collective prosperity. A "Nordic social democratic" OS might have robust built-in social safety net functions, whereas a "survival-focused" OS in a developing economy might have more advanced resource-sharing and informal economy features.

The sociologist Ann Swidler's concept of culture as a "tool kit" aligns with this idea—culture provides us with the tools (we might call them "apps") to construct our worldview and modes of action.[8] Culture shapes our basic assumptions about money, wealth, and economic relationships, often in ways we don't consciously recognize—much like how our choice of smartphone or personal computer OS subtly influences our engagement with the digital world.

The apps in this analogy represent the specific social scripts, behaviors, and strategies available to individuals within a given cultural context. In behavioral economics, these might be understood as the heuristics or decision-making shortcuts people unconsciously use. In sociology, we might think of these as the "repertoires" individuals draw upon to navigate social situations. These can include everything from family financial traditions and peer group norms to media influences and educational experiences. Crucially, just as certain apps are only available on specific operating systems, some economic behaviors or strategies may be more readily accessible or culturally consonant for particular individuals within particular cultural frameworks.

While behavioral economics has focused on individual decision-making processes, this book also sets itself apart from traditional sociological analyses of the economy. Sociologists look to the bigger picture—the maze of groups, institutions, and societal structures that shape economic interaction. Firms, markets, and the grand narrative of capitalism itself have taken center stage in economic sociology, often leaving the individual actor somewhat in the background. As Neil Smelser and Richard Swedberg, two pioneers in the field of contemporary economic sociology, bluntly put it: "The analytic starting point of economics is the individual; the analytic starting points of economic sociology are typically groups, institutions, and society."[9] They admit that this macrolevel focus tends to leave the individual out of the spotlight, favoring instead an examination of larger systems.

But it wasn't always this way. Rewind to the early days of sociology more than a century ago, and you'll find giants in the field like Max Weber and Emile Durkheim grappling with the connection between social structures and individual behavior.

Take Weber's *Protestant Ethic and the Spirit of Capitalism.* With meticulous detail, he traced how religious values, particularly the Calvinist belief in predestination, catalyzed the "spirit of capitalism," which profoundly shaped individual economic attitudes across the Western world.[10] These religious tenets didn't just dictate personal values; they wove themselves into the very fabric of society, fundamentally transforming the economic ethos of entire generations.

Weber's insight that societal structures, including religion and culture, profoundly shape individual behavior suggests that how we behave and how we react to the world around us cannot simply be reduced either to individual psychology or to rationality. Indeed, Weber elaborated on multiple forms of "rationality" that work on our decisions. One such form, which he called *instrumental rationality*, resembles the self-serving and calculating rational actor found in mainstream economic theories. Here, individuals undertake a straightforward analysis of costs and benefits to maximize their personal advantage and achieve their goals.

But as Weber astutely pointed out, there's more to the story. He introduced the concept of *affective rationality*, which recognizes the power that emotions hold over our decision-making. We might open our checkbooks to a charity after being moved by a heart-wrenching story, or refuse to lend money to a friend in need because of a lingering grudge, regardless of the potential financial gains. Then there's the force of *tradition*—those ingrained customs and rituals that guide our actions without our even realizing it. When we buy a turkey for Thanksgiving dinner or exchange gifts during the holidays, we're not necessarily making a rational choice but following long-established cultural scripts.

Weber also outlined the idea of *value rationality*, where our moral compass, rather than our calculator, steers our decisions. When we pay extra for fair-trade coffee or choose a career in social work over investment banking, we're prioritizing our ethical principles over pure economic gain. These choices serve as a powerful reminder that economic behavior is far from one-dimensional. Even when we believe we're acting independently and making personal choices for ourselves, various layers of social influence are quietly informing our decisions behind the scenes.

Parallel to Weber's work, Emile Durkheim was exploring a similar terrain but from a slightly different angle. He focused more on the role of social cohesion and collective consciousness in influencing individual actions. In his influential work on suicide, Durkheim argued that the degree of integration in a society—that is, how strongly its members are bound together—can affect even the most personal of decisions. From this, he developed the concept of *anomie*, a state of social detachment and normlessness, which, in our context, offers an alternative explanation for economic behavior that departs from rational calculation. Individuals may engage in things like reckless spending or excessive risk-taking, not out of a miscalculated pursuit of profit or self-interest, but because the societal norms that ordinarily guide economic behavior have somehow been rendered inoperative.

The mid-twentieth century saw French social theorist Pierre Bourdieu build upon these classical insights through his "theory of practice." Bourdieu expanded the view of how individual agency and social structures interact with one another to shape preferences and behaviors. While not known principally as an economic sociologist, his concepts of *habitus*, *field*, and *capital* provide an analytical toolbox that enables us to delve deeper into understanding economic behavior as both a personal and social phenomenon—one which will be explored in depth in chapter 2. Bourdieu argued that beyond just financial resources, people also accumulate cultural capital in the form of knowledge, tastes, and practices: the way you approach a financial decision isn't just determined by the size of your bank account but also by the cultural resources you bring to the table. Think about it: if you've spent years cultivating a deep appreciation for classical music or modern art, you're likely to view the economy quite differently than someone who earned an MBA or spent their days analyzing the stock market. Our position in the overlapping hierarchies of economic and cultural life profoundly shapes the way we see and think about the world. It's like we're all wearing different pairs of glasses, each tinted by our unique combination of financial and cultural resources. Where we stand in society—our class, education, profession, reputation—all color the lens through which we view our financial decisions. In this way, someone who has sought out cultural capital might prioritize investing in experiences or art, while someone interested in accumulating money might focus on maximizing financial returns.

Chapter 3 shifts focus from these macrostructures to the more mesolevel social networks and groups that connect us. Here, sociologist Mark Granovetter's theory of *embeddedness* offers a powerful critique of the notion that we are solely self-interested actors, unattached to the social world around us. Granovetter reminds us that our business dealings and economic choices are often less about finding the best deal and more about maintaining the trust and relationships we've built over time. Think about the people you choose to do business with. More likely than not, you gravitate toward those within your circles of trust or with whom you have built some rapport—friends, family, colleagues—rather than random individuals who might offer a better price. Our membership in certain social groups, whether based on kinship ties, ethnicity, profession, or other affiliations, also guides our economic behavior in powerful ways. You might feel compelled to support a local business owned by someone from your community or to steer clear of transactions deemed unacceptable in your professional network. But our social networks offer more than just a series of connections; they serve as conduits for social norms, key pieces of information, and peer pressures that can influence our choices. They can act as both road maps and roadblocks in our economic journey, providing valuable insights or setting constraints that shape our decisions in ways we might not even realize.

Next we look to our more intimate, interpersonal relationships. In chapter 4, I draw from Viviana Zelizer's trailblazing work on relational economic sociology, which emphasizes the actual content and history of our relationships at the individual level, rather than the arrangement of our social networks. In Zelizer's view, every economic transaction is more than an exchange of goods or services for money—it is also a social exchange of meaning-making between individuals. Think about the last time you made a financial decision that involved someone close to you. Maybe you were saving for a family vacation, or putting away money for a child's education. These transactions become infused with social meaning, emotional resonance, and the ongoing "relational work" required to navigate money matters among our intimate ties. When we budget with a partner, for instance, we're not merely crunching numbers. We're negotiating issues of intimacy, fairness, and domestic roles. Every line item in that budget is a reflection of shared values, common needs, and the delicate balance of power in the relationship. Similarly, when we put money into a child's college fund, we're not just making a financial investment—we're expressing hopes and dreams for their future, a commitment to their success and well-being, and our love for them as a parent. Zelizer's work reveals how even the most impersonal financial dealings can become deeply socialized through the injection of moral considerations, symbolic meanings, and emotional attachments. She challenges the notion of the market as a cold, calculating sphere detached from social life, and instead shows how economic activity is "lived" through our intimate relationships and moral negotiations.

These chapters show how economic behavior does not emerge in a social vacuum. Even something as personal as our risk tolerance or financial knowledge is profoundly shaped by the broader social and cultural contexts in which we find ourselves. Nowhere is this more evident than with gender. Chapter 5 investigates how gender identities and implicit cultural beliefs about masculinity and femininity in the economy influence individual financial behaviors and intersect with overarching norms, socialization processes, and cultural scripts that guide economic roles. It demonstrates that ascribed characteristics like gender cannot be separated from the rest of social life that constructs economic actors. Our choices emerge through participation in gendered worlds that establish certain expectations and perceptions of economic possibilities and proper conduct. And it's more than individual choices. Our economic behavior is also constrained by overarching norms and cultural scripts that dictate proper conduct for men and women. A woman who negotiates aggressively for a raise, for instance, might be seen as pushy or unlikable, while a man engaging in the same behavior is praised for his assertiveness.[11] These double standards create real economic barriers for women, limiting their opportunities and perpetuating gender inequalities. By framing the economy as an irreducibly gendered space, the chapter provides tools to understand and address enduring financial marginalization based on one's gender.

Sociological perspectives, in this way, can enrich our understanding of seemingly irrational economic actions by revealing the influence of social structures, relationships, and contexts. But such perspectives can also help us understand new ways in which human beings are becoming ever more "rational," despite our lingering cognitive and social limitations. The final chapter explores the potential for *nudges* and financial technologies (*fintech*) to engineer rationality in economic decision-making and behaviors. Popularized by Richard Thaler and Cass Sunstein in their influential book *Nudge: Improving Decisions about Health, Wealth, and Happiness*, nudges are subtle changes in the environment that influence people's choices without restricting their options or forcing them to do anything. The idea is that by designing the choice architecture in a certain way, we can guide people toward making better decisions for themselves and society. For example, making enrollment in a retirement savings plan the default option (with the ability to opt-out) has been shown to significantly increase participation rates compared to when people have to actively opt-in.[12]

Similarly, the rise of fintech has brought with it a host of new tools and applications that aim to automate and optimize our financial decisions. "Roboadvisors," for instance, are user-friendly apps that use algorithms to create and manage investment portfolios for individuals, often at a lower cost than traditional financial advisors. By codifying the principles of rational investing into these algorithms, roboadvisors can help people make more optimal financial decisions without requiring them to have extensive knowledge or constantly monitor the markets.[13] However, as the chapter notes, attempts like these to engineer rationality are not without their limitations and potential drawbacks. Nudges, for all their promise, can often fail or even backfire if they don't take into account the social and cultural contexts in which decisions are being made. What works in one setting may not translate to another, as people's choices are deeply influenced by their identities, relationships, and cultural norms.[14]

Moreover, the increasing reliance on algorithmic decision-making in finance raises important questions about human autonomy, financial literacy, and accountability. When our financial decisions are outsourced to machines, how does that change our relationship to money and risk? Who is responsible when things go wrong? And crucially, who benefits most from these innovations, and who might be left behind?[15] By grappling with these questions, the final chapter highlights the complexity of rationality, technology, and the social world. It reminds us that even as we strive for greater rationality in our economic decisions, we cannot ignore the deeply human contexts in which those decisions are made. Ultimately, the promise and perils of nudges and financial technologies point to the ongoing need for sociological perspectives in understanding and shaping our economic lives.

The Economic "Game"

If we are not rational, does it even matter? Of course it does. Whether it's overestimating our abilities, letting emotions cloud our judgment, or simply fumbling a decision, we've all had moments that remind us of our imperfections. These lapses in rationality are not just occasional glitches in our thinking; they're part of what makes us human. But sometimes these human errors can have serious consequences. From staying in a doomed relationship, to governments botching economic recovery plans, to companies pouring money into products no one wants—our capacity for less-than-ideal choices can be both impactful and costly.

Perhaps that's why the myth of the perfectly rational economic actor—what social scientists consider another species entirely: *Homo economicus*—continues to captivate us. We aspire to transcend our human limitations and become this idealized being who consistently acts with flawless logic to maximize profit. While this figure is a clear distortion of reality, it holds our attention for a compelling reason: in our hypercompetitive society, those who can closely mimic such rational behavior often emerge as the victors—or so we're led to believe.

In a world driven by relentless competition—corporations battling for market dominance, job seekers vying for the same positions, and consumers navigating an increasingly complex marketplace—rationality is touted as the ultimate advantage. The ability to make consistently logical decisions, free from emotional bias or cognitive error, is seen as the key to unlocking success in every arena of life.

This idealization of rationality is not entirely without merit. A single miscalculation, oversight, or failure of judgment can have far-reaching consequences. It could mean missing out on a once-in-a-lifetime opportunity, being overlooked for a crucial promotion, or falling prey to sophisticated marketing tactics. In a financialized economy where margins for error are razor-thin and competition is fierce, the costs of irrationality can indeed be steep.

Making better, more "rational" decisions is, therefore, not merely a topic of casual interest but of real importance. Sure, we might aspire to become skilled like a star NBA player or a master artist; but very few of us will face long-lasting penalties if we never quite figure out how to nail a three-pointer or paint like Picasso. That's because most of us simply do not play the "games" of basketball or fine art every day—and even if we do, they are not terribly consequential for us.

We do, however, play the *economic game* all the time—a game that we may not even realize we are playing. Every time we go to work, purchase things online, pay bills, or save money, we are, in a sense, playing this game. We partake when we engage with matters like the stock market, interest rates, and credit scores—and our aptitude in these kinds of matters can bring about differentials in personal outcomes: like whether or not you can buy that house you've always wanted, afford to send your kids to the right college, or achieve a comfortable retirement. We negotiate and bargain, borrow and lend, save and invest, day in and day out. We are involved in the game of the economy whether we like it or not—and it is one we didn't choose to play in the first place.

Take a moment to consider what would happen if you were to take a break from this game for a while—or to quit it entirely? What is at stake? What would you lose?

What sets this game apart is that there's no "Game Over"—no option to simply turn it off and walk away. Even if you decide to become a hermit in the woods, you're still playing—just on a different, more challenging terrain with limited resources and tougher conditions. Living "off the grid" still entails making difficult economic decisions about resource management, barter, and occasional interactions with the broader economy.

Most often, quitting the game is not an option. Financial obligations don't pause—bills still need to be paid, loans accrue interest, and essentials must be purchased. Stepping back could mean falling behind on payments, damaging your credit score, and accumulating debt. Without engaging in the economy, you would struggle to meet basic needs like housing, food, and health care. In our interconnected world, opting out of economic participation is virtually impossible without facing significant hardship.

This "game," of course, is only a metaphor for the economy; but it is also indicative of a social reality with real winners and losers, and tangible consequences for individuals and society. Like all games, there are incentives and rules of play with various moves and strategies that can be made, as well as those which are against the rules.[16] In a modern capitalist society, it's often a zero-sum game, where the winner takes all at the losers' expense. This system inherently rewards those who can accumulate the most economic resources: the self-interested, flawless calculators singularly focused on profit. These "winning" attributes mirror those of *Homo economicus*. However, by uncovering human irrationality, we reveal an unsettling truth: many of us are ill-equipped for this economic game, with some at a severe disadvantage. This perspective doesn't just illuminate individual shortcomings; it lays bare the harsh realities faced by individuals who cannot—or choose not to—conform to the mold of the rational actor. In doing so, it challenges the very foundations of our economic structure and raises pressing questions about fairness, equality, and the true nature of human decision-making in economic contexts.

A Behavioral Economics Refresher

Some behavioral economists have also used a "game" analogy. Dan Ariely, for one, suggests that "we are pawns in a game whose forces we largely fail to comprehend" (although for Ariely, these forces emerge not from society around us but from within the human mind).[17] Robert Shiller, another prominent figure, has likened market behavior to a speculative game, where players are driven by emotions and psychological biases rather than rational calculation.[18] Others propose that we are instead "misbehaving" or "straying" when the decisions we make amount to a bad move or strategy of play.[19] To be sure, behavioral economists and I are studying similar phenomena, but we are using different lenses and methods to analyze them. Navigating this intellectual terrain as a sociologist presents its own set of challenges, given that the dominant discourse has been largely shaped by economists and adopted as doctrine. This makes my endeavor not only an interdisciplinary one but also an exercise in challenging established perspectives.

It is within this context that we should appreciate the initial challenges faced by the field of behavioral economics. When it first appeared in the late 1970s and throughout the 1980s, its success was anything but guaranteed. Economists committed to the idea of humans as perfectly rational actors were initially dismissive and even confrontational toward this emerging field. In his recollection of these tumultuous early days, Nobel laureate Richard Thaler noted that making space for behavioral economics required defying the prevailing economic orthodoxy that overemphasized hyperrational behavior.[20] The struggles behavioral economics faced in gaining acceptance provide a road map for sociologists like myself who seek to bring a different set of analytical tools to the table.[21]

Of course, behavioral economics did ultimately manage to establish itself as a significant field of study, becoming a major research program that serves as a repository for the cognitive biases and errors that pervade economic life. The field generally follows three main strands, which will be called upon throughout this book: (1) Herbert Simon's concept of bounded rationality, (2) Daniel Kahneman and Amos Tversky's formulation of prospect theory, and (3) issues related to intertemporality, linked to the work of Richard Thaler and Hersh Shefrin. Lending weight to these ideas, Nobel Prizes in economics have been awarded to Simon (in 1978), Kahneman (in 2002), and most recently Thaler (in 2017) for his work on "incorporating psychologically realistic assumptions into analyses of economic decision-making."[22] For those unfamiliar with behavioral economics, here is a very brief overview:

BOUNDED RATIONALITY

Herbert Simon explored the intersection of psychology and organizational behavior. He noticed that in real-world settings, "human behavior is *intendedly* rational, but only *boundedly* so"—the human mind simply has biological limitations that constrain our ability to calculate and predict.[23]

Simon found that people instead use mental shortcuts, called "heuristics," to achieve what he calls *satisficing* (a combination of "satisfying" and "sufficing")—acceptable results or good-enough solutions rather than best ones—results which nevertheless help us to achieve our goals. His empirical work showed how corporate decision-makers did not really act like *Homo economicus*; instead, they sought a satisfactory outcome, for example, aiming for a "sensible market share," "reasonable profit," or "fair price." Simon's work on bounded rationality has been important in shaping behavioral economics, where ordinary individuals are found to satisfice in all aspects of economic life.

PROSPECT THEORY

Daniel Kahneman and Amos Tversky, working together at the Hebrew University in Israel, built on bounded rationality and developed their framework of *prospect theory*. They discovered that the way a decision is presented or "framed" could subtly shift a person's choice. If a situation is framed as a possible win vs. a potential loss, individuals will process each scenario differently, as opposed to objectively analyzing the final outcome. One significant result of their research is the identification of *loss aversion*—that potential losses matter much more to people than equivalent gains.[24]

Consider this: If you were offered a gamble on a coin toss, where tails would mean you lose $100 but heads would win you $150, would you take it? While a rational actor would always accept this gamble given its positive expected value, Kahneman and colleagues found that most people refuse, as the fear of potentially losing $100 overcomes the prospect of gaining $150.[25] Loss aversion can lead to a range of irrational choices, such as holding onto losing investments for too long, selling winners too early, or missing out on good opportunities. Kahneman surmised this behavior could be traced back to our evolutionary survival instincts, where dodging threats held more urgency than chasing opportunities.

Prospect theory proposes a "dual-process model" of cognition, or a two-stage decision-making process, that explains how people make decisions under conditions of uncertainty: *System-1* operates quickly and automatically, while *System-2* requires attention and mental effort, such as with complex calculations. According to the theory, the interaction between these two systems is what explains the systematic errors made when faced with economic decisions. In the case of loss aversion, System-2 might reject the gamble after some thought, but the emotional impulse leading to that decision is due to System-1.

INTERTEMPORAL CHOICE

Just as prospect theory reveals our tendency to make ill-advised decisions influenced by the present context, the concept of intertemporal choice explores our knack for making choices today that would be detrimental to our future selves. Conventional economic theories suggest that people's decisions should display a consistent and logical approach toward time. Yet real-world evidence often shatters this assumption, revealing our penchant for favoring the present moment over the future—a phenomenon known as *time-inconsistent preference*.

Imagine this: you are given a choice between receiving $100 today or $105 a month from now. Most of us would reach out for the instant gratification of $100. But what if the same question were posed differently? If asked to choose between $100 in a year or $105 in thirteen months, many opt to wait the month for the extra $5.[26] Even though the potential gain for waiting a month is the same $5 in both scenarios, our inconsistent reactions expose a tendency called "hyperbolic discounting." We tend to overemphasize the present at the expense of the future, which can lead to issues of impatience and a lack of self-control.[27] This pattern affects real-world behaviors such as breaking New Year's resolutions, not saving enough for retirement, and overspending on credit.

Issues of intertemporal choice have become an important part of behavioral economics, but again these tendencies have been linked to our limited cognitive capacity. As one behavioral economist claims, "the preference for immediate gratification captured in these studies appears to have identifiable neural underpinnings."[28]

*

In its early days, the main task of behavioral economics was to point out the errors and blind spots of traditional economic models. Psychologists armed with experimental evidence stepped into the halls of economics departments and declared, "Look! Your *models* are clearly broken!" This was, to put it mildly, a seismic shift. The neat, mathematical world of traditional economic models was disrupted by the messy, impulsive realities of human psychology. It spoke to a truth many of us recognize in our daily lives: we are complicated, fallible beings.

But, despite a common perception that behavioral economics still stands in stark contrast to mainstream economics, it has, in reality, become part of the broader mainstream discourse, incorporating its insights into traditional frameworks. Today's behavioral economics has not abandoned the foundational elements of neoclassical economics—such as the focus on individual decision-making, the ideal of rational choice, and a reliance on mathematical models. Instead of continuing to challenge core assumptions of mainstream economics, it has largely become a tool for fine-tuning existing models, adding a psychological veneer to the same old frameworks. Behavioral economics has become less about critiquing the standard model and more about critiquing us, the human beings in the world—from debunking *Homo economicus* to reshaping *Homo sapiens*. These days, behavioral economics often positions itself as a normative discipline, providing corrective measures to our supposedly flawed decision-making processes.[29]

The message, it seems, has become, "Look! You *humans* are clearly broken!" The implication being: not only are our models in need of adjustment, but perhaps more fundamentally, so too are we—and therefore we need expert guidance or paternalistic "nudges" toward making better choices as prescribed by economic theories. This shift from critiquing models to critiquing people reveals a problematic assumption: that the economic theories themselves are fundamentally sound and that the fault lies within us—it's only that pesky human irrationality that needs to be corrected. But what if the real problem lies not in our human fallibility but in the narrow lens through which these theories have viewed human behavior in the first place?

*

Let's take a moment to consider a counterargument. Some more economically minded readers might be thinking, "Hold on, can't we just distill these social aspects down to a simple cost-benefit analysis? Can't we just assign some numerical values to things like culture, identity, and fairness, and then plug them into our economic models?"

It's a tempting proposition. After all, if we could quantify social influences and express them in the language of economics, then we should be able to neatly incorporate them into existing frameworks. We could add a "social capital" variable to economic models alongside income and wealth, or factor in a "cultural discount rate" when calculating the net present value of an investment. But just like attempts to reduce culture and identity to simple variables, as mentioned earlier, this misses the point. It tries to force the square peg of social complexity into the round hole of economic reductionism.

In theory, economists do have a way of accounting for noneconomic effects in their models, and it's called the *utility function*. But before we see why this doesn't really work, let's take a step back and understand what this concept of utility means.

The utility function is a mathematical equation that's supposed to represent how people weigh their options and make decisions. The idea is that we're all trying to maximize our "utility"—a fancy word for the satisfaction or happiness we get from the choices we make. Think of the utility function as a mental scoreboard. Every possible option out there gets a certain number of points based on how much we think it will contribute to our overall well-being. The theory goes that when we're faced with a choice, we tally up the points for each option and go with the one that has the highest score.

So, let's say you're deciding whether to spend your holiday bonus on a flashy new watch or donate the money to charity. The utility function would suggest that you'll choose whichever option gives you the most "points." Maybe the desirability and usefulness of the watch is worth, say, 100 points at the outset, while the warm glow from the donation is only worth 50.

Economists might argue that social considerations are simply another set of factors that we add to this mental scoreboard. So in this example, you might factor in some additional "social" points, like 20 points for impressing your colleagues with the watch, or 30 points for being seen as generous by your community. But at the end of the day, it's still just a matter of adding up the numbers and going with the highest total. Sounds neat and tidy, right? Well, not so fast. It's an intellectual sleight of hand that gives the illusion of scientific precision while obscuring the true nature of human decision-making. Here's where the utility function starts to unravel when we look at it through a sociological lens.

Our social lives are not a contest of numbers that can be neatly slotted into a mathematical formula. How do we quantify the depth of a lifelong friendship or the comfort of a familiar tradition? What price tag to we give to the sense of belonging in a community? This is akin to trying to measure love in kilograms or quantify the beauty of a sunset in decibels. It's not just difficult; it's conceptually nonsensical. These are the intangible, yet invaluable, aspects of human existence that shape our identities, values, and ultimately our economic choices. Trying to reduce complex social phenomena to mere numbers in a utility function is like trying to describe a Beethoven symphony by simply counting the notes. You might capture the basic structure, but you miss the emotional resonance, the historical context, the way the music can stir your soul. You lose the essence of what makes the experience profoundly human.

Even if we could somehow quantify these factors, they're not static. The "utility" of a choice can shift and fluctuate wildly based on context, mood, recent experiences, and countless other variables. The expensive watch that seems appealing in the store might feel like a hollow purchase once you're home. The donation that feels burdensome now might bring unexpected joy later.

Economists' utility function treats these values as fixed, when they're actually in constant flux.

But perhaps most damning is that the utility function completely ignores how our preferences and values are themselves socially constructed. It treats our desires as given, when in fact they're born from our social contexts, cultural norms, and interpersonal histories. The very idea of what brings "utility" is itself a product of our social worlds.

Our preferences and the scores we assign to various options are not things we passively download from society into our minds; we actively negotiate them through our social interactions. We learn and adapt what to value and how to value them through observing others, through conversation, through media consumption. We adjust our preferences to fit in with certain groups or to distinguish ourselves from others. This interactive and iterative process of preference formation is entirely absent from the utility function model.

Imagine you're thinking about buying a house. Sure, you might get some personal enjoyment from having more space or a nicer kitchen. But isn't your vision of the "ideal home" also shaped by media representations and societal expectations of success, status, and domesticity? Or think about donating to charity. That warm feeling from being altruistic doesn't just come from within. Scholars across disciplines agree that individual factors alone cannot fully explain altruistic behavior—it's taught and reinforced by religious, civic, and community values around reciprocity, generosity, and caring for others.[30]

Even our most basic needs and wants are shaped by culture. Take food, for instance. The pleasure we get from a meal isn't just about nutrition or even taste. It's influenced by norms around what's considered edible, appetizing, or even prestigious. Caviar, anyone?

The point is, we don't come into this world with a preprogrammed set of universal preferences or goals. We have to learn what is valuable, what to strive for, and how to make tradeoffs through our interactions with the world around us. It's not something we're born knowing. From our earliest days, we're absorbing cues from our environment about what's worth wanting. We learn from our families what it means to be successful.

We pick up from our peer groups what's considered cool or admirable. We internalize from media and advertising what the ideal lifestyle looks like. All of these influences shape our understanding of what's valuable, what's worth striving for, what will make us happy.

When we realize that the utility function itself is socially constructed, it starts to lose its explanatory power. Its circularity becomes even more problematic when we recognize the social construction of preferences: Economists observe that in a certain society, people tend to buy flashy watches. They infer from this that flashy watches have high utility in that society. Then they use this inferred high utility to explain why people buy flashy watches. But this explains nothing! It merely restates the observation in different terms. What's missing is the recognition that the preference for flashy watches itself needs explanation. Why do people in this society value flashy watches? How has this preference been cultivated? What social meanings are attached to watch ownership? How does watch-buying behavior relate to other aspects of the culture? Why don't certain people conform to watch-buying behavior—and what are the consequences?

By recognizing the social construction of preferences, we open up a whole new angle of inquiry. We can explore how cultural norms, social status, and group identities shape our economic choices. We can examine how marketing, media, and peer influence create and reinforce certain preferences. We can investigate how historical, political, and economic forces have molded societal values over time (for instance, the transformation of lobster from a poor man's food to a universally recognized luxury dish).[31] Indeed, we can't really understand economic behavior at all without understanding the social world that gives rise to it.

This isn't to say that the concept of utility is entirely useless or that individual preferences don't matter. Of course they do. We all have our own unique histories, personal tastes, and quirky inclinations that inform our choices. But to talk broadly about maximizing happiness or success, we need to recognize that we're already operating within a broader social framework that sets the rules of the game, from what goals are worth pursuing to what counts as a win.

Bringing Sociology into the Economic Behavior Equation

In 1977, the renowned economist Amartya Sen wrote an important article called "Rational Fools," which criticized the narrow view of rationality in economics. He argued that assuming self-interest is the only thing that drives people's behavior not only is unrealistic but also limits our understanding of what truly motivates human beings.[32] He believed that people's choices are often influenced by moral and social factors, such as loyalty, fairness, and a sense of commitment.

Half a century later, Sen's ideas are as relevant as ever, even if not fully incorporated into mainstream economic thought.[33] The sociological perspectives discussed in this book heed Sen's call for a wider awareness: as he pointed out, to truly understand decision-making, we need to go beyond simply labeling behavior as rational or irrational. This requires a willingness to engage with the complex and often contradictory realities of human behavior, rather than trying to fit them into neat equations.

My intention is not for sociological insights and theories to be subsumed by economics in the same way behavioral economics has been. The aim is not to squeeze economic sociology into mathematical models or have it simply become another tool for "correcting" or "nudging." Instead, the goal is to bring a sociological perspective into the economic conversation as a complement, as an expansion pack, and as a challenge to current ways of thinking. This means not just looking at how people deviate from rationality but also examining how different forms of rationality are socially constructed and contested. It means not just identifying the biases that influence our choices but also exploring how these biases are shaped by our own social positions, experiences, and immediate context. And it means not just designing choice architectures to steer people toward better decisions but also interrogating who gets to define what counts as a "better" decision in the first place.

The sociologist Wolfgang Streeck argued pointedly that in its quest to discredit *Homo economicus* from mainstream economics, "behavioral economics stripped human beings naked of their social relations and connections."[34] What we need to do is reclothe them in social fabric and move beyond just tacking on factors to existing frameworks. We need an economic sociology that comprehensively confronts the irreducibly social nature of economic life on its own theoretical terms—an integration that is not about eroding the boundaries of the disciplines but about building bridges and illuminating some of the blind spots that remain.

The exciting thing is, by bringing sociology into the mix, we have a real opportunity to deepen and enrich the conversation that behavioral economists have started. They've already shed light on the fascinating ways our minds work (and sometimes fail us) when it comes to financial matters. Now it's time to zoom out and explore how our social ties, cultural traditions, and relational contexts shape those mental processes in the first place.

2 * The Economic Mindset: How Culture and Social Position Shape Our Dispositions

Economic . . . dispositions can only be understood by reference to the economic and social situation which structures the agents' whole experience. . . . Economic agents make choices systematically different from those predicted in the economic model: either they do not play the game in accordance with the predictions of theory, or they resort to "practical" strategies. . . . The field imposes on everyone, though to varying degrees depending on their position and capacities, not just the "reasonable" means, but also the ends, of economic action.

Pierre Bourdieu

Why do some people seem to have a knack for making smart economic decisions while others simply don't? Think about yourself and those around you for a moment—you probably know both types of people. Someone who always saves a portion of their income, invests wisely, and avoids unnecessary debt. Maybe they are skilled at negotiating things like salaries or raises and can spot a good deal when they see one. And you might also know someone who regularly overspends beyond their means, borrows excessively, and takes reckless chances with their money. Perhaps they fall for get-rich-quick schemes or make hasty purchases that they come to regret. These patterns often start early in adulthood and can be hard to break. And they often have significant implications for one's financial stability and overall quality of life.

What explains such differences in economic behavior and judgment—is it due to some natural ability or favorable genetics? Is it just the luck of the draw? Or is it an intuition honed through specific life experiences? Does the environment in which one grows up, complete with its set of norms, opportunities, and limitations, shape these behaviors?

There is something to be said for each of these possibilities. In this chapter, however, I make the case that our economic decisions and behaviors are not solely a product of individual traits or chance but deeply embedded in and shaped by our social position and cultural contexts.

In the introduction, I suggested that economic life resembles a sort of grand game, characterized by a distinct set of rules, strategies, and inevitable winners and losers. The game unfolds across multiple arenas, from household budgets to global financial markets—each different in scale and scope, but governed by the same overarching logic of competition, resource allocation, and rational decision-making.

Some individuals seem to possess an innate ability to excel in these environments, consistently making optimal decisions that maximize their gains. These economic virtuosos navigate complex financial landscapes with ease, turning challenges into opportunities and amassing wealth and influence along the way.

In stark contrast, others find themselves perpetually on the back foot, their economic journey marked by a series of missteps and missed opportunities. These individuals, despite their best efforts, often fall victim to the system's unforgiving nature, struggling to keep pace with their more adept counterparts.

The game of chess, with its clear objectives and structured strategies, offers an analogy to the economic game. Computers, as the epitome of rational chess players, outperform by evaluating every potential move to select the very best one. However, human chess masters counter with an intuitive understanding that transcends raw computational power. This intuition, honed through extensive practice and exposure to varied playing styles and strategies, mirrors in certain ways the economic intuition that some of us develop. A knack for making wise financial decisions isn't innately programmed within us as rational actors but rather shaped by our experiences, upbringing, and the place in society we come from.

Disparities in economic performance, therefore, aren't merely a matter of individual capability. It reflects a deeper, more systemic issue: an economic framework that rewards a specific set of skills and behaviors while penalizing others. The "rules of the game" are not neutral; they're designed to favor those who can most closely emulate the ideal of the perfectly rational, self-interested economic actor.

The implications of this system extend far beyond individual success or failure. They shape the very fabric of our society, determining access to resources, opportunities, and ultimately, quality of life. By recognizing this, we begin to see that what's often framed as a personal economic shortcoming may, in fact, be the predictable outcome of where someone is located within a system that's inherently biased.

Indeed, the economic "game" looks very different depending on where you're sitting in the stadium of society. If you are metaphorically sitting courtside versus in the upper decks, your experience and understanding of the game will vary drastically. From the front row, you can see the players' facial expressions, hear their sneakers squeak on the floor. You feel the energy of the game viscerally. In the upper decks, the players are mere specks, the game a distant abstraction. Likewise, the economy looks very different from the vantage point of the wealthy compared to those struggling to make ends meet. For those at the top, the economy is a realm of opportunity, a game to be strategized and won. For those at the bottom, it can feel like a rigged system, a daily struggle for survival.

Without a doubt, some of the disparities seen in economic intuition are linked to deep-seated structural imbalances within our society. Some of us are born into the game with more advantageous starting positions—an inheritance or family safety net, access to quality education, a network of influential connections. Others enter the game with fewer resources and face more obstacles from the outset. These initial conditions don't rigidly determine where we end up, but they do define the range of moves available to us and influence how we react to the opportunities and challenges we encounter along the way. Moreover, the economic game is not played on a level playing field. The rules and enforcement mechanisms that govern the game often reflect and reinforce existing power structures and inequalities. Some players get extra turns or bonus rounds, while others face penalties and are forced back to the starting line.

Consider the impact of family background: Children who grow up in financially stable homes, with parents who model responsible money management, are more likely to absorb those habits themselves. They might also inherit a safety net that allows them to take calculated risks or weather economic storms. On the other hand, those who grow up in financial precarity, where every penny is stretched and debt is a constant companion, may have a harder time developing a sense of control over their economic futures. These early experiences can shape later financial behaviors, influencing comfort with risk, the ability to delay gratification, and beliefs about what's possible for our economic future. Someone who has always known scarcity may develop an unconscious fear of investing or taking financial leaps, even if their circumstances improve later in life. Meanwhile, someone who has always had a cushion may be more willing to take risks like jumping into the markets or starting a business, knowing they have a fallback.

While it's tempting to think that our economic decisions are merely a product of whether we grew up rich or poor, the reality is far more nuanced and interesting—and it's not just about who has or had more money. It's also about where you fit into society more broadly—your connections, your education, the norms of your community, the role models you had access to, the kind of work you do, and even the beliefs and expectations others have of you. Someone employed in a stable but low-paying job might understandably be more risk averse, valuing security over opportunity. A freelancer making the same overall income—but more used to frequent ups and down in their income—may be more willing to make bold investments. But if that freelancer happened to grow up in a small community where everyone knows everyone else's business, they could, nonetheless, be more hesitant to take those risks, because failure in a close-knit community has social repercussions beyond just financial loss. Past influences often resonate in our present decision-making.

Now consider a third person, who again earns the same income, but who works in a creative field like art or music. This person sees money through an entirely different lens. For them, financial resources are a means to fuel creativity. They might invest in a vintage guitar instead of stocks, prioritize experiences that inspire new compositions over building a retirement fund, or choose lower-paying gigs that offer artistic growth. Their relationship with money is shaped by their identity as an artist, by the values and priorities of their creative community. So, even with similar incomes, individuals' approach to money can be strikingly different, influenced not just by how much they make but by who they are in the world.

With this in mind, it becomes clear that our economic choices are not entirely our own, nor are they made in a vacuum. They emerge from a blend of social, cultural, and psychological factors that mold distinct dispositions toward money, markets, and risk—depending on where we are located in society and from where we came. Consequently, economic behavior will tend to vary from person to person, conditioned by their distinct social position.

A concept that can help illustrate this idea is being "right-brained" vs. "left-brained," a theory popularized in the 1980s and 1990s that suggested people's brains are just "wired" differently. If you're analytical, objective, and methodical in your thinking, the theory says that you are left-brained. If, instead, you are more creative, artistic, intuitive, or emotional, you're right-brained. This would suggest that left-brained people, with their analytical orientation, might be better equipped to consistently make more objective, rational economic choices. Right-brained people, on the other hand, might be more prone to miscalculations and allow emotions or subjectivity to get in the way.[1] Think about it for a moment: Which "sided" brain are you?

Well, despite its persistence in pop psychology, being left- vs. right-brained has no actual scientific basis. In fact, research over the past two decades has largely debunked the left/right brain myth, revealing no significant differences in the structure or function of the brains of such people.[2] In reality, the brain is a highly interconnected organ, with both hemispheres engaged in nearly all tasks, both creative and calculative. Yet it is undeniable that many of us still exhibit personality traits, preferences, and talents typically associated with one "brain type" or the other. If we shift the lens from neurology to sociology, we can instead look to how a person's position in the *social structure* affects their underlying dispositions and orients them toward particular behaviors and interests. It's less about the inherent "wiring" of our brains and more about the "programming" we receive from our social environments and the roles we occupy.

Think of the social structure as an invisible lattice that holds individuals in their respective places in society.[3] The CEO of a large corporation will probably be situated in a wholly different position in society than a migrant worker; a tenured university professor occupies a position distinct from that of a freelance artist. This social lattice is not made of materials like steel or wood, but of power dynamics, wealth distribution, and the hierarchy of statuses. Along its frame runs the gamut of unwritten norms, deeply held values, and core beliefs that influence how people act, react, and interact within their communities. Where we fit in depends on a variety of factors: educational background, income (and parents' income), occupation and career trajectory, cultural knowledge, social connections, and even our hobbies and interests. These elements form a unique combination of "social coordinates" that point to our location within the structure. Just as a gardener tends to vines on a lattice, tucking new growth into available spaces or redirecting a branch, so too do our choices and opportunities—along with society's responses to them—continually adjust our position within this invisible framework. Whether we move up, slide down, or shift sideways isn't solely a matter of individual will or randomness; it's a back-and-forth between our personal attributes and the social forces at work around us. And, just as a vine may find it easier or harder to climb based on its position on a physical lattice, our place in this social structure affects our access to life's opportunities and challenges—and ultimately how we see ourselves and the world.

Bourdieu's Theory of Practice and the Economic Field

To better understand the influence of social structure on economic attitudes and behaviors, I look to the work of the French social theorist and public intellectual, Pierre Bourdieu.

Bourdieu spent many of his early years as a researcher studying the Kabyle people, a Berber ethnic group situated in the mountains of northern Algeria, and he witnessed the imposition of free-market capitalism during the 1950s and 1960s. There he documented how the French colonial state and its agents introduced market institutions and capitalistic values into Kabyle society, such as credit, land ownership, taxation, and bureaucracy.

He also saw striking contradictions between the Kabyle's traditional customs and the rapid integration of market structures brought upon them. The pursuit of monetary profits and the newfound need for applied calculation created practical mismatches between the existing set of dispositions historically found in Kabyle culture and those demanded by the free market. When thrust into this new economic logic, the Kabyle appeared wholly irrational to outside observers.

Bourdieu's observations of Kabyle street vendors, who consistently showed up to market despite suffering daily losses, serves as an eye-opening case. Their seemingly illogical economic choices actually have roots in the Kabyle community's traditional mindset, which doesn't distinguish between "productive" and "unproductive" work. Raised to see hard work as virtuous and idleness as a moral failing, these vendors viewed even a loss as better than no work at all. Bourdieu noted of them, "To work, even for a minimal income, means, both to oneself and to the group, that one is doing everything in one's power to earn a living by working, in order to escape the state of unemployment."[4]

The Kabyle example makes it clear our views on things like profit or work are not universal truths, but come from a specific cultural upbringing. Bourdieu dug deeper by looking at how the different contexts we occupy, even within the same society more broadly, can mold our mindsets. From this, he proposed a model of social stratification that incorporated economic, cultural, and symbolic dimensions. He devoted much of the rest his career to studying how class divisions are perpetuated through the allocation and transmission of these social resources. He was particularly interested in linking the architecture and dynamics of various social domains—which he termed *fields*—to the individual choices, tastes, and perceptions that unfold within them, a concept he called the *habitus*.[5]

*

Think of fields as "social game boards" where each of us is a player, strategizing to accumulate wins and climb the leaderboard. Common fields you'll encounter are that of the economy, culture, politics, religion, education, the industry or sector you work in, and even the competitive hobbies or sports you partake in, among others. In each of these arenas, people vie for a particular kind of currency—or form of "capital"—that is vital to succeeding in that specific field. In the economy it's typically money, but with one's education, for example, it would instead be grades earned or degrees held.

Capital accumulation is not merely an end in itself but a powerful means to enhance one's standing and influence within a given social arena. Those with the highest levels of capital—be it world leaders who leverage their political capital to shape national and international policies, or sports icons who use their athletic capital to attract fans and inspire millions to take up the game—these individuals embody the pinnacle of success within their respective fields.

Crucially, each field operates according to its own distinct internal logic for how its specific form of capital is to be acquired and deployed—regardless of one's overall position within that field's social hierarchy. This field-specific logic governs the actions of all participants, from the most influential players to those just starting out. In politics, for instance, the currency is influence and the ability to effect change. The logic for accumulating this political capital—through efforts like coalition building, public communication, and strategic positioning—remains consistent whether you're a seasoned senator or a first-term mayor. The scale may differ, but the fundamental rules of engagement do not.

Likewise, in the field of academia, intellectual capital is paramount. The logic of its accumulation—through rigorous research, peer-reviewed publications, and contributions to scholarly discourse—applies equally to a tenured professor and a doctoral student. The volume and quality of output may vary, but the underlying principles remain the same. Even in creative fields like art or music, where capital often takes the form of recognition and artistic credibility, the logic of accumulation remains constant across all levels of success.

This consistency across different positions within a field is critical to understanding how these social arenas function. It reveals that the "rules of the game," as well as what is worth pursuing in the first place, are fundamental operating principles of the entire field. And it suggests that, regardless of one's current position, the path to success involves mastering the field-specific logic and strategically accumulating the relevant form of capital. A novice politician, for example, isn't playing a completely different game than an experienced one; they're playing the same game, just at a different level.

In this chapter, I'll focus on just two key fields: *economy* and *culture*. They similarly have their own internal logic and rules that shape the behaviors and aspirations of individuals operating within them. The economic field is where we engage in activities related to wealth accumulation, investment, and financial decision-making. It's a realm that operates on the currency of money, assets, and purchasing power. Here, your ability to understand market trends, allocate resources wisely, and seize profitable opportunities can set you apart. Whether you're a Wall Street professional, an individual investor, or a budget-conscious individual, the principles of the economic game remain largely the same, even though the stakes might differ.

The cultural field, in contrast, is concerned with the production, evaluation, and appreciation of things like art, literature, science, and heritage. Here, what really matters is your cultural capital—the depth of your understanding, the extent of your education, a discerning eye, and your ability to engage critically with various cultural forms.[6] In this arena, the markers of success aren't typically monetary; they're measured in terms of reputation, taste, and the ability to enrich society's cultural fabric, among other intangibles. The acquisition and display of cultural knowledge, refinement, and expensive tastes serves an important social function—it allows the upper crust of society to signal their status and differentiate themselves from the rest. This parallels the concept of "conspicuous consumption," first recognized over a century ago by the sociologist Thorstein Veblen in his influential 1899 book, *The Theory of the Leisure Class*.[7] Veblen argued that the "leisure class"—the wealthy elite of his time who didn't need to work for a living—engaged in conspicuous consumption and leisure as a way to signal their superior social standing. This wasn't really about flaunting expensive possessions but more about cultivating and displaying rarified cultural tastes and pursuits. By consuming luxury goods and engaging in cultural activities that were inaccessible to the working classes, elites could reinforce their position at the top of the social hierarchy.

Just as owning a yacht or a mansion telegraphs one's wealth and economic pedigree, so too for the field of culture do being able to intelligently discuss philosophy, appreciate fine art, or partake in refined hobbies like golf or horseback riding. Though it may appear as harmless connoisseurship, the strategic display of cultural refinement is often a form of social posturing.

Cultural capital extends beyond personal tastes, habits, and knowledge. It can materialize in objectified forms such as works of literature and art. Possessing extensive libraries, walls of paintings, or a collection of vintage vinyl creates an aura of cultivation. But one must also be able to perform the work of explicating, contextualizing, and illuminating the real import of these items. The curation of cultural artefacts requires a kind of performative discernment—explaining, for instance, what makes a particular artwork daring or part of a master's oeuvre. The returns from cultural capital lie not simply in ownership but in imbuing material objects with symbolic meaning. Beyond purchasing power, the true measure of success in the cultural field is the accumulation of symbolic profits rather than material ones. Acknowledgment from peers and audiences alike serves as the ultimate validation of one's cultural contributions and insight. Whether you're an acclaimed author, an underground musician, or someone who simply enjoys attending the theater, the underlying objective remains the same: to achieve mastery, distinction, recognition, and respect. Cultural capital might not buy you a house, but it can certainly open the right doors.

Both cultural and economic capital are vital in their respective fields, yet they operate by fundamentally different principles and yield different kinds of rewards and influence. Therefore "culture" and the "economy" can be understood as two clear-cut aspects of social life, each with its own rules and measures of success.[8] Think of them like *Pictionary* and *Monopoly*. They're different games, each requiring its own skills and strategies—what counts as a win in one field may not even register as relevant in another.

Why do the fields of culture and economy stand out as particularly salient when compared to others like sports, religion, or even politics? The answer lies in their ubiquity and influence over the broad spectrum of human experience. Culture and economy are foundational pillars that underlie virtually all other social activities. While you might never engage directly in the world of politics or sports, it's nearly impossible to go through life without participating in both the economy and some form of culture (whether it's attending the opera or binging reality TV). They are the common denominators in almost every social interaction, from buying a cup of coffee to dishing on the latest Netflix series. Cultural currents influence our political ideologies, our religious affiliations, and even our conduct toward sportsmanship. Meanwhile, economic power—or the lack thereof—can determine our access to resources across other fields. Financial wealth provides the footing for pursuing political office, elite education, ascetic religious devotion unencumbered by work, and so on. In essence, culture and economy act like the levers and pulleys of the grand social machine, setting the basic terms and conditions under which everything else operates. Additionally, the tension and interplay between these two realms provide an almost inexhaustible source of social dynamics. Every decision we make—where to go to school, what career to pursue, even which social circles to join—is a calculus that weighs both economic sense and cultural meaning. Bourdieu thus invoked what he called a "principle of division" between that which is *economic* and that which is *cultural*, emphasizing a kind of essential boundary between the two fields.

Throughout his work, Bourdieu was particularly curious about why certain social groups seem to gravitate toward cultural tastes that include things like opera and fine dining, while others prefer fast food and pop music. The point of this research was not merely to highlight the obvious lifestyle differences between social classes but to dig into how patterns of cultural choices actually function in society. In his influential book, *Distinction*, Bourdieu argued that our tastes and preferences do more than reflect our place in society—they actively reinforce it. By mapping out how culture is passed on and transformed, he shed light on how everyday attitudes and preferences become mechanisms that perpetuate social divisions and reinforce the exercise of power.[9]

The economic/cultural divide that Bourdieu noticed reveals a profound sociological phenomenon: the emergence of distinct cognitive-social ecosystems that shape individual perceptions alongside entire collective realities within society.

If you're the type of person who excels in accumulating economic capital, your mindset and way of life may likewise be geared toward measurable outcomes, objective probabilities, competition, and personal gains. You could see the world in a more utilitarian manner, "for what it is." You may even think of yourself (mistakenly) as "left-brained." While these dispositions may serve you well in the economic realm, they could, in fact, make for an awkward fit in the cultural sphere, where success is less about mathematical precision and empirical description and more about symbolic and interpretive richness.

Conversely, if you are immersed in the cultural field—perhaps an aspiring artist or armchair philosopher—your instincts may guide you toward more abstract thought, expressive nuance, or aesthetic appreciation. Such deeply rooted dispositions could affirm your place in the social structure among others who similarly value intellectual engagement, artistic expression, and emotional depth. These very qualities, which are assets in the cultural realm, might cause you to make what are perceived as irrational choices in a strictly economic context, where there is little latitude for interpretation or emotional reflection. Such people's decisions and actions may sometimes seem like random or risky choices when viewed through the lens of pure economic rationality. However, these behaviors often make perfect sense when you consider the symbolic meanings, emotional factors, and cultural values that are important to the individual but are not captured by economic models. Just as a financially minded person might find artistic inspiration strange and foreign, someone who is attuned to cultural accumulation might find economic reasoning equally confusing and unfamiliar.

This dichotomy is not meant to divide society neatly into the wealthy on one side and the cultured on the other. In reality, individuals often navigate multiple fields simultaneously, drawing on different forms of logic and adapting their strategies to suit the specific rules and expectations of each arena. Indeed, most people will have stock in *both* economic and cultural capital (as well as other forms) and in varying amounts. It is the relative composition of these capitals that matters. At one end of the spectrum, you'll find society's elites—individuals who are rich in both cultural and financial terms. At the other end, people in marginalized communities, unfortunately, often lack both types of capital. Somewhere in between are the rest of us, holding various mixtures of these capitals.

Bourdieu saw that cultural capital and economic capital could, at times, complement each other in gaining social and economic advantages. When they work in tandem, they can amplify each other's influence, both materially and symbolically. Consider an entrepreneur who also has a deep appreciation for fine art. They have not only the financial resources to acquire valuable specimens but also the cultural acumen to understand what makes each piece significant. Their economic capital allows them to purchase high-quality artworks, while their cultural capital guides them in selecting pieces that are both meaningful and likely to appreciate in both value and notoriety. The synergy enriches their personal collection in a way that either form of capital alone couldn't achieve.

However, Bourdieu also observed that economy and culture often act as counterweights, even working in opposition to one another. This opposition becomes especially salient when individuals do not possess equal weightings of both forms of capital, leading to an imbalance in their social and material capabilities. Take someone with a great deal of cultural competence but little in the way of money. They can effortlessly navigate intellectual conversations and make a strong impression in academic or artistic settings, yet find themselves confined to the gallery when the auction begins. On the other hand, a person flush with cash but culturally unaware could use their money to open doors, but might find those doors only lead to rooms where they aren't fully accepted due to a lack of sophistication or refinement.

Between these scenarios lies a fundamental tension, one that captures the sometimes incompatible logics that contribute to these two forms of capital. The economic field, with its emphasis on quantification, calculation, and material value, can sometimes clash with the cultural field's focus on symbolic meaning, aesthetic quality, and intellectual sophistication. Think of another business owner, this one a nouveau riche who is not an aficionado, just a hobbyist art collector. They may be able to estimate the value of a painting and amass an impressive portfolio of works, yet be unable to tell a Monet from a Manet. In a setting where the value of an art piece truly lies in its emotive power or conceptual audacity, financial calculation offers little guidance. This type of person might stand in front of a painting, bewildered, trying to quantify its worth or predict its investment potential—completely missing the point of the artistic experience.

Likewise, individuals who are more culturally attuned might find economic decisions frustrating or nonintuitive—not necessarily because they lack rationality but because their way of thinking and seeing the world is oriented toward a different set of objectives and values.[10] Imagine a history teacher or theater director tasked with selecting a retirement portfolio. They may be astoundingly good at interpreting nuance, understanding narrative structure, or inspiring others. Yet, when faced with numbers, charts, or talk of marginal tax rates, they feel lost or overwhelmed. They could have a hard time transferring their finely honed skills of emotional intelligence, creativity, or pedagogy into a framework of risk assessment, long-term investment, and financial growth. They might approach investing and money matters as an emotional or even moral enterprise, seeking companies to invest in that align with their values, and feeling frustrated when those choices don't pan out money-wise.[11] It's not that they can't make good decisions; it's that their usual criteria for decision-making don't apply in the same way.[12] And this isn't necessarily a flaw, but it does highlight a different set of priorities influenced by a distinct set of guiding principles that may lead certain people to consistently commit what are seen as "irrational" errors in the economy.

The amount (i.e., how much) and composition of one's capitals (the particular blend of economic and cultural assets one possesses) is not, therefore, just a laundry list of one's assets or attributes; it acts as a kind of fingerprint that relates an individual's dispositions or underlying tendencies (their habitus). Accordingly, the form of capital that you hold relatively more of should be a key indicator of your primary field of influence—whether you are more aligned with cultural or economic norms and sensibilities. So, whether you're optimizing for maximum financial gain or pursuing intellectual and symbolic ambitions, your actions and decisions are apt to be shaped by the type of capital you are after—and guided by the different principles used to obtain it. To put it another way, the blend of resources you've accumulated—be it varying amounts of money, education, and cultural savvy—can reveal, in a sense, the unique lens through which you view the world and make decisions.

Both cultural sociologists and economists have arrived at complementary insights, albeit from their distinct vantage points. Sociologists have shown that having cultural capital corresponds with a preference for more refined taste and high-end consumption;[13] and economists show that income and wealth often correlate with more "rational" decision-making that hews more closely to traditional economic logic.[14]

What remains unexplored is the intriguing cross-disciplinary question: Do individuals who are rich in cultural capital but comparatively less endowed with economic resources exhibit uniquely "irrational" patterns in their economic choices? Specifically, might their economic decisions appear suboptimal when evaluated through the lens of conventional economic rationality?

Admittedly, depicting social life as just a combination of economic and cultural assets is oversimplifying things quite a bit. People are complex, and merely having these resources doesn't guarantee smooth sailing in either the economy or cultural pursuits. Bourdieu himself cautioned against such reductive thinking. He, as well as many others, have contended that a myriad of factors, not just economic and cultural ones, come into play in shaping our lives and how we live them. Emotional intelligence, social networks, personal circumstance, and even dumb luck, among many others, can have significant impacts. However, simplification can be a useful tool when trying to understand complex phenomena. By narrowing our focus to the interaction between cultural capital and economic decision-making, we can gain new insights into how different types of resources influence our choices.

So, if you've ever wondered why you make certain choices that seem at odds with your own economic interests—but which still resonate with your values, understanding the role of culture might offer a new lens through which to view your decisions. It's an opportunity to see that what's often labeled as "irrational" might, in a different light, be a form of wisdom or a reflection of values that conventional economic theories have yet to appreciate.

Playing the Economic and Cultural Games

I wanted to test whether the theoretical tension between pursuing cultural and economic capital actually confers different, or even oppositional, outcomes (see fig. 2.1). To this end, I fielded an original study to examine the relationship between a person's performance on two simulated tasks, each embodying some of the distinctive skill sets commonly associated with the economic and cultural fields: blackjack, and a task of aesthetically rating photographic images.[15]

I chose blackjack ("21") as the economic task because it is a common and simple card game that combines elements of both skill and luck, and which simulates some of the features and challenges of real economic decisions. In blackjack, players compete against the dealer to get a hand of cards that is as close as possible to twenty-one without going over, where they choose to hit (take another card) or stand (keep their current hand). These choices require players to weigh the probabilities and payoffs of different outcomes and to manage risk and reward—conditions that resemble some of the complexities and risks inherent in the

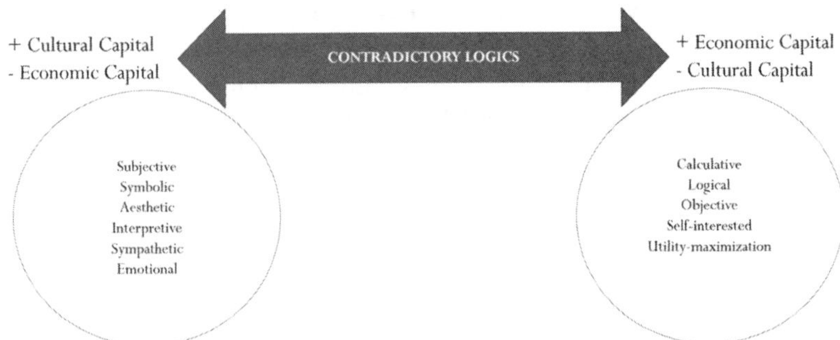

Figure 2.1: The opposing logic of the economic and cultural fields

actual economic field. Indeed, blackjack is not so much a game of pure chance—there is a definite optimal strategy to win consistently over several hands.[16] For these studies, respondents each played twenty consecutive hands of blackjack.[17]

I hypothesized that individuals with comparatively more economic capital, whose dispositions ought to be more closely aligned with the economic field, would intuit such a strategy from the game's odds and rules (even if unconsciously), leading to a greater number of wins.[18] Blackjack skill may not directly translate to effective decision-making in business or finance, but it does encapsulate some of the underlying principles and abilities that are relevant for economic life. Research has even found a correlation between blackjack skills and tasks like retirement planning, job hunting, and entrepreneurship.[19] Additionally, blackjack is sometimes used as an instructional tool in economics and business classes to exemplify concepts such as expected value and risk aversion, suggesting a logical connection between the principles of blackjack and economic decision-making.[20]

For the culture game, I drew inspiration from the opening chapter of Bourdieu's book *Distinction*, where he asked respondents to reflect on a series of photographs and rate them as either *beautiful*, *interesting*, *meaningless*, or *ugly*.[21] These images, which included an old woman's hands, an industrial gasworks at night, a tree's bark, folk dancers, and a self-portrait by the artist Frida Kahlo, among others, were displayed to respondents in random order.[22] I then developed an index of aesthetic disposition (from zero to twenty), assigning higher scores to those respondents who rated the images as beautiful or interesting, and lower scores for meaningless or ugly. It stands to reason that participants with a stronger connection to the cultural field would attain higher scores, appreciating the aesthetic value over utility. On the other hand, those with comparatively more economic capital may score lower as they could evaluate these images more for their practicality than their artistic merit.[23]

Evaluating photographs is a good example of a cultural task because it requires respondents to engage with visual art, which is a fundamental aspect of cultural experience and expression.[24] Photography, in particular, has a long and influential history as an art form, and it continues to be a relevant and popular medium today. By evaluating photographs, respondents are asked to consider and express their opinions about the aesthetic merit and artistic value of the images, which requires them to use their cultural knowledge and skills.[25] This type of task can measure an individual's ability to engage with and appreciate different forms of art and reveal their cultural tastes and preferences.

In addition to this task, I also asked the respondents to write a few words to describe three of the images: the old woman's hands, the gasworks at night, and the Kahlo self-portrait. The responses were closely analyzed and categorized as either *descriptive* or *interpretive.* Descriptive responses focused on the literal content of the images, such as the physical features of the subjects or the setting. Interpretive responses, on the other hand, went beyond the surface level and attempted to ascribe meaning, symbolism, or emotional qualities. The self-portrait was instead categorized as *descriptive* or *recognition* of the artist. I hypothesized that individuals with more economic capital would tend to provide more descriptive responses, while those with more cultural capital would offer more interpretive ones and show recognition of the artist. If we find a negative association between proficiency in the economic game and the cultural game, it would validate the notion that the two fields operate according to different principles and reward different forms of capital. This would justify further investigation into the influence of the field of culture on economic rationality.

Of course, these two tasks cannot fully capture the complexity of culture and economy in the real world. They are simplified scenarios that focus on just two specific forms of capital and may not reflect the full range of skills and dispositions available to individuals as they make economic decisions. However, they can still provide a useful starting point for investigating the relationship between economic and cultural logics and how they shape individuals' perceptions, judgments, and behaviors.

*

Before diving into the relationship between economic and cultural capital, I first wanted to establish that each form of capital is indeed a strong predictor of performance in its respective game. This initial validation is crucial because it directly tests the core assumption that economic capital is relevant to "success" in the economic game and that cultural capital is relevant to "success" in the cultural game.

To test this, I measured economic capital by respondents' household net wealth.[26] Cultural capital was evaluated in three forms: embodied, objectified, and institutionalized. *Embodied* cultural capital, which encompasses the preferences and tastes that are internalized through personal engagement with cultural activities, was measured by asking respondents about their participation in various cultural activities over the past few years, like attending the theater or reading a book for pleasure.[27] *Objectified* cultural capital represents the cultural items that an individual possesses, and so respondents were asked about their ownership of certain objects such as artworks, musical instruments, media, and the number of books they owned.[28] *Institutionalized* cultural capital refers to the educational qualifications and credentials an individual acquires, which can pave the way to higher social positions. This was measured by inquiring about respondents' level of educational attainment. By checking that each form of capital is predictive of a proficiency in its own game, we can be more confident that any observed tensions between them are also meaningful.

Here's what I found: When controlling for factors such as age, gender, marital status, educational attainment, and race, those respondents with greater economic capital indeed won more hands of blackjack, on average. This finding is consistent with existing research in economics and psychology, which demonstrates that economic capital correlates with more rational and strategic decision-making in economic contexts.[29] While blackjack is a stylized proxy for real-world economic decision-making, it nonetheless captures key elements of economic rationality, such as probabilistic reasoning, risk assessment, and strategic decision-making.

I also found that cultural capital is positively associated with scoring well in the photographic evaluation, regardless of how cultural capital was measured. This aligns with what Bourdieu himself showed in his studies of French society in the 1960s and 1970s: that those rich in cultural capital typically exhibit a higher degree of aesthetic appreciation and understanding.[30]

So what happens when the type of capital and game are mismatched? To answer this, I compared respondents' blackjack scores with their aesthetic image ratings, while controlling for variables like age, race, and gender, and adjusting for total capital amount. The results point to a strong and significant negative relationship between these two tasks (see fig. 2.2). People who excelled at blackjack tended to give lower ratings to the photographs. At the same time, those who appreciated the beauty in the photographs generally performed more poorly in blackjack.

Our dispositions—the habitual ways of thinking, perceiving, and acting—appear to correspond with the type of capital we most possess. When people try to apply the dispositions associated with accumulating one type of capital to a game that requires a different logic, they may perform poorly.

Recall that I also asked respondents to describe three of the images: the old woman's hands, the gasworks at night, and the self-portrait of Frida Kahlo—coded as either *descriptive* or *interpretive*—to see how these descriptions would correspond with their blackjack performance. For example, one descriptive response to the old woman's hands was: "A black-and-white photo of an old woman shown from the waist down, focusing on her hands." An example of an interpretive response to the same image was: "It makes you think she has worked hard in her life

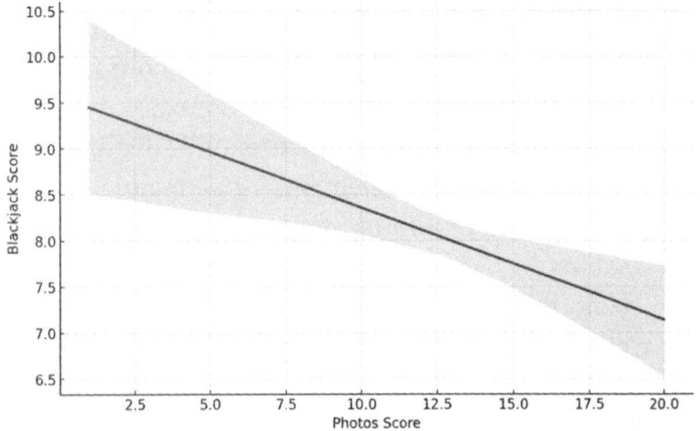

Figure 2.2: Regression line: blackjack scores vs. photo ratings scores

and her hands have some arthritis. She's maybe warming them over a fire or outside stove."

My hypothesis was that participants who excelled at blackjack would tend to give more descriptive responses, focusing on concrete details and facts. Conversely, I expected that those who provided more interpretive responses, touching on subjective meanings and emotional reactions, would be those who generally performed worse in blackjack. I also coded responses to the Frida Kahlo self-portrait as either *descriptive* or *recognizing* the artist. The latter code was used when respondents mentioned Kahlo's name or indicated recognition. Again, I predicted that having the cultural capital required to identify the artist would be negatively correlated with blackjack performance.

These analyses reveal a consistent and significant negative association between interpretive descriptions or recognition and blackjack scores across all three cases, even after controlling for other variables.[31] Figure 2.3 illustrates this relationship, based on a series of logistic regression models. Across all three images, a clear pattern emerges: as blackjack scores decrease, the likelihood of providing an interpretive response increases.

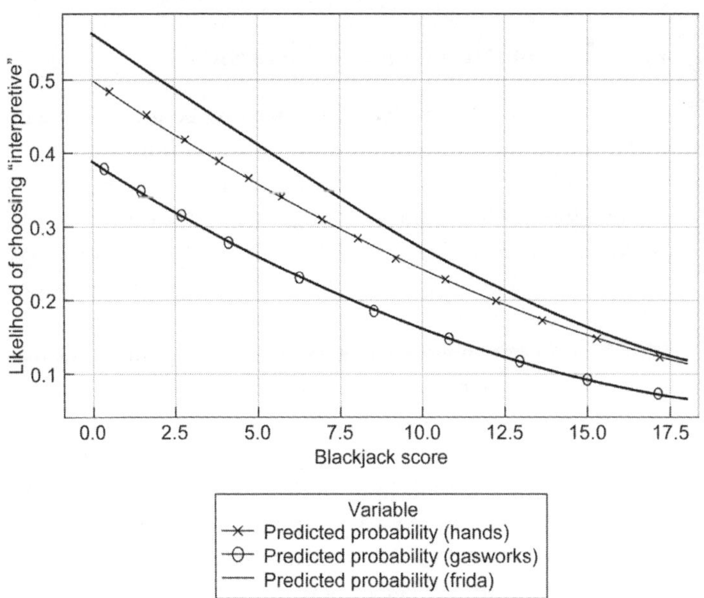

Figure 2.3: Likelihood of choosing "interpretive" vs. blackjack score

While these results are certainly intriguing, we should approach them with some degree of caution. Although they suggest a general opposition between cultural and economic attitudes, there are always exceptions to the rule. There are undoubtedly individuals who thrive in both domains, just as there are those who find both challenging. Bourdieu, too, recognized the existence of intermediate positions in the social structure, or those rich or poor in both types of capital. Nevertheless, these findings suggest a general cultural vs. economic opposition that is present in contemporary American society.[32] The tasks in these studies, moreover, are simplifications that might not directly predict how people would perform in real-world economic or cultural activities (e.g., does financial behavior really correspond with opera attendance?).

To further investigate the role of cultural dispositions on real-world economic choice, I next look to the relationship between an individual's degree of *loss aversion* and their composition of capitals. The aim is to see whether patterns similar to those observed above in the simulated games of blackjack continue to surface in the context of a bias that is already well known in behavioral economics.

Composition of Capital and Loss Aversion

Loss aversion is a concept first introduced by behavioral economists Daniel Kahneman and Amos Tversky, and it highlights our inherent tendency to value potential losses more than equivalent gains. Imagine finding $100 on the ground—it's a pleasant surprise. Now, imagine losing $100. Research shows that the distress from losing $100 outweighs the joy of finding it. As Kahneman and Tversky succinctly stated, "Losses loom larger than gains."[33]

This fear of loss can lead us to make less than optimal decisions or even engage in harmful behaviors—like excessive risk-taking in an attempt to recoup impending losses (such as doubling down at a casino with the hopes of breaking even) or clinging to floundering investments for too long while hastily selling profitable ones.[34] Individuals who are particularly sensitive to loss aversion may avoid taking even reasonable risks, overlook promising opportunities, and resist change or new ideas.

Traditional economic models state that rational individuals should not differentiate between a gain or a loss of the same amount. Whether or not you have a high or low overall risk tolerance, losses should loom equal to gains. Loss aversion contradicts this model, showing that people often go to great, often irrational, lengths to avoid realizing losses.

Loss aversion is so powerful it can even influence our preference between two options that are mathematically equivalent—simply because one is framed as a loss and the other as a gain. This was demonstrated by Tversky and Kahneman in a thought-provoking exercise involving a hypothetical public health crisis. One group of study participants saw the following:

> Imagine that the U.S. is preparing for the outbreak of an unusual disease, which is expected to kill 600 people. Two alternative programs to combat the disease have been proposed. Assume that the exact scientific estimate of the consequences of the programs are as follows:
>
> - If Program A is adopted, 200 people will be saved.
> - If Program B is adopted, there is 1/3 probability that all 600 people will be saved, and 2/3 probability that no people will be saved.
>
> Which of the two programs above do you favor? [A or B]

A second group was shown the same premise as above, but with a slightly different formulation for the proposed programs:

> - If Program C is adopted 400 people will die.
> - If Program D is adopted there is 1/3 probability that nobody will die, and 2/3 probability that all 600 people will die.
>
> Which of the two programs would you favor? [C or D][35]

The outcomes in either case are the same: 200 out of 600 people will survive, regardless of whether it is framed as a gain (200 will live) or as a loss (400 will die). Nevertheless, a striking 72% of participants in the first group chose the sure thing to save 200 people in Program A; but 78% in the second group opted for the riskier Program D. People gravitated toward certainty when the situation was framed was a gain, but preferred to take a risk when the same situation was framed as a loss. This incongruity, argue Kahneman and others, is a "cognitive error," rooted in our evolutionary past where "organisms that treat threats as more urgent than opportunities have a better chance of survival."[36] Loss aversion has since been demonstrated time and again by researchers and is now well established as one of the foundational concepts of behavioral economics.[37]

Curiously, loss aversion isn't a universal trait across individuals. Economist Adrian Bruhin and his team conducted experiments and discovered that around one-fifth of the people in their study actually behaved like rational maximizers, while one-third exhibited significant deviations from the standard model.[38] The remaining half displayed a moderate degree of loss aversion. Other researchers have found similar variations.[39] Even Kahneman acknowledged that, "of course, some people are much more loss-averse than others."[40]

Considering the relationships observed in the blackjack experiments, perhaps one's inclination toward or against loss aversion may also be shaped by the kinds and amounts of capital individuals hold. Individuals with comparatively more economic capital would then exhibit behavior closer to rationality, and thus be *less* loss averse; while those weighted more to cultural capital might be *more* loss averse. This hypothesis aligns with the idea that those with higher cultural capital might rely more on intuition and subjective impressions, which could indeed increase their susceptibility to loss aversion.

To test this idea, I took a cue from Kahneman's original loss-aversion research and asked respondents a simple question: How much money would you potentially need to win in order to take a gamble where you could lose $100 on the flip of a fair coin?[41] In addition to a $100 gamble, I also proposed the same question to respondents but with somewhat lowered stakes (a potential loss of $25) to ensure that the dollar amount of the potential loss wasn't skewing the results, and then averaged the two amounts.[42]

The higher the amount required, the more wary they are of losing. Studies show that people generally require a potential win of $200 to $300 to risk losing $100 on a 50/50 gamble, but some people, of course, require more or less than others.[43]

What I found was revealing: Individuals with more economic resources were indeed less sensitive to losses, as expected. However, it was striking to observe that those with a greater proportion of cultural capital were more averse to risk, behaving in ways some might deem more "irrational."[44] This held true regardless of how cultural capital was measured or defined.[45] Additionally, the results remained consistent when also controlling for other factors that could influence risk-taking behaviors, such as age, gender, race, marital status, general willingness to take risks, and respondents' stated affinity toward gambling.[46]

Figure 2.4 illustrates these findings, showing that as one's weighting to cultural capital increases, individuals are more likely to shy away from losses (indicated by the lines appearing to the right of the zero-line). At the same time, greater economic capital corresponds with individuals being less loss averse.

These patterns reveal how one's degree of loss aversion isn't just an individual psychological trait—it seems to also correspond to the social games we play and where our capitals lie—and these, in turn, correspond to where we are located within the social structure. Those of us focused more on the cultural game simply see the world a little differently, perhaps prioritizing interpretive richness and creative expression over mathematical computation and precision.

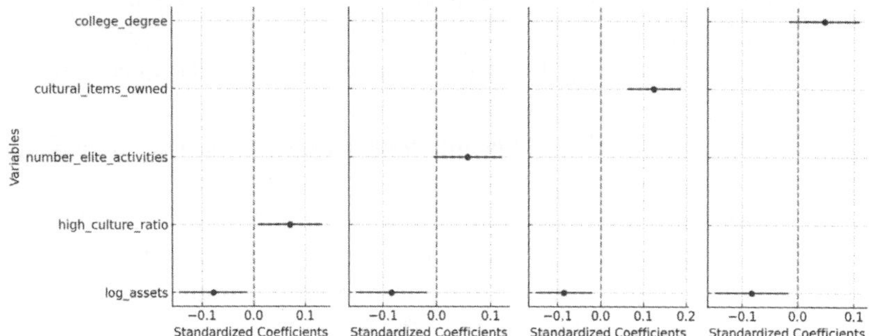

Figure 2.4: Individual loss aversion as it varies by economic capital and various measures of cultural capital

FRAMING EFFECTS

What counts as a loss? One of the key insights from behavioral economists' studies of loss aversion is that subtle differences in how a choice is presented or "framed" can sway our decisions in predictably irrational ways. As Tversky and Kahneman's "disease" experiments showed, people respond very differently to logically equivalent situations depending on the framing: 72% of respondents preferred a medical program that "saves 200 lives" compared to just 22% who preferred an alternative where "400 people die." Positive versus negative language triggers very different associations to guide our choices, even when the underlying information is effectively the same.

Still, a cognitive explanation does not fully capture the depth of how people perceive losses and gains. Sociologists argue that frames are not just personal worldviews but are derived from social contexts—they originate from and propagate through social structures and networks of relationships.[47] Losses could invoke greater emotional distress, not only because of an evolutionary predisposition to avoid threats and prioritize survival but because they threaten power and status within society. What constitutes a "loss" versus a "gain" is itself culturally defined. While money and personal health are among the most salient indicators of success and well-being in contemporary Western society, what represents a loss for someone depends on collective representations about what resources, attributes, and identities confer social value and esteem. In other words, the social and cultural context determines what is worth protecting, and thus what losing means.

Across history and cultures, losses of things like ancestral lands, sacred objects, social recognition through titles, or personal characteristics like beauty and strength have been framed negatively because they undermine social standing.

This might explain why Tversky and Kahneman's disease scenario elicits such asymmetry between saving lives or letting people die. One connotes heroic gains in moral status while the other signals an ethical failure. Outcomes framed using culturally resonant frames can trigger strong instincts that override calculative rationality. If "lives" were replaced with generic units without moral baggage (like "widgets" or arbitrary points), responses might very well be more consistent. The disproportionate weight we assign to gain vs. loss frames derives not just from hardwired cognitive biases (which, to be sure, explain part of it) but also from collectively recognized metrics of social advantage.

The way a choice is framed, therefore, depends a great deal on shared narratives, cultural motifs, and the positions of relevant reference groups. Choices about home ownership in the United States, as mentioned earlier, carry strong symbolic weight due to a pervasive narrative around the "American Dream" that emphasizes financial independence and wealth creation in securing stability and prosperity for oneself and one's family. Decades of societal messaging through media portrayals, politics, and commercial advertising have framed home buying (as opposed to renting or living with family) as a rite of passage and solid investment—an ultimately rational choice. Owning a home is often seen as essential for providing a secure environment for raising children, ensuring they have access to good schools and a stable community. In essence, the cultural framing of home ownership in the United States elevates it as a benchmark of personal success and family well-being, influencing individuals' decisions and perceptions about what constitutes a good investment.[48] These positive connotations, however, can also lead individuals to underestimate or minimize potential drawbacks of home ownership like upkeep, illiquidity, or overleveraging.

The experience of the 2008 subprime mortgage crisis and bursting home price bubble, which triggered an unprecedented housing market meltdown, altered the framing around home ownership for many younger Americans. This event exposed systemic risks and highlighted the personal consequences of owing more than your house is worth. Both the pre-crisis hubris and post-crisis wariness stem from collective frames about how people perceive the costs and benefits of buying real estate. Similarly, choices about attending college, taking on personal debt, or even purchasing luxury goods are framed by notions of social mobility and status seeking.

The subjective nature of how a frame resonates with an individual will depend on their social position, personal experiences, family values, and immediate context. Indeed, the very same person may make a completely different decision, change their evaluation, or take another course of action if a policy is framed as, say, either saving the "environment" vs. the "wilderness," or the "economy" vs. "jobs"—or a business strategy framed as "boosting efficiency" vs. "cutting costs," a protest characterized as "civil disobedience" vs. "unlawful behavior," a new technology presented as "innovation" vs. "disruption," or a candidate campaigning on "law and order" instead of "justice for all."

Given this sociological perspective on framing, it is not surprising to see variability in loss aversion when it appears in the behavioral economics research.[49] And while scholars have noted that wealthier individuals often exhibit comparatively less loss aversion, the role of sociological factors like cultural capital have been overlooked. Studies also find that women are more loss averse than men, on average (which is also found in my own research), but this is often attributed to things like hormones, genetics, or some other biological differences rather than differences in socialization practices and culture.[50] We will return to the matter of gender and its complex role in shaping economic behavior in chapter 5.

Attitudes toward risk and loss aren't universal truths; they're subjective and vary among different social groups. Depending on one's position in the economic field, losing face may be more consequential than losing a job. For others, losing to a competitor is worse than failing on one's own. Those working on Wall Street might see the loss-aversion task as a reasonable gamble, while an English professor might not. Indeed, financial professionals and university-trained economists are found to be more calculative, behave less cooperatively, and display more otherwise rational outlooks than the rest of us.[51]

Average levels of loss aversion should also vary across cultures. For instance, a man situated in a society that strictly maintains traditional gender roles may internalize a greater concern with financial loss as the expected breadwinner than a woman in the same society. Or we could expect loss aversion to be greater across the board in societies that prioritize individual autonomy or self-responsibility, since the consequences of a loss would more directly impact one's position in the social hierarchy. Indeed, recent research that compares loss aversion across more than fifty countries finds that people who live in nations ranking higher on dimensions of both individualism and masculinity do, on average, show increased loss aversion.[52] While cross-country studies like these do not examine individual-level differences or variations within a given country, they do signal a welcome shift toward acknowledging the influence of social forces like culture in explaining variability in economic behavior.

Time Inconsistency and the Social Construction of the Future

Before concluding this chapter, I want to consider another facet of economic decision-making where Pierre Bourdieu's theory of practice might be usefully applied to behavioral economics: in particular, the behavioral economics concept of time-inconsistent preferences and an inclination for immediate gratification, also known as *present bias* or *hyperbolic discounting*.

During his time in Algeria, Bourdieu observed that the Kabyle people who had not yet adapted to the free-market system had radically different perspectives toward time.[53] What he found is instructive. Unlike the typical Western view of the future—as a linear progression from one period to the next—the Kabyle saw it as a continuation of what came before. Their perspectives were shaped not by abstract calculations of risk and reward but by the tangible, cyclical rhythms of agricultural life. In the Kabyle world, the future wasn't an open field of probabilities but a cycle that mirrored the past. Their preparations for what lay ahead were grounded in practices of planting, harvesting, and storing. While serving as a practical measure for survival, the stockpiling of food wasn't so much a calculated hedge against future scarcity as it was a culturally ingrained response to the cyclical nature of agrarian life.

This stands in contrast to mainstream economic models that portray the future as a definable set of opportunities, each with its own probability and potential payoff. But as we all know, life often proves more unpredictable than any model can capture. Yogi Berra perhaps put it best when he said, "It's tough to make predictions, especially about the future."[54]

Sociologists argue that our perception and usage of time are not just basic properties of nature, like a clock ticking away in the background, nor are they simply psychological phenomena of individual experience. Instead, how we perceive and understand time is to a large degree shaped by tradition and cultural norms.[55] Eviatar Zerubavel's work, *The Seven Day Circle: The History and Meaning of the Week*, demonstrates how the week, a fundamental unit of time, is a social invention that varies across cultures, influencing how people structure their activities and rhythms of life.[56] Why do we consider a nine-to-five job routine? Why don't many of us work on the weekends? Why do we usually pay our bills at the end of the month? Why is the retirement age sixty-five—and how does this age affect our decisions about savings and investment? These numbers and patterns aren't really dictated by nature or any essential human characteristic, but are rather social creations that we internalize and come to accept as "normal."

But history could have just as easily created a world where the timing and order of our economic lives were different: perhaps a fragmented workday instead of the continuous nine-to-five, or work hours spread evenly throughout the week, including weekends. Indeed, the COVID-19 pandemic and subsequent lockdown measures have already prompted us to rethink what a "normal" work routine is. Many have shifted to remote work, which allows for greater flexibility and autonomy over our schedules. Some employers have adopted either a four-day workweek or a hybrid model of in-office and remote work, which studies show have actually improved the productivity, well-being, and work-life balance of employees.[57] These changes, which persist even after the pandemic, challenge traditional norms of work and show that there are alternative ways of understanding time.

The future itself, much like our perception of time as it passes, can be thought of as socially constructed. It's not just an extrapolation of the past and present, in this view, but a particular set of possibilities that are shaped by institutional frameworks, collective beliefs, and shared narratives. The "American Dream" is one such narrative. It motivates individuals to pursue higher education, buy homes, and seek career advancements. These actions, in turn, reinforce the narrative, making the dream seem attainable and real.

Our ability to imagine or dream different futures, and to act upon those visions, is a powerful driver of economic behavior today. Such "fictional" expectations (as opposed to rational ones)—far from being fantasies—are grounded in available cultural frames. They often become self-fulfilling prophecies, as the beliefs we hold about the future influence our actions and, ultimately, the outcomes we experience.

In his book *Imagined Futures: Fictional Expectations and Capitalist Dynamics*, Jens Beckert explores how these fictional expectations shape economic actions.[58] He argues that economic actors are guided by visions of the future, which influence their decisions in the present. For example, entrepreneurs invest in new ventures based on their imagined success, not on certain outcomes. This expectation creates a reality where innovation and risk-taking are normalized and rewarded. Another example Beckert discusses is the stock market. Investors make decisions based on their expectations of future profits and market trends, which are influenced by narratives about economic growth, technological advancements, or geopolitical stability. These collective expectations drive market behavior, creating feedback loops that can lead to booms or busts.

So how do different social groups frame the future? Individuals in more privileged positions, such as those with greater capital, often have a more expansive view of the future. They can envision a wider range of possibilities and have the resources and networks to pursue them. This advantaged position allows for more strategic and long-term thinking as well as greater resilience in the face of setbacks. Moreover, the advantaged often benefit from a sense of agency and self-efficacy that comes with their social position. Having grown up with an array of options and opportunities, they may develop a belief that their choices and actions can meaningfully shape their future prospects. This internalized sense of control can fuel motivation and persistence in the face of challenges, as they believe in their ability to influence outcomes and overcome obstacles.

Other people, however, such as those entrenched in a cycle of poverty, may struggle to imagine a future that diverges significantly from their current reality. For them, the future appears only dimly on the horizon, with limited opportunities for change or improvement. This harsh reality can lead to a focus on short-term survival over long-term planning—and at the same time limit agency and creativity as well as the ability to cope with unexpected challenges or opportunities.

Unfortunately, this perception isn't helped by institutional structures that reinforce "short-termism" in the economy. As it stands, today's economy often rewards immediate gratification and encourages credit-fueled consumption, favoring short-term profits over the so-called patient capital and cautious saving. From quarterly earnings reports that incentivize a corporate focus on short-term gains rather than long-term investments, to the proliferation of high-interest payday loans and revolving credit card debt traps, the system is rigged against the future.[59] This creates a vicious cycle where individuals, particularly those with less capital, are further encouraged to adopt a short-term perspective in order to keep up within these systems.

Economists do observe that lower-income individuals are much more likely to seek immediate gratification than wealthier ones, but they argue poverty perpetuates itself by undermining one's ability to exercise self-control.[60] But it's not always about individual self-control; rather it reflects how time horizons are shaped by social position and access to resources. Those in disadvantaged positions face numerous structural barriers that constrain their ability to plan for and invest in the future, such as limited access to quality education, health care, and stable employment. Sociologists Neil Fligstein and Adam Goldstein support this fact by showing that people of lower socioeconomic status often adopt short-term, defensive financial strategies to cope with their situations, while those with greater wealth and income use finance as a way to enhance their lifestyles through long-term investment.[61] Indeed, what may appear as irrational behavior is often a necessary response to the constraints and challenges faced by those with limited resources and opportunities. When survival is uncertain and the future appears bleak, prioritizing short-term needs and seeking immediate relief is a logical necessity.

This is also consistent with Bourdieu's theory of habitus, where he wrote "[t]he peasant knows that, whatever he may do, he will not succeed in making ends meet, and he resigns himself to living day by day."[62] Bourdieu's peasants—just like the contemporary poor—tend to have dispositions oriented toward the present and not toward the future; so behavioral economics says that they are present-biased. But it's essential to realize this isn't just a matter of personal psychology. To overcome present bias and plan for the future, people need to have some minimum control over their present situation.

While having or lacking economic capital clearly influences time preferences, the role of cultural capital is less clear-cut. For one, cultural proficiency might confer beneficial qualities when it comes to time, such as patience, restraint, and foresight—and a greater imaginative capacity toward the future. I carried out a small study to explore the relationship between economic and cultural capital and their impact on immediate gratification. Consistent with behavioral economics research, my findings did confirm a strong association between a lack of economic wealth and an increased tendency toward short-termism. However, any differences based on cultural capital appeared to be inconsequential. Despite expectations that higher cultural capital might correlate with greater patience and long-term thinking due to an enhanced imaginative capacity and greater foresight, the data did not support a significant impact. This suggests that while one's cultural disposition can influence certain aspects of economic behavior, its effect on temporal decision-making may be minimal compared to the powerful influence of one's economic situation.

*

Many of our economic habits—like stopping for expensive morning coffee, leasing a new car every three years, or over-insuring for low-probability risks—are not often the result of careful, rational calculations. Instead, they map on to particular locations within our culture and society that have shaped particular habits and instincts over time. We don't wake up each day and objectively deliberate whether coffee-buying or car-leasing behaviors maximize individual utility in some narrowly defined economic sense. Rather, our perceptions of needs and wants are crafted through shared symbols, norms, and pressures that make certain consumer choices feel more "rational" than others by transforming them into perceived individual necessities instead of indulgent status markers. Making coffee at home is much quicker and cheaper in the long run. In fact, drinking coffee at home could save you upward of $2,000 a year![63] But going to Starbucks is more than just about the coffee; it's about participating in a social ritual that has been normalized and valorized by our society.

But not all of us share such desires equally—our social positions and cultural orientations result in varying perceptions of "rational" choices. Where one person sees reasonable financial management, another sees meaningless self-denial over daily joys that lend meaning.

In a complex society like ours, it makes sense that our tastes, attitudes, and actions aren't purely our own, nor are they entirely universal. They are a blend of historically established beliefs originating from shared understandings and interactions with other individuals and institutions. This diversity underscores the importance of considering the broader sociocultural context in our analysis of economic behaviors. It's easy to lose sight of the fact that we all inhabit different social positions, which, in turn, shape our default modes of thought. The ways we think, act, and react to economic opportunities are greatly influenced by social structures and the distribution of resources in society. The different dispositions that they impart produce a range of rationalities and how responsive we are to economic incentives, effectively constraining and directing our choices.

By pointing this out, I do not mean to ignore or downplay the role of agency, personal preferences, or individual goals in explaining economic behavior or decision-making. Even those of us occupying an equivalent social position will have our own unique personal histories and experiences that result in distinct personalities and worldviews. While structure and culture play an important part in influencing our choices, individuals also exercise agency within these boundaries, often in creative and extraordinary ways. Indeed, those among us who are aspiring artists, academics, and bohemians, too, must find ways to balance cultural orientations with unavoidable budget constraints and financial obligations. After all, involvement in the economy is not a matter of choice but a fundamental aspect of human existence.

Paradoxically, the standard model of rational choice, by assuming that people always make the single "best" decision, actually strips away our agency and limits freedom of choice. In this way of thinking, the perfectly rational *Homo economicus* doesn't really have any options—they are expected to always pick just the very best one. If they do anything different, their actions are either ignored or simply called irrational—the rational economic actor is paradoxically constrained by the model's limited definition of what counts as "good behavior!" By insisting on a single, rigid standard of rationality, the mainstream model ironically denies the very thing it claims to uphold: the human capacity for reason and self-determination. In this sense, the rational choice model is not just descriptively inaccurate but also prescriptively dangerous. By holding up *Homo economicus* as the standard to which all behavior should converge, it creates a kind of economic peer pressure that stigmatizes and punishes anyone who doesn't fit the mold. It says, in effect, "You're not rational enough, so you're not good enough."

True rationality, one could argue, lies in embracing the full spectrum of human experience and decision-making, not in conforming to a predetermined ideal: a spectrum that accounts for all the different positions within the social structure, along with the various choices, opportunities, and constraints that these positions afford. It reminds us that what may appear irrational from one perspective can be deeply meaningful and purposeful from another. The artist who forgoes a stable income to pursue their passion, the parent who sacrifices their own comfort to provide for their children, the activist who risks their livelihood to stand up for their beliefs—these choices may not align with the narrow definition of economic gain, but they are rich with personal significance and reflect a broader understanding of what it means to live a fulfilling and rational life.

3 * The Influence of Others: The Role of Social Networks and Group Identities

Who are you? It's a deceptively simple question that can be surprisingly difficult to answer. Are you your job title? your hobbies? your relationships with friends and family? Are you what others think of you? Or are you something deeper, more elusive, more fundamental? One way to think about this is to consider the broad social categories and groups to which you belong, like being a member of a particular gender, ethnicity, religion, or nationality. These overarching identities often have a large impact on our underlying attitudes, beliefs, and behaviors. And what about involvement in smaller groups, like clubs, cliques, and various other social circles? These affiliations also influence our more immediate attitudes, beliefs, and behaviors and play into the larger social networks from which they are formed. In this chapter, we will explore these and other issues at the intersection of identity, social networks, and the *embeddedness* of economic behavior.

Social networks are the web of relationships that connect us to other people. They can be based on all sorts of things, like kinship, shared interests, living in the same area, going to the same school or workplace, and so on.[1] Networks help shape parts of our self-concept by reinforcing the worldviews and norms of the groups to which we belong. If your circle of friends or family prioritizes saving, you'll probably be more inclined to adopt a frugal mindset, even when faced with temptations to splurge. On the other hand, if they attach great importance to spending and showcasing wealth, you might find yourself following suit—even if it strains your budget or undermines your long-term financial well-being.

We all hold on to different identities, shifting between them depending on the situation at hand. The one we choose to emphasize can change how we think, feel, and act.[2] For instance, at the office, we may put on our professional hat and focus on our tasks, goals, and responsibilities. We may adopt a more formal tone, dress code, and etiquette. And we probably interact with our colleagues, clients, and managers in a respectful and courteous manner. We might also avoid disputes or making risky decisions, so as not to lose our job or inflict reputational damage. In contrast, when surrounded by close family or friends, we bring forward the more informal and spontaneous elements of our persona, sharing genuine emotions and candid opinions. Our priorities shift and we might find ourselves more open to debate or receptive to new ideas or take risks, especially if encouraged by others in the group. This chameleon-like behavior, where we alter our actions and choices to match the social settings we find ourselves in, is known as *identity switching.*[3]

Picture this: you're at a dinner party, and someone you don't know very well approaches you with an investment opportunity. They're enthusiastic about their new business venture, promising considerable returns. Although you're not entirely convinced, their personality is charming, and it feels impolite to simply dismiss them. So, how do you navigate this? Do you take the risk and invest your hard-earned money based on their charismatic pitch? Or do you politely decline and risk offending this person? But maybe you are swayed if you learn that several of your friends at the party had already committed their funds—or conversely, if they had all decided against it? Now consider a slightly different scenario: you're at a company retreat, and one of your bosses approaches you with the same business idea. They make the same enthusiastic promises and claims—but this time, you have a professional rapport with them. Would your response differ in this case? Maybe you'd consider your existing workplace dynamics and the potential impact on your career progression. Would their senior position in the company weigh into your decision-making? Will you make the rational choice in each scenario?

Social context matters. Who's asking, the nature of your relationship with them, who else is involved (directly or indirectly), and the broader social setting all play a role in shaping your response. Our decisions, in this way, aren't always entirely our own. We are constantly interacting with and checking in on others, and these interactions subtly influence our preferences and choices. Consider the power of social validation. As social beings, we look to others to gauge what is acceptable or smart, what is a risk and what is an opportunity. We might not even realize that we're doing it, but it's a powerful force. In the first investment pitch, the knowledge that your friends are investing could tip the balance in favor of taking the financial leap, without crunching the numbers. Or otherwise: knowing that they had all turned down the offer may cause you to steer clear of the investment regardless of its potential merits. The situation plays upon the natural human tendency to trust the wisdom of the crowd or to avoid standing out as an outlier. At the company retreat, the proposition is the same as at the dinner party, but this time, the stakes somehow feel higher. The person proposing the business idea isn't just anyone, but a boss—someone who holds professional power and influence over your work life and career progression. This power asymmetry could pressure you to consider the investment more seriously than you would have otherwise. Your decision now involves more than just potential financial gain or loss; it carries social and professional consequences within the hierarchy of the workplace. Subtle differences in social context can alter our thinking in ways that might seem irrational or suboptimal from a strictly economic standpoint—and also in ways that can go against our baseline dispositions discussed in the last chapter.

Take the *bandwagon effect*, a cognitive bias taken from behavioral economics.[4] This describes a subconscious tendency to sign on to what others around us are thinking and doing—even if we wouldn't normally agree or think it's a good idea upon personal reflection. It's a domino effect that can drive fads and fashion trends, the acceptance of peculiar beliefs, or even the rise of certain political figures. But it can also lead people down paths that aren't necessarily the most financially responsible. We may find ourselves swept up in the momentum of the crowd, jumping headlong into inappropriate financial strategies or investments without thorough and thoughtful analysis.

The strength or closeness of our social connections significantly impacts how much we allow others' opinions to sway us. When we share a deep bond with someone, we're more susceptible to phenomena like the bandwagon effect. We trust these people, and, often subconsciously, want to align with their choices and ideas. But even weaker and more diffuse ties, while less influential on a personal level, can transmit social validation, normative expectations, and conformity pressures that lead our thinking astray. Looser connections, while providing a broader range of viewpoints that can give us different types of information and opportunities than those found in our inner circles, also serve as a barometer for wider societal acceptance of behaviors and the momentum of trends. Weak ties act as conduits, channeling whispers of "what everyone's doing" that gradually seep into our own opinions and behaviors.

This social dynamic of connectedness and influence underpins the theory of the *embeddedness* of economic life within society, an idea advanced by the sociologist Mark Granovetter in the 1980s.[5] Granovetter argued that economic action is inextricably bound up with the networks of relations that create opportunities and impose constraints on individual choice. He challenged the view of economic behavior as occurring between isolated individuals driven solely by profit. Instead, he argued that economic actions are shaped by the norms, expectations, and reputation concerns that arise from our social networks.

Granovetter's perspective categorizes economic interactions into two types: those conducted at "arm's-length" and those that are "embedded." Arm's-length transactions occur between strangers or anonymous others, relying mainly on "economic" factors such as price, quality, and availability in the absence of personal rapport. These impersonal, market exchanges align more closely with traditional economic assumptions of self-interest. Embedded transactions instead happen within our networks—among family, friends, or associates. In these relationships, loyalties, trust, and a sense of mutual aid come into play. Consequently, we're more likely to prioritize the group's well-being and maintaining those relationships rather than haggling over prices or agonizing over unfair terms. Furthermore, actions seen as self-serving, stingy, or unethical within these interconnected networks can lead to social sanction and disapproval, endangering prospects for future collaboration and assistance.

Consider the choice of where to buy your morning coffee. If you have a personal connection with the owner or barista at a local coffee shop, you may feel obligated to patronize their business regularly. Even if a chain coffeeshop offers lower prices or better amenities, you might hesitate to switch, knowing that your absence could be noticed and interpreted as a slight. The owner might mention your defection to mutual friends, leading to subtle forms of sanction, such as gossiping or questioning your loyalty. You might even feel guilty for not supporting your friend's business, regardless of the economic rationality of the choice. In this way, your decision about where to buy coffee is not simply a matter of individual taste or price but deeply embedded within a network of social relations and expectations. The potential social costs of going elsewhere, if it were to get back to the owner or barista, may outweigh any purely economic benefits.

Empirical research, for example the organizations scholar Brian Uzzi's study of the New York City garment industry, provides evidence of the embeddedness theory in action.[6] He found that companies that cultivated close, embedded relationships within their supply chains actually saw greater profitability and success compared to those that strictly adhered to impersonal, arm's-length transactions. The keys to this success were increased trust, cooperation, and information exchange. But Uzzi's study also finds that relying *too much* on embedded ties can have a negative effect, such as insularity and less exposure to new ideas and opportunities. Overreliance on embedded ties can also cloud our reasoning, with emotional attachments interfering with better judgment. So while these trusted relationships can contribute positively to a company's success, they also need to be balanced with more impersonal, external, market-based interactions.

The concept of embeddedness goes beyond just business dealings—it significantly shapes how we all make economic decisions in our daily lives. Think about a major purchase like buying a used car or a home. Researchers have found that for these kinds of infrequent, high-stakes transactions where there's a lot of uncertainty about the quality or value of the item being purchased, people greatly prefer to buy from people they know and trust within their social network.[7] Having an existing relationship with the seller provides a level of comfort and assurance about the deal. Our social ties bind the transaction with a set of tacit guarantees and potential consequences if things go awry. We know the seller has a vested interest in upholding their end of the bargain to preserve the relationship and their standing in the community. For more routine purchases like groceries where the stakes are low, people tend to just go with the most economically advantageous option regardless of their connections to the seller. Social embeddedness matters less in those transactional contexts.

Interestingly though, the same researchers found that people are often hesitant to sell high-value items to close friends or family. The concern is that if something does go wrong with the sale, it could damage their relationship. So in these embedded social contexts, the very trust that facilitates transactions for buyers and affords them peace of mind can also create reluctance or anxiety for sellers. This highlights how social embeddedness cuts both ways—our social ties confer personal protections when we try to make a deal, but also bind us with mutual obligations.

This dynamic also comes into play in the hiring process. Many times, getting a job is much more about *who* you know than what you know. Friends, family, and close colleagues can provide a foot in the door by leveraging their positions or influence to recommend you directly to hiring managers.[8] People tend to trust recommendations from those they know personally, making a referral from a close contact a valuable asset. These direct connections can advocate on your behalf and share insights about your skill set, work ethic, and personality that might not be immediately apparent from your résumé or during an interview. A personal endorsement can be instrumental in distinguishing you from other candidates and securing opportunities that might otherwise be inaccessible. However, if the person hired based on that personal recommendation underperforms or is a bad fit, it can reflect poorly on the recommender. Their reputation and standing become linked to the hire's success or failure. So while recommendations from trusted connections can be hugely valuable for candidates, they also raise the stakes for the recommenders should things go wrong.

Interestingly, Granovetter also showed that even casual, superficial contacts—our "weak ties"—should not be underestimated when it comes to unlocking potential resources and opportunities. Weak ties such as old classmates, former colleagues, distant relatives, or friends-of-friends may seem tenuous, but can actually play an equal, if not more important, role than strong ties in certain situations. That's because these loose acquaintances connect us to entirely separate social networks from our own close-knit circles. While strong ties bind us in relatively insular communities with redundant information and the same set of opportunities, weak ties serve as bridges to new and otherwise disconnected social groups with diverse perspectives and different information. Since our casual contacts travel in different worlds professionally and personally, they can expose us to knowledge and connections we'd otherwise miss by relying solely on our strong ties. A job lead from a best friend may not tell you anything you don't already know, but an old high school classmate who works out of state or in a different industry can expose you to unique opportunities. Granovetter demonstrated this "strength of weak ties" through a survey asking people how they found their current jobs.[9] He discovered that a majority of people found their jobs through personal connections but, surprisingly, not through their closest friends or family but rather through acquaintances—those weak ties.

Weak ties often facilitate freer exchange of resources and information due to lower emotional stakes and there being fewer social risks if things go awry. We may be more open with acquaintances than close friends about sensitive career matters, fearing potential strain on core relationships. While reconnecting with casual contacts was challenging in the past, social media and professional networking platforms like LinkedIn have greatly expanded our ability to maintain and leverage weak ties. These digital tools amplify weak ties' power by providing easy access to job opportunities, industry insights, and potential collaborations aligned with our skills and interests, allowing for strategic use of these connections when needed.[10]

Socially Bounded Rationality

Our social networks constrain the information we receive and the opportunities we pursue. We often take the path of least resistance, asking a friend for a quick recommendation rather than thoroughly researching all options. Instead of conducting an exhaustive search for the optimal choice, we rely on friendly tips, recommendations from others, and opportunities arising from our existing contacts. By leaning on our social networks, we're essentially outsourcing some of our decision-making. This strategy reflects an innate drive to simplify complex choices and cope with information overload. Let's take a closer look at the behavioral economics concept of *bounded rationality*, which was briefly touched upon in the introduction. Pioneered by Nobel laureate Herbert Simon, bounded rationality says that while our intentions may be to act rationally, we are held back by the biological limitations of our brains. Simply put, our minds can only process and store so much information, which hampers our ability to make the most optimal choices.

Instead, we *satisfice*—a fusion of "satisfy" and "suffice." It captures our tendency to settle for decisions that are good enough, or, at the very least, acceptable. Satisficing explains why we often opt for what's right in front of us, rather than undertaking an exhaustive search for all possible choices, whether that's choosing a job, making an investment, or buying a car. Take car buyers. The last time you were car shopping, did you research every car brand and every model available? You probably limited the search to just a handful of makes and models, perhaps based on recommendations from friends, previous experience, or prominent advertisements. To search for all available car options would be incredibly time-consuming and mentally taxing. You'd need to research hundreds of models, compare their features, prices, reliability ratings, and safety records. You'd have to visit numerous dealerships, take multiple test drives, and negotiate with various salespeople. This process could take weeks or even months and, by the time you finished, new models might have been released, forcing you to start all over again. While not guaranteed to find the absolute best car for your needs, *satisficing* usually results in a pretty good purchase without spending an exorbitant amount of time and energy.

Similarly, investors, even the professionals, would be completely overwhelmed by the enormous amount of financial data and potential investments available in global markets. Their workaround? Concentrating their efforts on a smaller range of assets or a specific investment style. Indeed, many investors today satisfice by simply holding an index fund that tracks a broad benchmark like the S&P 500.

Satisficing becomes a go-to strategy when our brains get overwhelmed, exceeding their natural abilities. But it's important to recognize that our social environment also plays a crucial role in shaping these decision-making processes. Our social networks not only provide us with readily available information and recommendations, but they also influence our perceptions, preferences, and even the options we think to consider in the first place. Group and social identities, along with the norms and expectations associated with them, can place their own restrictions on decision-making. They can limit the options we think about and the information we give precedence to. In this light, our rationality is bounded not just by our brain's capacity but also by our social environment and context—a kind of *socially bounded rationality*.

Pierre Bourdieu, whom we met in the previous chapter, applied this idea to emphasize the power of socially situated frames in guiding our decision-making process. These frames focus our attention on certain things while ignoring others, thus narrowing our range of possibilities. Bourdieu observed, "Rationality is bounded not only because the available information is curtailed and because the human mind is generically limited and does not have the means of fully figuring out all situations, especially in the urgency of action, but also because the human mind is *socially bounded*, socially structured and determined, and, as a consequence, limited."[11]

Imagine a scenario where the CEO of a cleaning products company is contemplating buying up a competitor, and wants to gather as much intel as they can about the potential target. Now, the janitor at the company might have some valuable insights into the competitor, as they also work at the competitor's premises and might have overheard or noticed certain things. Importantly, this person has hands-on experience with the competitor's cleaning products and how they fare in the real world. But would the CEO ever consider asking the janitor for their insights? Highly unlikely! Just as it would be equally improbable for the janitor to approach the CEO for advice on new cleaning products, even though the CEO oversees the production of those very items. In fact, the janitor and the CEO would not likely talk to each other at all, let alone seek the other's advice. As a result, the two do not even recognize each other as potential sources of useful information. From a conventional bounded rationality viewpoint, both parties could have benefited from each other's knowledge (however improbable), especially since they work in the same office building. Yet socially bounded rationality practically eliminates this possibility. The result is often a highly structured and segmented set of worldviews that keeps certain ideas and knowledge out of reach.

Bourdieu's study of the Kabyle in Algeria offers another example of this principle of socially bounded rationality. There, he observed an informal credit system where a farmer who didn't have enough money to buy an ox could borrow one from another farmer, repaying the loan by plowing the lender's land with the same ox at a later time, without any written contract or formal obligation, but based on trust and honor. This exchange, known as *s'fella,* is based not on equal value but on mutual recognition and respect.[12] The lender gains prestige and influence by helping others in the community, and the borrower gains access to a valuable resource and a potential ally. In a traditional economic framework, the rational thing to do when lending the ox would be to negotiate terms that maximize the owner's personal benefit—perhaps by charging interest or by obligating the borrower to some future favor. But, rather than maximizing *or* satisficing, the Kabyle farmers adhered to strict social limitations that discouraged profit-seeking altogether. So, when Bourdieu points out that, "when self-interested calculation is openly revealed, it is sharply reproved," he's illustrating a form of socially bounded rationality.[13]

In this context, what might be considered the "best" financial course of action is bounded not by cognitive limitations but by social ones.

AVAILABILITY AND CONFIRMATION BIAS

Socially bounded rationality also applies to certain phenomena found in behavioral economics, such as the *availability bias*. Also known as the *recency bias*, it is our tendency to give more importance to recent or easily retrievable information, irrespective of its actual significance. This bias can result in poor decisions, as we underestimate older or harder-to-access, yet valuable, information. At the same time, it can lead us to overestimate the probability of recent events recurring, regardless of their actual likelihood. For instance, following reports of a plane crash or a shark attack, we may suddenly fear flying or swimming in the ocean. Yet, if you look at the numbers, flying is much safer than driving on a per-mile basis, and far more people succumb to drowning than are eaten by sharks.[14] In the same way, we may be drawn to buy shares of a trendy stock simply because it is making headlines, and not because it's actually a good investment.

Alongside recency, behavioral economists have identified another, similar irrational tendency known as *confirmation bias*: we have a propensity to seek out, prioritize, and affirm information that aligns with our already-held views, while we disregard or minimize anything that contradicts them. Consequently, our perception of reality can become quite skewed, reinforcing preexisting beliefs that may not accurately reflect the world around us. An investor already convinced that a specific stock is a lucrative buy may choose to read only news articles or analyst reports that support this belief, neglecting or discounting any information suggesting that the stock might be overpriced. Such confirmation bias can furthermore cause individuals to dig their heels deeper into their beliefs when they're confronted with new, contradictory evidence, as a sort of defense mechanism.[15] This can have serious implications for both individuals and society, as it can lead to the spread of misinformation, polarization, and divisiveness.

But where do these existing beliefs come from? Much like our preferences, our beliefs—even those we consider factual or scientific—are shaped by our social environments and interactions. From an early age, we absorb ideas, values, and "facts" from our families, schools, peer groups, the internet, and wider cultural contexts. These influences lay the foundation for our worldviews, determining what we consider credible, important, or even possible. Social boundaries can make certain information stand out while keeping us oblivious to other details, shaping our understandings of things like aviation safety, sharks, or the stock market. People often do try to make smart, informed decisions about the world, but their social networks and group memberships can bound their rationality, by essentially curating the types and sources of information that they are exposed to. For example, Americans with conservative political views might predominantly tune into Fox News, while those with liberal views may lean toward MSNBC. People naturally gravitate toward these particular news outlets as they align with their preexisting worldviews. Consequently, it becomes increasingly difficult to question the veracity of the information viewers receive, especially when others within their social circles follow the same channels. And accepting new or contradictory information becomes that much harder when it comes from less favored sources.

This urge to confirm and conform can result in "groupthink," where group loyalty supersedes independent thinking. Under such circumstances, even individuals with differing views might choose to suppress their personal opinions to preserve group harmony. As time passes, the spectrum of acceptable perspectives narrows until everyone aligns. To this point, in the United States these days, it's highly unlikely for a staunch conservative to even consider watching MSNBC or for a liberal to watch Fox News.

This sort of phenomenon extends beyond just news consumption—it can influence financial decisions too. Take the frenzy around "meme stocks" in 2020–21.[16] Online communities, like the *r/WallStreetBets* subreddit, championed the idea of buying and holding stocks from struggling companies like video game retailer GameStop and the movie theater chain AMC Entertainment. Despite the bleak financial outlook of these companies, their stock prices saw an unexpected surge as thousands of individual investors followed the online hype and bought shares. Initially, the group's goal was to engineer "short squeezes" to punish big institutional investors who were betting that these stock prices would fall.[17] It was a show of strength, asserting the collective influence of the little guy over Wall Street giants. But soon the meme stock craze turned into a speculative bubble, fueled by greed, fear of missing out, and herd mentality. As more and more novice investors jumped on the bandwagon, these stock prices became ever more detached from their fundamental values, creating an unsustainable situation that was bound to burst sooner or later. At its peak, the movement's ranks swelled to several million users, with the desire for social conformity and the sway of group norms playing an increasing role in the irrational exuberance that drove these stocks to extraordinary heights and kept them there for months.

Despite earnest warnings from financial experts and large investors, these online communities dismissed contradictory information as manipulation or "fake news" from threatened elites, creating an echo chamber that amplified and fortified their beliefs. Dissenting voices were ignored or silenced. Billionaire investor Leon Cooperman's public criticism of the GameStop surge, for example, was met with scorn and mockery by community members who saw him as representative of the very financial elite they were challenging.[18] Similarly, any group member urging caution about the unsustainable rise of a stock faced hostility, labeled as having "paper hands" (a derogatory term implying weakness and readiness to sell) and accused of betraying the group.[19]

Those rallying around meme stocks, in this way, even developed their own vernacular and codes of conduct. Community members started to refer to themselves in solidarity as "apes," borrowing the line "apes together strong!" from *Planet of the Apes*. They developed additional slogans (accompanied by corresponding emojis) like "diamond hands" 💎🙌 for holding firmly onto a stock despite short-term price drops, and "to the moon" 🚀🌙 to express their hopes for prices to skyrocket ever higher. These and other modes of behavior served more than just entertainment; they persuaded community members to cling to financially unsound investments and resist selling, even when these stock prices eventually started to tumble.

In this scenario, socially constructed boundaries played a pivotal role in defining the scope of available information that shaped investment decisions. These boundaries, reinforced by powerful group norms and a shared identity, circumscribed which facts were considered relevant and which options were perceived as viable. They not only filtered and curated the information that these investors were exposed to but also influenced how they interpreted and acted upon it. As a result, the decisions made within these boundaries were not simply the products of misguided individual choice but the outcome of the social context in which they were embedded.

Falling prey to these social dynamics can lead to dire consequences. By early 2023, the tale of these meme stocks unfolded as many had anticipated: GameStop shares had plunged to levels below their prefrenzy prices, and AMC shares, once soaring near $60, dwindled to around a mere $5 per share—costing those shareholders collectively billions of dollars—exactly what many financial experts had warned would happen.[20]

The Imitation Game

What happened with the meme stocks frenzy is not entirely new. Yes, social media and personal investment apps made the rapid assembly and mobilization of like-minded individuals more feasible than ever before. But the underlying "bandwagon" dynamics of this movement echo a much older, deeply ingrained pattern in the fabric of economic behavior: *imitation*.

In the 1800s, writers like Gustave Le Bon and Charles Mackay described how people swept up in a crowd lose their individual thinking and willingly adopt the collective mindset. This phenomenon, often referred to as "herd mentality" or "crowd psychology," has been observed in various economic contexts throughout history.[21] For instance, during the Dutch Tulip Mania of the 1630s, people frantically bought tulip bulbs at increasingly inflated prices, driven by the belief that others were profiting and that they would otherwise miss out. Similarly, the South Sea Bubble of 1720 saw investors pouring money into a company based on little more than rumors and the observation that others were doing the same.

In more recent times, we've seen this behavior manifest in the dot-com bubble of the late 1990s, where investors rushed to buy shares in internet-based companies, many of which had no clear path to profitability. The housing bubble that led to the 2008 financial crisis is another example, where the widespread belief that housing prices would continue to rise led to unsustainable levels of speculative investment and risky borrowing.

This tendency toward imitation is not just a quirk of financial markets but a fundamental aspect of human behavior. In the field of psychology, researchers have studied how imitation is important for learning new skills, communicating with others, and developing a sense of self. The discovery of "mirror neurons" in the 1990s showed that we are wired to empathize with and learn from others by observing and copying their actions.[22] Psychologists have found that mirroring is crucial for personal development, as it allows individuals to read others, form social bonds, and develop a sense of self in relation to the world around them.

Sociologists like Charles Horton Cooley have also pointed out that our sense of identity is formed through our interactions with others and our perceptions of how they see us. This "looking-glass self" concept emphasizes the social nature of identity formation, where imitation not only facilitates the adoption of certain behaviors and attitudes but also engages in a form of social reflection, seeing one's self as part of a larger community and understanding one's place within it.[23] In this way, imitation serves as a bridge for cultural transmission, enabling the spread of norms, traditions, and knowledge across generations.

The French social philosopher René Girard offers a provocative theory of imitation (which he called *mimesis*) that goes beyond mere copying. He argues that imitation is the very foundation of human desire and, to a certain degree, society itself.[24] According to Girard, we don't want things just because they're objectively good or useful, but because we see other people wanting them. Girard called this "mimetic desire." Imagine two children playing in a room full of toys. One child picks up a toy and starts playing with it. Suddenly, the other child, who wasn't interested in that toy before, now desperately wants it. The kids start fighting over the toy, each one claiming they wanted it first. The appeal isn't based on how great the toy is but on the fact that the other child wants it. Mimetic desire has placed the children in competition with one another, seeding various degrees of envy, rivalry, exclusion, and conflict over the coveted object.

This doesn't just happen with kids and toys. Think about the phrase "keeping up with the Joneses." It captures the pressure people feel to have the same nice things as their neighbors or friends. If your neighbor gets a fancy new car, you might feel like you need to get one too, even if it means going into debt. People even buy homes they can't really afford because they want to live in the same neighborhood as their peers. It's not just about the house itself but about the status and lifestyle it represents.[25] They may keep up with the Joneses but not with the mortgage.

This constant cycle of wanting what others have can lead to some pretty irrational behaviors. People might buy or upgrade to the latest gadgets or fashion trends, not because they really need or like them but because they don't want to feel left behind.[26] People may even pursue certain professions or work in industries not because of a genuine passion or aptitude but because they see others succeeding in those fields and want to emulate that success. The result is unsatisfying and unfulfilling career choices as individuals pursue paths that aren't well suited to their skills or interests.

When left unchecked, Girard believed that the drive for imitation could lead to serious conflict and destabilization within a society. If everyone is competing for the same things, it can create a lot of tension, resentment, and even lead to violence. To prevent this, he proposed that societies adopt "scapegoating mechanisms," where these hostile impulses are channeled onto a sacrificial victim rather than back onto themselves.[27] From medieval witch hunts to persistent racial discrimination and anti-Semitism to contemporary cancel culture, the scapegoating mechanism has manifested in various forms throughout history and across cultures. By uniting against a perceived common antagonist, groups are able to release pent-up tensions and restore social order.

But mimetic desire isn't always a bad thing. Girard also saw imitation as the glue that holds societies together. When people want the same things and follow the same trends, it creates a sense of belonging and solidarity—it is through shared desires and the construction of common enemies that communities are formed and maintained. From religious rituals to sports fandom to fashion statements, cultural institutions provide an outlet for the "violence" generated by mimetic rivalry and help channel imitation into socially acceptable forms. These institutions give people a way to compete and express themselves within a set of shared rules and meanings. When you wear your team's jersey or participate in a cultural festival, you're not just imitating others but also affirming your place in a community.

Of course, these cultural mechanisms aren't perfect. They can also reinforce social hierarchies, exclude people who are different, and sometimes mask deeper problems. And as Girard points out, the scapegoating mechanism can lead to terrible violence and injustice when the effects of mimetic rivalries are channeled onto vulnerable individuals or groups.

But Girard's theory has important implications for how we think about economic behavior and decision-making. It challenges the idea that we always make choices based on our own individual preferences and self-interest. Instead, it suggests that our economic desires and behaviors are deeply influenced by what we see others doing and wanting. This can help explain phenomena like bubbles and crashes in financial markets. When investors see others getting rich from a particular stock or asset, they may feel a strong desire to jump on the bandwagon, even if the underlying fundamentals don't justify the price, which eventually leads to inevitable corrections and panics.

Similarly, with consumption patterns, imitation can lead to wasteful and irrational spending. Are we buying things because they truly enrich our lives, or because we see others doing the same? Imitation, in this way, can fuel unsustainable levels of consumer debt and contribute to environmental problems like overconsumption and waste.

The forces of imitation do not stop at the level of individuals and their communities; they also shape the behavior of formal organizations and markets. We may think of businesses as being the pinnacle of rationality, driven purely by the profit motive, but companies have been known to rush to enter a market or launch a product just because their competitors are doing it.[28] They may even dive in without fully understanding the market, resulting in costly failures and wasted resources. The dot-com bubble is a classic case. Even companies that had nothing to do with technology rushed to invest in internet-related ventures, not because these companies had a clear plan or business model but because they were afraid of missing out on the digital gold rush. More recently, we've seen a similar phenomenon with the rush to adopt "green" or socially responsible business practices. While the goal of sustainability is laudable, many companies have jumped on the eco-friendly bandwagon without fully understanding what it entails or how it fits into their overall strategy. Some have even been accused of "greenwashing," making superficial environmental claims to boost their images without making substantive changes.

Imitative corporate behavior doesn't just affect product strategies. It can also shape fundamental business practices like hiring and even organizational structure. Many companies, especially in competitive fields like tech, will copy the hiring practices of industry leaders, even if those practices haven't been proven to be effective. For example, a lot of firms now use brainteasers and complex problem-solving tasks in their interviews, mimicking the hiring approach of giants like Google and Facebook. But there's little evidence that these methods are actually good at predicting job performance.[29] Similarly, the use of unpaid internships has become widespread in certain industries like finance and the media, largely because it's seen as the norm. But this practice often favors privileged candidates who can afford to work for free, and the internships may not provide much actual training or value.[30]

Academia is not immune to imitation either. Elite universities, in an effort to boost their prestige and rankings, will hire Nobel Prize laureates and other academic "superstars," even if these individuals are nearing the end of their careers and may contribute little in terms of teaching, research, or advising. While the presence of a Nobel laureate on the faculty can initially increase a university's visibility and funding, these effects are short-lived and do not necessarily translate into long-term institutional benefits.[31] Despite their high salary costs and the uncertain returns associated with these hires, universities continue to pursue them, in part because having a Nobel laureate on staff has become a marker of elite status in the academic world. Instead of focusing on developing and supporting promising young scholars or investing in innovative research programs, universities may be tempted to chase after big-name hires in a bid to keep up with their competitors. This can create a self-reinforcing cycle, where the perception of prestige becomes more important than actual impact.

The common thread in these examples is that organizations are imitating practices not because they are necessarily efficient, effective, or meaningful in their specific context but because they have become taken-for-granted expectations in their field. This kind of organizational mimicry, which scholars call "isomorphism," can be amplified by institutional pressures. Companies may feel like they *have to* conform to certain norms and expectations in order to be seen as legitimate in the eyes of investors, customers, and other key stakeholders.[32] They might implement a formal performance review process, not because they believe it will genuinely improve employee performance but because it's seen as a standard practice that any reputable company should have. Or they could develop formal codes of conduct and an employee handbook, not necessarily because they anticipate significant behavioral changes but because such documents are viewed as a basic requirement for a trustworthy organization. Deviating from such norms of legitimacy can be seen as risky or amateurish, even if the practices themselves are somewhat arbitrary, costly, or suboptimal.

"Irrational" Norms

Norms have been mentioned already several times, but what are they exactly? From a sociological perspective, norms are the informal rules, shared expectations, and compliance with cultural regimes that guide and constrain human behavior within a society or group.[33] These unwritten rules shape how individuals interact with one another, influencing everything from everyday etiquette to major life decisions. Sociologists view norms as a fundamental component of social structure, helping to maintain order, stability, and cohesion within communities.

This understanding differs somewhat from the psychological use of "norms," which tends to focus more on how individuals internalize and respond to social expectations.[34] Psychologists are most interested in the cognitive and emotional processes that underlie norm adherence or violation, and how norms interact with personal traits, motives, and beliefs. Sociologists are more concerned with why norms come to be and the broader patterns and consequences of normative behavior.

The sociological view also emphasizes that norms are socially constructed and collectively upheld, rather than being individual choices. Norms are seen as a key mechanism of socialization, through which individuals learn to participate in social life—they serve as a kind of social glue, providing a shared set of expectations and guidelines that allow individuals to coordinate their behavior and work together toward common goals. In this way, sociologists have argued that norms can help to solve various collective action problems, where otherwise individually rational behavior would lead to suboptimal outcomes for the group as a whole.[35] For example, norms of reciprocity and fairness can encourage individuals to contribute to public goods, even when they could personally benefit from free-riding on the contributions of others. Similarly, norms of trust and honesty can facilitate economic transactions by reducing the need for costly monitoring and enforcement mechanisms.

The social philosopher and political theorist Jon Elster wrote extensively about the tension between social norms and individual rationality.[36] Norms around civic responsibility encourage people to contribute to the public good even when it is not in their immediate best interest to do so, but because they feel an obligation to contribute. Norms that encourage people to give up their seats on public transportation for the elderly or disabled, or those that promote blood donation, may cause temporary discomfort for the individual, but society benefits from a more supportive environment that prioritizes the well-being of vulnerable members. Similarly, practices like tithing or philanthropy impart a personal expense but generate a societal gain. Norms developing around environmental responsibility, such as recycling, conserving water and energy, or reducing one's carbon footprint, also fit this pattern. While these actions may involve personal inconvenience or expense, they contribute to the long-term sustainability and health of the planet.[37]

Another type of social rule that can make people act apparently against their own best interests revolves around norms of reciprocity. This ingrained expectation compels us to return a favor or act of generosity—even if doing so requires a significant investment of time, effort, or resources. While this norm can nurture positive relationships and goodwill, it can sometimes lead people to act in ways that seem counterintuitive. A business manager might choose to work with a supplier who has given him a favorable deal in the past, even if a better offer is on the table from a new vendor. Similarly, in social situations, the norm of reciprocity may lead us to attend events or gatherings that we would rather avoid, simply because we feel obligated to return the invitation. We may also feel compelled to give gifts of comparable or even greater value to those we have received, even if doing so strains our budget or goes against our preferences. In the workplace, the norm of reciprocity can lead employees to take on tasks or responsibilities that are not formally part of their job description, simply because a coworker has helped them out in the past.[38]

The compulsion to reciprocate can even set off a cycle of escalating exchanges, with each party feeling obligated to outdo the previous gesture, culminating in a situation where the expense of reciprocation outstrips its initial social benefit. Imagine a scenario where a neighbor helps you fix a leaky faucet, spending a couple of hours of their weekend to lend a hand. Feeling indebted, you might bake them a cake as a token of appreciation. They, in turn, may feel obligated to return the favor by mowing your lawn or helping you paint your fence. As this cycle of reciprocation continues, the favors can become increasingly time-consuming and costly, potentially leading to a situation where both parties are investing significant resources into maintaining the exchange—even though the original issue (the leaky faucet) was relatively minor. In extreme cases, the escalation of favors can cause resentment or a sense of being overburdened, straining the very relationship the norm of reciprocity was meant to strengthen.

Elster also identifies norms that that seem to exist without benefiting anyone at all. He gives this example: Suppose you could pay someone to let you take their spot in a line. This would not hurt anyone. The other people in line would not lose their places. The person who got the offer could simply say no. Plus, if this were allowed, some people would be better off—but there is a norm against paying for someone's place in line—so that makes some people worse off (i.e., the person who wanted to pay and the person who wanted to take the money).[39] Another example is the taboo against discussing your salary with coworkers. Because people may feel uncomfortable talking about their income (some may suspect they are being paid more than they deserve, while others might fear they earn less than their colleagues), this norm can prevent them from discovering potential pay disparities or negotiating better compensation. By maintaining silence around salaries, employers stand to benefit from less pressure to address wage inequalities, so both individuals and society suffer from a lack of transparency (such as with the gender wage gap that often exists between men and women who have the same job title and duties). Or think about the norm against regifting, or passing along a gift you received to someone else. From a purely practical perspective, regifting could be seen as efficient: if you receive a gift that you cannot use or do not want, giving it to someone who would appreciate it more could maximize its utility. However, the stigma around regifting often leads people to hold onto unwanted items out of a sense of obligation or to avoid appearing ungrateful.[40] The result is a wasted resource as well as perhaps a missed opportunity to bring joy to someone else.

Interestingly, there are norms that people sometimes follow that seem to harm both the individual *and* society. Consider the norms around honor and revenge that persist in some cultures. The expectation that individuals must respond to perceived slights or insults with retaliatory violence can lead to cycles of escalating aggression and loss of life.[41] At the individual level, those who engage in honor-related aggression face violent recourse against themselves or their families, legal consequences, social stigma, and psychological trauma. At the societal level, these norms perpetuate a culture of violence, strain the criminal justice system, and hinder social cohesion and trust. Similarly, in some communities, norms of masculinity that emphasize toughness, aggression, and emotional suppression (e.g., "machismo") can harm both men and the society they live in.[42] Men who adhere to these norms may engage in risky behavior, neglect their health, and have difficulty forming deep emotional connections.[43] These norms also contribute to societal problems like domestic violence, sexual assault, and the stigmatization of mental health issues.[44]

Despite these potential drawbacks, norms often have a positive impact on society. Without norms, social interactions would be far more unpredictable and potentially chaotic. And by promoting mutual support and collaboration, norms help weave a tighter social fabric—even if it sometimes comes at a personal expense. But the cost of *not* following norms can be even steeper, including disapproval from peers, social isolation, and fractured relationships. The penalty for violating norms can range from mild discomfort to severe punishment, depending on the context.[45] These sanctions serve as a way of enforcing conformity and discouraging deviant behavior. The fear of social disapproval can indeed be a powerful motivator.

Note, however, that not all norm compliance is driven by the fear of sanction—we tend to follow certain norms even in the absence of any external enforcement or threat of punishment. We may conform to conventions—like greeting acquaintances, saying "bless you" after a stranger sneezes, or wearing the proper attire for specific occasions—simply to fit in or to be perceived as a good member of the community. This voluntary conformity underscores the deep-rooted human desire for acceptance and belonging. At other times, we abide by norms we've internalized as simply being the "proper" way to behave, even when there aren't any tangible consequences for noncompliance—like not wearing white after Labor Day, leaving a generous tip at a restaurant we'll never return to, or tapping a wine glass before making a toast.

These examples highlight the fact that norm compliance is not always a matter of conscious cost-benefit analysis. Much of our normative behavior is automatic and intuitive. We often follow norms without really thinking about why we're doing so, simply because it feels right or natural. This automatic, unreflective adherence to internalized norms has some significant advantages. It allows us to navigate the complexities of social life with relative ease, without having to constantly stop and deliberate over every action.[46] It provides a kind of social autopilot, freeing up mental resources for other tasks.

But unthinking, uncritical adherence to norms can lead to a kind of social inertia, where suboptimal practices persist simply because they are familiar and expected. This is where Elster's work can be particularly relevant. He points out a crucial difference between rational action and norm following: rational action is always concerned with achieving certain outcomes, while norms are not. Rationality might then be expressed as: "If you want to achieve a specific goal, take the action that will lead to that goal." In contrast, social norms are expressed as simply: "Do this specific action," or "Don't do this specific action," without reference to any particular outcome. More complex norms might be conditional: "If you find yourself in this situation, do this specific action," or "If others are doing this specific action, you should do it too." The key point is that these norms are justified not by their consequences but by their perceived appropriateness, regardless of personal discomfort or cost.

By layering Elster's framework onto anomalies identified by behavioral economists, we can develop a richer understanding of why people so often act in ways that seem irrational through a purely economic lens. Take the *status quo bias, regret aversion*, and *loss aversion*—closely related biases that lead us to maintain the current state of affairs. Our tendency to stick with the familiar and avoid losses is likely exacerbated by social norms around stability, loyalty, and risk-taking. The fear of being seen as flighty, disloyal, or reckless can amplify our natural reluctance to make changes or take risks, even when doing so could lead to better outcomes. This could help explain why people stay in suboptimal jobs, relationships, or investments long after the rational choice would be to move on.

Similarly, the *sunk cost fallacy*—the irrational commitment to continue with a losing course of action because of what we've already put into it—may be exacerbated by standards of commitment, loyalty, and "sticking it out." With norms around grit and perseverance that cast quitting as a character flaw, the pressure to throw good money after bad can be immense. Whether it's staying in a dead-end job, pouring resources into a failing business, or refusing to abandon an expensive but unused gym membership, the fear of being labeled a flake or a failure can keep us trapped in suboptimal situations even if the rational choice would be to cut our losses.

Or consider how the *endowment effect*, which is our natural tendency to overvalue what we already possess (and which we will see again in the next chapter), might be amplified by attitudes against wastefulness, norms of sentimentality, and the sanctity of personal property. In a society that places a high value on cherished possessions and frowns upon wastefulness, people may cling to outdated or inefficient items not just because of an irrational aversion to loss but also to signal their alignment with these deeply held views. The subconscious fear of being perceived by others as callous or wasteful can amplify our reluctance to part with things, even when doing so would be economically beneficial.

Elster's observation that norm following is often divorced from rational outcomes is particularly noticeable here. Many of our economic behaviors are guided not by a careful weighing of pros and cons but by an automatic, unthinking adherence to social expectations. We may miss out on bargains, forgo lucrative opportunities, or engage in financially suboptimal practices simply because it's "what people do," without ever pausing to consider whether these norms are truly serving our interests.

Social Capital's "Credit Slips"

We've discussed the roles of economic and cultural capital in the last chapter. Now, let's focus on *social capital*, which refers to the resources you can tap into through your social relationships and connections. These resources can be anything from valuable information and emotional support to opportunities and favors that people in your network may provide. The amount of social capital you possess is therefore closely linked to the quality and extent of your social connections. The sociologist James Coleman, a key theorizer of social capital, noted that it is unique in that it exists within the relationships *between* people, rather than being a property of the individual or of physical assets.[47] In other words, while economic and cultural capital are both things you possess, social capital is built on what you share in your relationships with others.

Coleman thought of social capital as like a system of credit slips, or IOUs accumulated through interactions with others. If you perform a kind act for someone, it's often assumed that they'll return the favor someday. This sense of future reciprocation forms a sort of obligation to be redeemed—a social "I owe you"; the more IOUs you have and the more varied their sources, the richer your social capital. This type of social wealth can then be leveraged to meet your objectives by calling in favors when needed.

Take a moment to ponder: Who could you turn to if you urgently needed to borrow a car? Who do you know that could provide assistance if something in your home broke? Do you have any acquaintances who could alert you about job openings if you were to lose your job? How many people could you convince to meet you at a bar to commiserate on short notice?

If you had no trouble naming names, then you probably have plenty of social capital at your disposal. On the other hand, if you found this exercise difficult or felt uncertain, it might signal a need to broaden and deepen your social connections. Ultimately, the amount of social capital available and how much advantage it can grant depends on the structure and features of your social networks themselves.[48]

Like other types of capital, social capital is not evenly distributed among society's members. Those with more robust social networks tend to have greater access to opportunities, resources, and support systems. This can reinforce and magnify existing disparities. Coleman points to the example of a tight-knit farming community, where "one farmer gets his hay baled by another and where farm tools are extensively borrowed and lent—the social capital allows each farmer to get his work done with less physical capital in the form of tools and equipment." Meanwhile, "in other social structures where individuals are more self-sufficient, depending on each other less, there are fewer of these credit slips outstanding at any time."[49] Individuals within a particular social structure also differ in terms of the amount of social capital which they can draw on at a given time. For instance, in an extended family structure with a clear hierarchy, the patriarch might hold a significant number of these social IOUs, capable of calling them in at any moment to achieve his goals.

The "credit slips" of social capital, unlike tangible resources, can be more difficult to quantify or exploit. Their worth is highly context-dependent and can change over time as relationships evolve. A favor owed by a childhood friend might be more valuable in a personal crisis, while a professional connection might be more useful when seeking job opportunities. Furthermore, it's important to note that social capital is not just about "taking." One of the most effective ways to build social capital is to "give"—to be generous with your time, resources, and support. By doing so, you are investing in a kind of communal wealth that goes beyond just economic riches.

The social capital perspective emphasizes the ways in which social networks and relationships can create value that traditional economic models or individual psychological processes cannot easily account for. But we can also think about how people can exploit social capital in a self-interested way. Some people may extend informal "IOUs" knowing that they can later be leveraged for personal gain. By doing favors (even unwanted ones), they create obligations, and this can be seen as a type of insurance policy with inexpensive premiums that may provide valuable benefits in the future. For example, someone might regularly offer their time and expertise to colleagues, not just out of goodwill but also with an understanding that these colleagues could be more inclined to support them when they need assistance on a project or result in greater job security in the future. At the same time, a self-interested individual may choose to avoid receiving favors from others to prevent the creation of a social debt that they would rather not have to repay. Or such individuals may choose to repay favors only when it suits them best, rather than when the other person needs it the most.

*

Concepts like imitation, embeddedness, social norms, and social capital offer a broader perspective on economic behavior than traditional behavioral economics, emphasizing the crucial role of social context. While behavioral economics focuses on individual cognitive biases, these socially oriented concepts highlight how our economic decisions are shaped by our social networks, cultural norms, and collective behaviors. For instance, social imitation explains how trends cascade through markets, embeddedness theory shows how economic actions are intertwined with social networks, and social capital theory demonstrates how nonfinancial assets influence economic outcomes. By integrating these social concepts with insights from behavioral economics, we can develop a more comprehensive understanding of economic behavior that accounts for both individual psychology and the complex social environments in which we operate, explaining phenomena that individual-focused approaches might overlook. This social dimension of decision-making becomes particularly evident when we consider how people distinguish between "us" and "them" in their economic choices.

In-Group/Out-Group Bias

Imagine you're walking down the street and you see someone in need of help. Maybe they're struggling to carry some heavy bags or asking for spare change. How likely are you to help them? Your decision, of course, will be influenced by a number of factors, including your mood, if you are in a hurry, and whether other people are around who might be able to help instead. One particularly powerful influence on our behavior in such situations is our perception of whether that person is part of our "in-group" or "out-group."

In-group bias is the tendency to favor and help those who are members of our own social groups, even if we have never met them before or have little in common with them beyond group membership. Think of it as a deep-seated tribal mentality, where you might inherently favor someone just because they share your nationality, political views, or even your devotion to a particular sports team. Let's consider a few examples. Research has revealed that alumni from the same institution are more inclined to recommend one another for job opportunities.[50] Likewise, voters often cast their ballots in favor of a candidate from their political party, despite lacking full understanding of the candidate's policies or their alignment with personal values.[51] On a less serious but equally fascinating note, diehard sports fans often experience a strong bond with fellow fans of their home team, sharing collective highs and lows that correspond with the team's victories or defeats. In some extreme instances, this solidarity can even drive fans to act aggressively toward supporters of rival teams.[52]

Such negative attitudes and behaviors toward those external to the group are known as *out-group bias*. The tendency here is to be more critical and less helpful toward those who we perceive to be members of different social groups, which can result in animosity, discrimination, and a host of other social repercussions. These biases are significant because they can fuel serious societal issues such as racism, xenophobia, and exclusion. Because of this, social scientists have sought to better understand their impact on decision-making through the use of experimental games like the Dictator Game and the Prisoner's Dilemma, both used extensively in behavioral economics. In these "games," participants are placed in simulated situations where they must make decisions that can either benefit themselves or benefit others to varying degrees.

In the Dictator Game, one player (the "dictator") is given a sum of money and has the power to decide how much, if any, of that money to give to another player. The receiving player has no say in the matter and is simply given whatever amount the dictator decides. This setup is frequently used to study concepts such as fairness, altruism, and generosity. Several studies show that when the "dictators" are told they are part of the same group as the other player (e.g., the same nationality, ethnicity, or even something as simple and arbitrary as being on the "blue team" vs. the "red team"), they are more likely to behave altruistically, even when it comes at a personal cost. However, when the dictators see the other player as belonging to a different group, they more often lean toward self-interest, keeping a larger share of the money for themselves. Research has found that the distinction between being in-group and out-group can be based on a wide range of categories, with family and kinship ties being the most powerful source of identity.[53] Other impactful groupings include political and religious affiliations, cultural beliefs, club memberships, a shared workplace, and sports team allegiance.

Notably, gender does not appear to serve as a basis for oppositional identity.[54]

The Prisoner's Dilemma is another classic economics game that has been widely used to study cooperation and strategic thinking. This scenario involves two players who are faced with a hypothetical choice of either cooperating together or defecting, and their combined decision determines their payoffs (the original example involved two "convicts" deliberating whether to rat the other out or remain silent). An individual's payoff is maximized if one player defects while the other cooperates, but mutual cooperation results in the highest combined payoff. The temptation to defect, though, is strong, since a player can receive a higher amount by betraying their partner—but if both act in their own self-interest, each will end up worse off. This makes the Prisoner's Dilemma a handy device to explore what influences decision-making when self-interest is in tension with prosocial or mutual interests. As with the Dictator Game, individuals have been found to favor members of their own group in the Prisoner's Dilemma, leading to higher levels of cooperation within groups and greater competition between them. Individuals also tend to believe that partners who are in their in-group would likewise be more cooperative with them.[55]

The impact of identity-based favoritism and discrimination extends into everyday life, carrying serious implications. It has been found to influence where people make charitable donations and who they vote for. It also biases jury decisions.[56] In-group preference has been found among corporate hiring managers for both job candidate recruitment and promotion.[57] It appears among hospital administrators during resident selection.[58] Supposedly self-interested venture capitalists, too, prefer to fund start-ups whose teams share a similar professional background and education to their own.[59] And in India, a team of researchers discovered that borrowers belonging to the same caste as loan officers receive better terms—lenders who share cultural similarities with borrowers were more likely to approve loans, assign them higher credit ratings, and offer lower interest rates.[60]

Collectively, this research illuminates how our group identities and biases can have a potent influence on our behaviors, even when self-interest might seem more important. Often, in-group and out-group biases are so deeply ingrained that we are not consciously aware of how they affect our decision-making. This can be particularly concerning in situations where individual decisions aggregate to have significant economic or social impacts on others.

The Many Faces of Economic Behavior

The goal of this book is to shed light on the often underappreciated ways in which social factors shape the our economic thinking. However, this isn't an attempt to dismiss the valuable contributions from fields like traditional economics, behavioral economics, or psychology. Rather, think of it as expanding our ability to examine economic behavior by building bridges and making connections with perspectives offered by sociology.

Economic behavior is, therefore, far from being a one-dimensional issue. And it's not something can be explained by one theory alone—psychological, sociological, or otherwise. It's an amalgam of many elements: individual self-interest, cognitive biases, social networks, interpersonal relationships, and cultural contexts, among others. These elements, while they may be practically siloed in their respective academic disciplines, are rather interconnected when it comes to real-world decision-making. When making decisions about money or resources, people draw from and blend these diverse factors. And this blend isn't set in stone; it adapts depending on the circumstances. For instance, in some situations, the drive for personal gain might guide us toward a more rational-seeming choice. In other scenarios, cultural expectations or the opinions of our friends and family might weigh more heavily. As we navigate different situations, the blend shifts, reconfiguring how much each factor contributes to our decision-making process.

How can we understand this composite nature of economic behavior? It's not always clear which considerations take priority when we're making money choices. How can we distinguish just which factors come to the fore, and when? So far, this understanding has remained elusive—the layers of complexity and dynamism in decision-making make it challenging to isolate and measure the relative importance of each factor. And disciplinary boundaries that have been drawn between economics, psychology, sociology, and other fields have hindered the integration of different perspectives. But what if we could take a more unified, interdisciplinary approach? What if we had a tool that could help us peel back these layers and shine a light (even if it's still a dim one) on the underlying mechanics?

Enter *conjoint analysis*, a statistical technique that allows researchers to examine just how individuals weigh and prioritize the different elements involved in a complex choice. It does this by presenting people with hypothetical options that combine various attributes in different ways and asking them to make choices between these options. For example, imagine you're looking to buy a new smartphone. You'd likely consider several factors simultaneously like brand, battery life, price, storage, color, and more. Conjoint analysis can evaluate the often unconscious trade-offs people make between those attributes and determine which of them tips the scales. We may find that price point matters a lot, but brand name dominates in overall importance for the purchase decision, while color is comparatively the least important consideration. By systematically varying the attributes of the options presented and analyzing the patterns in people's choices, researchers can uncover the relative importance of each factor in the decision-making process in a data-driven manner.[61]

Conjoint analysis has been used extensively in marketing and consumer science but less so in sociology and economics. Still, we can adapt this method to explore the interplay between various influences when it comes to economic decision-making. Let's say you're buying household furniture from a private seller. Would you just go for the cheapest option? Or might you pay more to a seller you know and trust? Both economic costs and social relationships likely matter—but to what degree? What if you are buying a car instead of a sofa—do the priorities shift? When lending money, is friendship quality more vital than interest rates?

By incorporating economic considerations like price alongside sociological factors like the embeddedness of ties, interpersonal dynamics, demographic characteristics and more into the hypothetical exchange scenarios, conjoint analysis can shine a light on these hidden corners of our decision-making processes, revealing what truly matters to us when money is on the line.

In the early 2000s, two sociologists, Vincent Buskens and Jeroen Weesie, ventured into similar terrain. They used conjoint methods to understand what influences people's decisions to buy from used car dealers, offering hypothetical scenarios with varying dealer attributes while emphasizing their degree of embeddedness. What they found was enlightening. Prospective car buyers weren't merely driven by price. Instead, they showed a preference for dealers with whom they shared social connections—those embedded relationships acted as a sort of safety net, allowing potential buyers to tap into others' past experiences and hold the dealer accountable if any issues occurred post-purchase.[62] Who you're dealing with matters when making economic decisions.

The level of social embeddedness is, therefore, likely a critical factor—most people would probably feel more at ease lending money to a close friend versus a passing acquaintance or a complete stranger. The quality and current standing of the interpersonal relationship is also prone to carry significant weight: you may typically be willing to lend money to a close friend, but what if you've had a recent falling out or a breach of trust? Chances are that would give you serious pause. This suggests it's not just about familiarity or tie strength alone. Societal biases and characteristics like race, gender, politics, and religion could also subconsciously shape informal economic decisions, even if we wish it were not the case. People may feel an instinctive inclination to transact with those they see as part of their same demographic in-group. What's unclear is just how much such social factors or biases might matter when weighed against more objective economic factors like the financial terms or dollar amounts involved.

To explore these dynamics, I designed a conjoint study that presented participants with a set of hypothetical informal economic scenarios. In each scenario, participants were shown ten pairs of potential exchange partners, each with varying social and economic attributes. Social attributes included social proximity (e.g., immediate family, close friend, stranger), relationship quality, and demographics like race and gender. Economic attributes included price, quality of goods, and financial terms. Each attribute contained multiple levels to represent different possible values or states. For instance, the "price" attribute might have levels like $500 vs. $100, while "relationship quality" could range from "excellent" to "poor." These levels allowed for a comprehensive exploration of how different combinations of attribute values influence decisions. Participants then chose their preferred exchange partner from each pair. By analyzing patterns across these choices, I could measure and parse how people prioritize the trade-off among social and economic factors in their decisions. (For an example, see fig. 3.1.)

While not a perfect solution, conjoint analysis provides a unique quantitative lens for focusing on the motivations, both "economic" and "social," that guide our actions and choices. It inevitably simplifies complex theories about economic behavior by distilling them down to just a handful of stylized elements. However, the goal here isn't to comprehensively test or validate entire theories in their purest, most comprehensive forms. Rather, the aim is to extract key insights from various theoretical perspectives and explore how they manifest and interact in realistic informal economic settings. The attributes and levels represented in the conjoint study serve as approximations, allowing us to deconstruct the complex process of economic

(7/10) you are interested in buying a used car. Below are some characteristics of each potential seller. Choose your preferred option below:

	Seller 1	Seller 2
Relation to you:	A close family member or friend	An old acquaintence
Personal impression of seller:	You like them a lot	You don't like them very much
Reputation of the Seller:	2 stars on a website that rates sellers	5 stars on a website that rates sellers
Quality of the car	Luxury vehicle	Low-end economy vehicle
Race:	Latino	Asian
Religion:	Jewish	Jewish
Gender:	Male	Male
Politics	Centrist independent	Centrist independent
Price offered by the seller:	$8000.00	$5000.00
	○	○

Figure 3.1: Example conjoint analysis pair evaluating potential used car sellers

decision-making in a more tractable way. The elements don't need to capture the absolute nuances of each theory, but they do need to provide enough fidelity to identify their relative influences when economic choices intermingle with social contexts and interpersonal dynamics.

INFORMAL EXCHANGE: WHAT REALLY MATTERS WHEN WE BUY AND SELL

Imagine you're browsing through an online marketplace for some household furniture. You find two private sellers: one is a family friend offering a nice sofa but at a high price; and the other is an affable stranger with a 5-star rating offering a similar sofa at a lower price. Whom do you choose? Does your choice change if the stranger's seller rating is only 3 stars? Does the price of the sofa trump everything else? Unlike surveys that ask respondents to self-report their preferences, conjoint analysis measures revealed preferences by confronting subjects with realistic trade-off scenarios.

In the first of a set of conjoint studies, I asked hundreds of respondents to imagine a scenario where they were either buying or selling a used sofa from another individual for cash (as opposed to a furniture store or financed purchase).[63] Several details varied systematically—like the price and quality of the sofa, the seller's online reputation rating, how much they know and how well they liked the seller personally, their gender and race, religion and politics.[64]

The results showed that for this type of transactional decision, objective economic considerations tended to dominate—but social factors nonetheless played a meaningful role (see fig. 3.2a and fig. 3.2b). Sofa buyers cared most about getting a quality product at a fair price, but they also significantly valued purchasing from a seller with a good reputation. Sofa sellers were likewise motivated primarily by getting the best possible price. However, they too exhibited significant concern about their social standings and how others perceived them.

Interestingly, I found sellers weren't just singularly trying to off-load lower quality goods for a quick buck. They demonstrated a notable preference for selling higher quality items

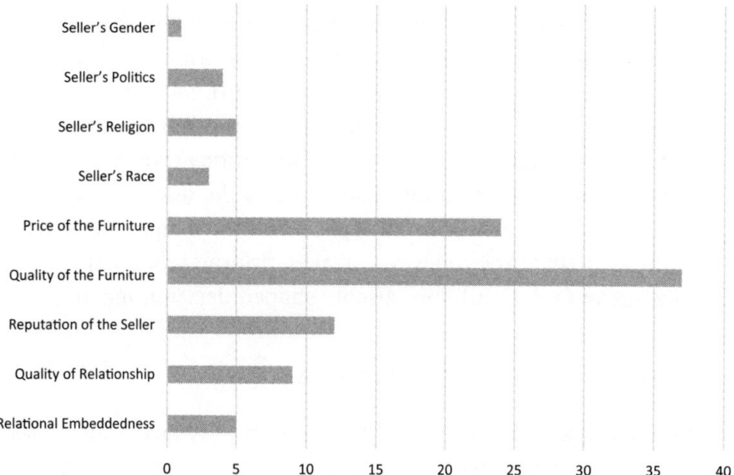

Figure 3.2a: Conjoint preference share (%) when buying a used sofa

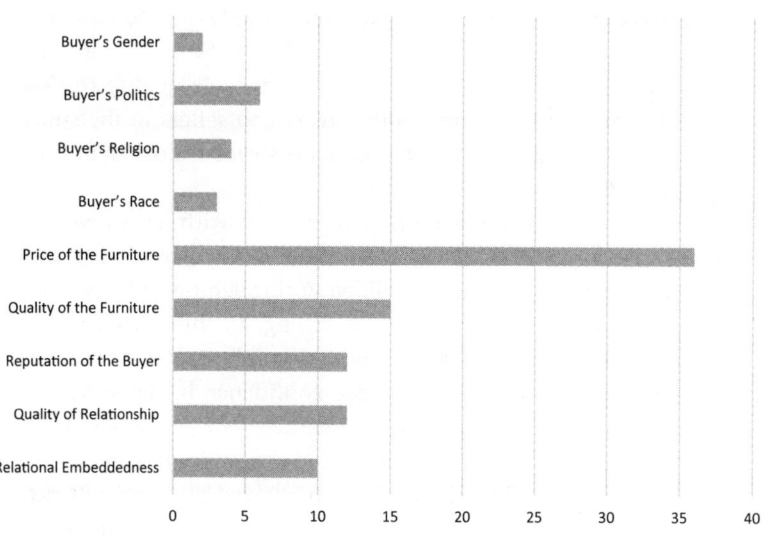

Figure 3.2b: Conjoint preference share (%) when selling a used sofa
Note: Preference share totals add up to 100%.

as well—suggesting seller motivations extend beyond just economic gain. Maintaining a positive reputation and avoiding strained relationships appeared to be additional priorities.

In contrast, demographic factors like the buyer's or seller's gender, race, religion, and political affiliations proved to be relatively minor considerations compared to the other variables.

So while the core financial aspects like price and quality were paramount in a relatively low-stakes transactional setting like this, social factors still measurably shaped decision-making.

RAISING THE STAKES: THE CAR MARKET

Now consider a scenario where you're in the market for a used car from a private party in an all-cash deal (as opposed to purchasing from a dealership or getting it financed).[65] Buying or selling a car represents a bigger financial decision compared to something like a sofa. Cars are more expensive, these deals occur less frequently, and there's greater uncertainty around potential mechanical issues or unseen wear and tear. So in the private-party used car market, while price and vehicle quality remain paramount considerations, both buyers and sellers in the study placed significantly more emphasis on social factors than they did for sofas.

Buyers want confidence they're dealing with a trustworthy seller. And sellers, too, care about the buyer's credibility and reliability when it comes to following through on full payment. Regardless of whether buying or selling, in this higher-stakes transactional context there's a notable preference for transacting with parties that inspire more confidence in the social dimensions of the deal. We like to interact with people we deem trustworthy, even if it sometimes costs a bit more money or nets a bit less profit. The relationship's perceived quality itself carries intrinsic value that can outweigh just the purely financial aspects. Here, demographic factors like gender, race, religion, and politics fade even further into the background compared to these more personally relevant social considerations (see fig. 3.3a and fig. 3.3b).[66]

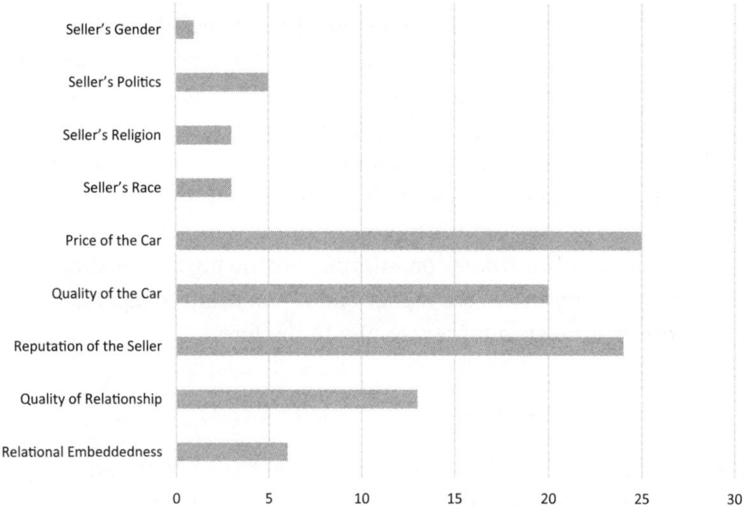

Figure 3.3a: Conjoint preference share (%) when buying a used car

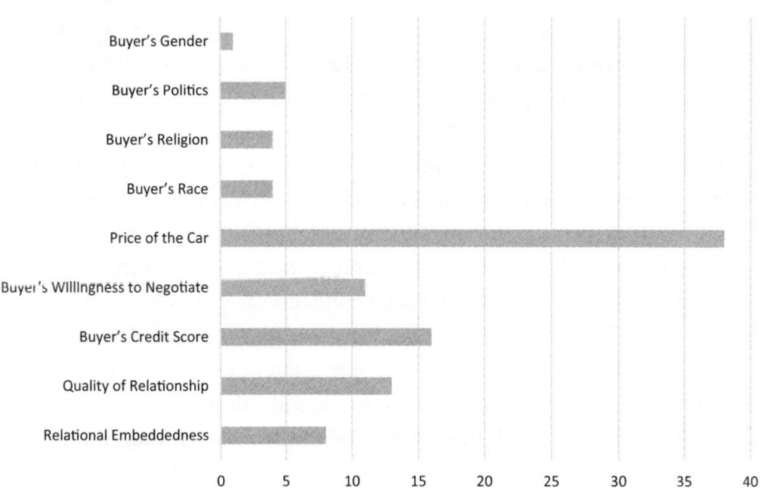

Figure 3.3b: Conjoint preference share (%) when selling a used car
Note: Preference shares add up to 100%.

While straightforward economic incentives like price and quality still loom large, the elevated stakes of a used car transaction compel people to more heavily prioritize and place value on the social aspects of the exchange relationship. So when economists or sociologists debate whether "social" or "economic" factors are what matters in effecting transactions, the truth is that they both do, and that it depends.

The next set of studies on informal borrowing and lending reveal that when stakes are higher and relationships deeper, social factors emerge even more strongly to the fore.

INTERPERSONAL LOANS: IT'S A DIFFERENT GAME

Let's examine a context of informal exchange that can carry even higher personal stakes than buying a used car: borrowing or lending money from people you know.[67] When it comes to interpersonal loans, the relationship itself takes center stage, often overshadowing concerns around financial terms like interest rates or repayment amounts. Unlike one-off transactions, loans create lasting obligations between the parties involved. We're not just evaluating dry economic factors but grappling with the significant emotional and social implications of owing (or being owed) money to (by) someone we know personally.

As a result, the study shows that people tend to strongly prefer borrowing and lending within their close social circles, where levels of trust, mutual understanding, and implicit responsibility run deepest. Both borrowers and lenders prioritize the quality of their past relationship and direct social connection, even above securing the most favorable terms. The degree of personal familiarity and positive prior history with a potential lender or borrower becomes more influential than purely economic self-interest would predict.

Additionally, both borrowers and lenders weigh the moral dimensions behind a loan request. Lenders consider the legitimacy of the loan's purpose—being more willing to help for essentials like medical bills versus perceived indulgences like vacations. Meanwhile, borrowers hesitate asking from those already financially stretched themselves. There are implicit social norms that appear to be activated around the appropriateness of both requesting and granting these personal loans.

It's worth noting that borrowers, perhaps driven by a more pressing need to secure a loan, appear somewhat more sensitive to the financial aspects compared to lenders. However, borrowers still place a high value on the social rapport and closeness with potential lenders. Both sides recognize that treating these personal loans as cold and impersonal can risk jeopardizing the relationship over the long term, where preserving mutual trust and interpersonal understanding supersedes dollars and cents (fig. 3.4a and fig. 3.4b).

Unlike simpler, more transactional contexts, personal loans can upset the balance of power, influence reputation, and shake up status within a social network.[68] We all probably know someone who has developed a reputation for unreliable repayment. Their poor track record becomes common knowledge, garnering side-eyes at social gatherings and undermining their standing within the group. On the flip side, someone who lends money readily when asked and doesn't aggressively demand repayment tends to gain a certain respect. Their generosity accentuates their social capital and perceived trustworthiness within the group. Of course, this can be taken advantage of too. It's a tricky balance.

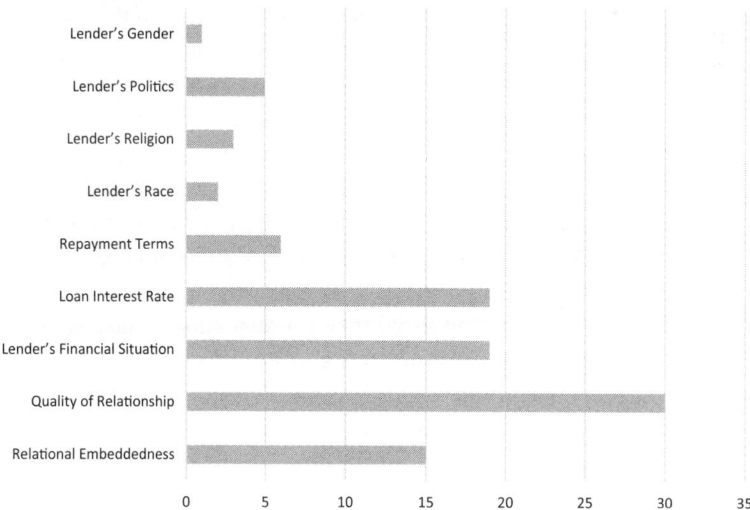

Figure 3.4a: Conjoint preference share (%) in the context of informal borrowing

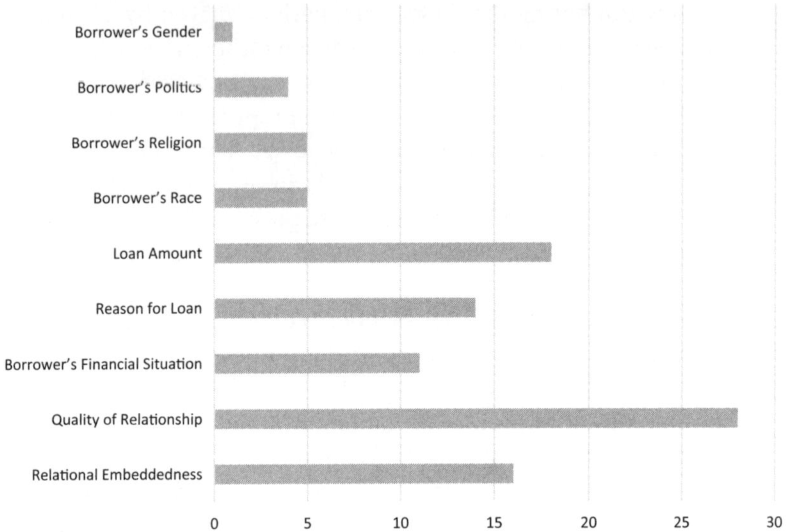

Figure 3.4b: Conjoint preference share (%) in the context of informal lending
Note: Preference shares add up to 100%.

Our relationships and moral views clearly shape economic decisions, and different theoretical traditions offer pieces to this puzzle. Each approach has its merits, and together they paint a fuller picture of why we make the choices we do. For instance, both embeddedness and relationality (covered in the next chapter) agree that social relationships matter for economic behavior, but they approach it from different angles: embeddedness considers how people are connected in a network, while relationality looks at how people interact with each other one-on-one. So, they both would agree that social relationships matter but disagree on exactly what makes them important.

When we combine the insights of rational choice and behavioral economics with elements of sociology, we get a more well-rounded and nuanced picture of why people behave the way they do. This cross-pollination invites us to challenge our assumptions, expand our perspectives, and ultimately develop a more holistic approach to analyzing economic phenomena in the real world.

*

Economic behavior does not occur in a social vacuum. Group identities and social networks profoundly influence our economic attitudes and actions. Through mechanisms like imitation, social validation, and norms, our social circles shape preferences and sway behaviors. Factors like trust, reputation, and relationship concerns often override pure self-interest, especially among close network ties. Empirical evidence affirms this, where shared social connections strongly guide behaviors from hiring choices to used car purchases and lending preferences.

Our social environments also filter information in ways that bolster certain beliefs while dismissing others. Concepts like socially bounded rationality demonstrate how group norms delimit which ideas are considered relevant or viable. Peer pressure and effects like "groupthink" can further entrench suboptimal behaviors. As a result, critical views can get suppressed in order to maintain group coherence. The prevalence of in-group favoritism and out-group discrimination provides further evidence that social groups and identities unconsciously shape behaviors. A range of experimental games reveals systematic preference for one's own identity groups, a favoritism that surreptitiously influences outcomes from charitable giving to corporate hiring and resource allocation.

In addition to economic and cultural resources, we also can utilize social capital—the value inherent in the relationships and networks that we have with others, and the resources and benefits that we can access through them. Social capital can help us to achieve our personal and professional goals, to enhance our well-being and happiness, and to contribute to the common good of society. By calling in accumulated "favors" or "credit" through network ties, social capital furnishes a form of advantage invisible to traditional economic accounting. However, the distribution of social capital is uneven, concentrated around well-connected individuals and groups who can effectively leverage it for personal gain.

In the economic game, what looks like irrational behavior might be perfectly reasonable within the context of someone's social environment. They might spend a large portion of their paycheck on an expensive status symbol, like designer clothing, or else invest a significant amount of time and resources into a seemingly unprofitable business venture. To an outside observer, these might seem like wasteful, irrational choices. But within the context of the individual's social circle, say, where status is heavily tied to visible displays of wealth or entrepreneurial risk-taking, the choices make sense. They are playing by the hidden rules of their particular social games, even if those rules are not apparent to outsiders.

4 * A Relational Balance Sheet: The Art and Science of Mixing Friends, Family, and Finances

In the previous chapters, we looked at how our economic choices are greatly influenced by overarching social structures: the culture we grow up in, our place in society, and the social circles we belong to. These inescapable circumstances create a sort of subconscious default setting in our minds, guiding economic actions in generally predictable directions, with our lived experiences acting like a feedback loop, confirming or challenging these presets and subtly altering our views and actions over time. This is why someone raised in an entrepreneurial family may internalize certain assumptions about risk-taking and start a business, while someone from an hourly wage background might have a more cautious personal financial philosophy. It helps explain why a recent college graduate surrounded by peers with student loan debt and gig economy jobs would have different consumption habits than their parents, who came from a generation where stable, full-time employment right out of college was the norm.

While we cannot escape the gravity of these broader social currents, our economic lives ultimately play out through a myriad of more microlevel, interpersonal interactions and relationships. This means that economic choices and behavior will change depending on who the person is that we are directly dealing with: friends, family, coworkers, or casual acquaintances. Relational categories like "friend," "spouse," "colleague," or even "stranger" each carry their own socially encoded scripts around expected economic behaviors. Being cast into the role of "old friend" may compel us to act with generous flexibility when negotiating a deal, while "coworker" primes us for more formality and adherence to organizational protocols. On an interpersonal level, it is not the network position or strength of the tie itself that primarily guides behavior but rather the negotiated meaning and situational norms attached to each relation.

Our interpersonal connections are moreover colored by specific relational histories—how long we've known that particular person, the intimacy of the relationship, our subjective feelings toward them, whether we like them or not. This relational context temporarily alters our baseline sense of identity, priorities, and motivations when interacting, which has a direct impact on how we think and what we feel appropriate in various situations.

Take dining out as an example. You might normally opt for a steak when eating alone, but if you're sharing a meal with a vegetarian friend, relational awareness may lead you to go for a pasta option instead. You adapt your food preference not only to be polite but to send certain social cues in the moment that reinforce the type of relationship you have (or hope to have) with your companion. Even the tip you leave after the meal can shift significantly based on who you're with. You might match a good friend's 15% tip to signal equal status and mutual respect. Or if out with a new romantic interest, a generous 25% tip could convey your generosity, financial capability, or overall desirability. On the other hand, if dining with notoriously frugal relatives, leaving anything above 10% might draw unwelcome comments about being careless with money. Who you are dining with subtly modulates your behavior—your companions' very presence fundamentally transforms your available options, priorities, and motivations in the moment—often without even realizing the contextual subtleties at play.

Micro adjustments in economic behavior based on relational context are so common that they become almost second nature. Yet they underscore how our economic selves are not fixed, monolithic entities but rather dynamically constructed based on the specific situations we find ourselves in. Continuing with the dining out example, you might be more inclined to split the bill evenly when out with colleagues, even if you ordered less, to maintain workplace harmony. When dining with a respected elder or mentor, you might allow them to pay for the meal without protest, respecting their seniority or expressing gratitude for their guidance. With family, you might insist on paying the entire bill to show care or assert your financial independence. We're constantly adjusting our in-the-moment rationalities to fit the granular relational cues and interpersonal dynamics at play when money is involved.

Whether it's splitting the bill, lending money, or buying gifts, our exchange partners are frequently people we know and who are the closest to us. This chapter spotlights how these interpersonal relationships and the relational work involved in maintaining them play an often unseen role in shaping financial decision-making. The sociologist Viviana Zelizer offers a solid framework for exploring this angle. Her perspective reveals the myriad ways in which money and economic transactions become intertwined with the social relations involved, and her work challenges the traditional view of money as merely a neutral medium of exchange.

Zelizer argues that individuals engage in "relational work" to negotiate the often thorny terrain of mixing money with friends and family. This work involves setting boundaries, managing expectations, and negotiating the emotional and symbolic meanings attached to financial transactions with friends and family. We earmark funds for specific people or purposes based on its origin and the relationships involved, adhering to unspoken rules about appropriate monetization in different social contexts. Moreover, we use economic exchanges as a tool to send social signals, reinforce bonds, and define the nature of our relationships—often serving purposes far beyond mere economic utility.

These relational considerations can lead us to make financial decisions that deviate from classical economic rationality. For example, we may choose to hire a less skilled family member over a stranger who is more qualified for a job. We may insist on treating a close friend to a shared cab ride home but meticulously split the fare with a casual acquaintance. We might hesitate to charge a family member interest on a loan, even if we would readily do so with a friend. Or we may put extra thought and spend more time on a sibling's birthday gift than a wedding present for a colleague, even if the objective value of the gifts is similar.

People tend to load money with specific relational meaning, transforming it from a neutral medium of exchange into a symbol of social bonds and emotional commitments. This process of "earmarking" imbues financial resources with significance far beyond their monetary value, tying them inextricably to particular relationships or shared aspirations. When parents open college savings accounts for their children, they are making an emotional and symbolic investment in their children's future. The money becomes relationally earmarked from parent to child, carrying with it the weight of parental love, sacrifice, and aspirations for their success. Those monthly deposits come to represent hopes and dreams far more than mere dollars and cents. Similarly, when these parents are planning a dream vacation together, they aren't just budgeting income and expenses—the spare change put into the vacation jar becomes earmarked for one another, deepening their bonds of intimacy and shared commitment by imagining future memories.

These relational earmarks also shape priorities and trade-offs in financial decision-making. That couple might gladly use up their vacation savings and then take on credit card debt to fund their dream trip if needed. However, they wouldn't dare dream of touching their child's college fund. From a traditional economics perspective, this behavior seems irrational. After all, using existing savings (like the college fund) to avoid high-interest credit card debt—especially in the case of an emergency—would be the most cost-effective choice.[1] These choices do not always make "economic sense," but they're perfectly understandable when you factor in the emotional, moral, and symbolic significance of those earmarked monies.

Economics has long operated under the assumption of "fungibility"—the idea that all money is perfectly interchangeable and substitutable: a dollar set aside for retirement should be no different than a dollar for paying utility bills or buying groceries. A dollar earned from your employer should similarly be worth the exact same amount as a dollar gifted by a grandparent. Earmarking, and the relational perspective more broadly, upend this assumption. Indeed, the dollar with a grandparent's earmark is likely more "valuable" than the employer's. We routinely infuse different money with symbolic meaning and emotional energy based on its social connections—filling some dollars but not others with a sense of moral obligation, urging us to use them in a way that honors the giver's intentions and values. A dollar can be worth "more" or "less" to you than $1 because of who it's connected to.

Relationally Endowed: What Can We Learn from a Coffee Mug?

David Rockefeller, grandson of John D. Rockefeller and former CEO of Chase Bank once said, "I am convinced that material things can contribute a lot to making one's life pleasant; but, basically, if you do not have very good friends and relatives who matter to you, life will be empty and sad and material things cease to be important." Many people, no doubt, agree with this idea, that forging social bonds and experiencing life with friends and family are more important than material things. Nevertheless, psychologists have found time and again that people indeed do attach great importance to the material things they own. In fact, we often attach a surprising amount of personal value to items simply because we have them, regardless of how they came into our possession. This could be a gift we received, an inherited piece, something we bought, or even a found item. This quirk in our perception of value was noticed as far back as Aristotle in ancient Greece, who observed, "Most things are differently valued by those who have them and by those who wish to get them: what belongs to us, and what we give away, always seems very precious to us."[2] This tendency means we often resist selling or letting go of our possessions, even when there's no obvious reason for us to hold on to them. Behavioral economists call this the *endowment effect.*

Daniel Kahneman, Jack Knetsch, and Richard Thaler illustrated this concept by way of a humble coffee mug in a study first conducted in the 1980s. They handed out mugs they had purchased from the campus bookstore to half their students, leaving the other half empty-handed.[3] Conventional wisdom tells us that an object, like a mug, should have the same value to both prospective buyers and sellers whether they have one or not—that's Economics 101. However, they discovered something different: when asked for how much they would exchange the mug, students who had received one required a price more than double what their mugless classmates were willing to pay ($5.25 compared to $2.50). One economics professor who reruns the classic mug experiment each year with his undergraduates confirms, "Every time I have done this activity, a comparison of the willingness-to-pay prices to the willingness-to-sell prices shows the average for the willingness-to-sell price to be significantly higher."[4] Indeed, this type of experiment has been repeated many times using all sorts of objects, and it consistently shows the same thing—on average, people value what they own more than what they don't.

This surprising gap between willingness-to-accept and willingness-to-pay, of course, is problematic for the standard economic model. But the endowment effect can also explain a host of seemingly irrational behaviors across many contexts, like hoarding, avoiding reverse mortgages, staying in an unsatisfying job, or even keeping underperforming players on sports teams.[5] Many successful sales strategies exploit this bias by instilling a sense of ownership in potential customers. Tactics include allowing in-home trials, offering test drives, and promoting "freemium" subscription models (". . . you can cancel at any time!"). The irrational tendency to overvalue already-held assets can also prove costly to investors. One piece of financial industry research suggests that more than one full percentage point in returns is lost each year to the endowment effect, costing investors in excess of $6 billion annually.[6] That's a lot of coffee mugs!

But what if the mug carried more than just mere ownership value? What if it could hold additional significance due to its relational origins—whether it was a gift from a friend, a partner, or even an ex? This question brings us back to Zelizer's concept of relational work and the social meaning of money and objects. A mug gifted by a loved one isn't just a vessel for coffee; it becomes a symbol of that relationship, also endowed with memories and emotional value. The added layer of meaning could significantly increase the gap between willingness-to-accept and willingness-to-pay. This perspective challenges the principle of "source independence," which remains prevalent among economists—a principle that suggests the value of an object should remain unaffected by its origin or the identity of the giver.[7]

Consumer scientists like Peter McGraw and Philip Tetlock have examined how the relationship between giver and recipient affects an item's sentimental value, influencing buying and selling decisions.[8] They focus on four distinct types of relationships that people generally have with others: equal partnerships, hierarchical structures, relationships based on give-and-take, and those built on a sense of communal sharing.[9] Their findings reveal that the type of relationship from which a gift originates significantly colors how individuals assess the value of that item. For instance, they found that participants were more reluctant to sell gifts from close relationships (like those from the communal sharing model) compared to those from give-and-take relationships. When forced to sell such gifts, people in the communal sharing condition demanded much higher prices—often several times the original purchase price. Moreover, participants expressed greater moral distress when asked to replace a gift from a communal relationship with money, compared to gifts from other relationship types.

The impact of relational history doesn't stop at objects like coffee mugs; it extends to money itself. You'd probably treat a $100 gift from your grandparents a bit differently than $100 won from a bet with an acquaintance. Zelizer has noted that "[f]or each distinct category of social relations, people erect a boundary, mark the boundary by means of names and practices, establish a set of distinctive understandings that operate within that boundary, designate certain sorts of economic transactions as appropriate for the relation, [and] bar other transactions as inappropriate. I call that process relational work."[10] From this perspective, not all dollars are equal. By extension, not all coffee mugs should be equal either—even if they are ostensibly identical items. So, whether it's a mug or a dollar bill, its value isn't just a number. It's a more complex equation involving the quality and closeness of our social ties, the emotional investment, and relational history.

According to economic sociologist Nina Bandelj, the way money is allocated in different situations is less about economic practicality or general cultural norms and more about the careful balancing, or *matching*, of the meanings we attach to both social relationships and financial transactions.[11] When this balance is achieved, it facilitates the economic aspects of the relationship;

when it's off, it can create obstacles. For instance, a married couple might comfortably draw money from a shared bank account, but it would be unusual for roommates to have the same financial arrangement despite living under the same roof. Similarly, the most fitting medium of exchange may differ depending on the relations involved. In a work environment, for example, a cash bonus could be the best method to show gratitude for outstanding performance. But in a close friendship a thoughtful gift or favor would be a more meaningful exchange, conveying a deeper understanding and mutual respect between parties. What's considered "appropriate" is deeply influenced by the underlying relationship rather than a universal economic logic.

The relational significance we attach to money influences our spending decisions, even in private. For example, a gift card from a close friend might be spent more thoughtfully on something special, due to the emotional connection involved. In contrast, a paycheck of the same value from an employer—a more impersonal relationship—is more likely to be used for routine expenses without much thought. The source of money, and our relationship to that source, can shape our spending behavior, regardless of whether others are directly involved in the transaction.

In addition to the type of relation involved, the quality of the interpersonal relationship between giver and receiver dramatically influences how economic decisions are made. While sharing a joint bank account works well for a married couple on good terms, it could become a point of contention if the relationship sours. In that situation, each party might hesitate to make withdrawals or might scrutinize the other's spending habits more closely. Similarly, asking to borrow money from a close friend when the relationship is strong and trusting is far different than making the same request when ties have frayed. The same objective transaction takes on entirely different meaning and holds different implications based on the subjective state of the relationship at the time.

A good relational match can lead us to value certain funds or items more, even to the point where we're reluctant to part with them. A mismatch, however, can have the opposite effect, making it easier to let go of that money or sell items for less. I believed that this dynamic could play a role in magnifying, minimizing or, in certain cases, even reversing the endowment effect, showing just how entangled our social relationships are with our economic choices.

WHAT A RELATIONALLY EARMARKED COFFEE MUG CAN TELL US

To test this hypothesis, I designed a study centered around the classic coffee mug experiment. However, I introduced a new dimension by randomly assigning participants to slightly different scenarios, each representing a distinct relational context for the mug's acquisition.[12]

In one scenario, respondents were simply asked to state how much they'd be willing to pay for the mug in figure 4.1. This sets the baseline willingness-to-pay. In a second scenario, some respondents were assigned to a baseline willingness-to-accept condition, where they were told that they had received the mug as a gift generically from "a friend," and were asked for the lowest amount they'd sell it. These two scenarios essentially replicate the original Kahneman, Knetsch, and Thaler experiment described above. Participants assigned ownership of the mug demanded significantly higher prices to sell it compared to what nonowners were willing to pay: on average, participants wanted $4.59 to sell the mug, but would only pay around $3.66 to buy it—about a 25% gap (fig. 4.2).

But here's where it gets more interesting: In addition to the baseline scenarios, I introduced three new conditions, each attaching a unique relational significance to the mug based on the friend's relationship with the participant. One group of participants was informed that the mug was a gift from a friend who had previously

Figure 4.1: Coffee mug image used for the endowment effect study

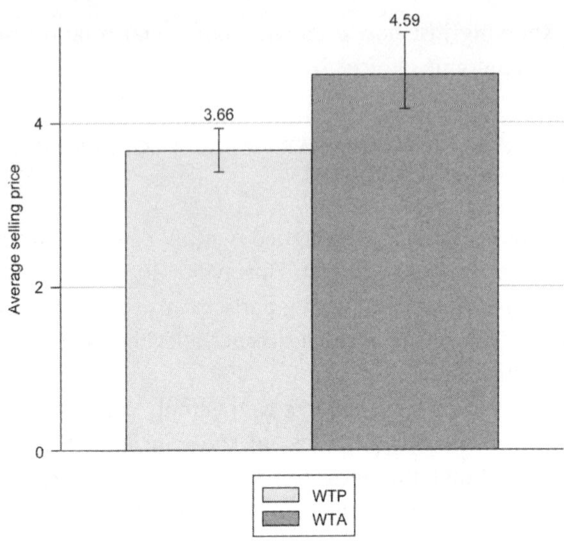

Figure 4.2: Willingness-to-pay (WTP) vs. willingness-to-accept (WTA)

provided helpful support. Others were told that the friend had, sadly, passed away. A third group learned that this so-called friend was cheating on them behind their back. How did these varied relational contexts impact the perceived value of the mug?

People who imagined they received the mug from their helpful friend now demanded a price 40% higher than those in the baseline who were told it was generically from a friend ($6.45 vs. $4.59). And those mourning a loss? They valued the mug more than 2.5 times the baseline price at around $12. But, for those betrayed by a friend, the mug's value plummeted to just $2.28 (see fig. 4.3), even lower than the amount people were initially willing to pay for it—erasing the endowment effect altogether!

The next time you look at that mug on your kitchen counter, think about who gave it to you. It might just change how much it's worth to you.

FROM MUGS TO MANSIONS

If a simple coffee mug can stir our emotions and hold relational weight, what happens when the stakes are much higher—like owning and selling a home? Indeed, behavioral economists have detected the endowment effect in the housing market, where

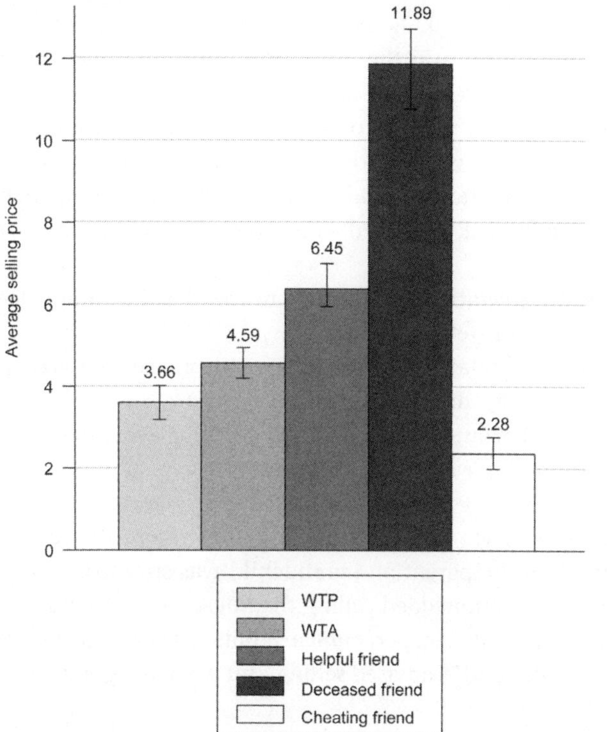

Figure 4.3: Willingness-to-accept (WTA) with relational conditions

home owners tend to overvalue their properties.[13] Could relational earmarks attached to the home also change how we value it? To explore this possibility, I collaborated with housing sociologist Max Besbris and designed an experiment where participants were presented with the following scenario:

> Imagine your friend inherits a modest one-bedroom home from a late grandparent. **[condition]**
>
> The value of the house has been stable and not expected to change much in the coming years. Your friend has two choices:
>
> - Sell the house immediately for a bit less than its market value and move on.
> - Keep the house and rent it out, although this could be costly in the long run.
>
> Which option should your friend choose?[14]

Economically speaking, neither of these choices seems to hold a clear advantage over the other, as both entail some sort of cost. However, the relational history tied to the grandparent could potentially tip the scales based on what each choice implies.

Participants were randomly divided into three groups, each exposed to a different relational backstory between the friend and the grandparent, indicated where **[condition]** appears above:

1. **Positive relational history**: Your friend and their grandparent had a warm, close relationship.
2. **Negative relational history**: Your friend and their grandparent had a rocky, distant relationship.
3. **Control group**: No additional information about the relationship was provided.

Here's what we found: In the situation where the relationship between grandparent and grandchild was strained, 71% of participants recommended selling the house rather than keeping it. This was a full ten percentage points higher than the control group, where 61% advised selling. But when the grandparent and

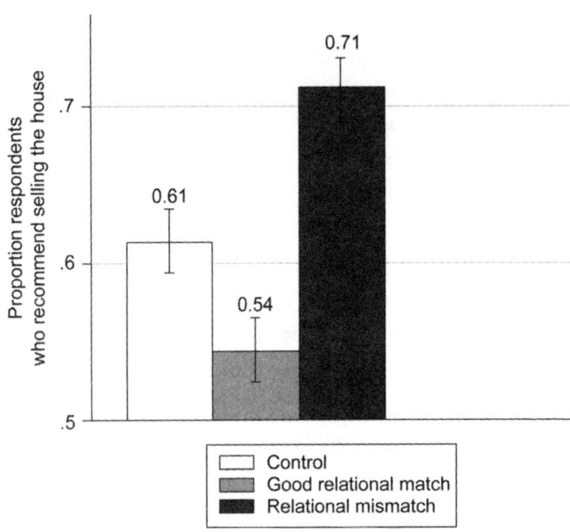

Figure 4.4: Relational earmarks and whether to sell an inherited home

grandchild had a strong, loving relationship, only 54% suggested selling (fig. 4.4).[15]

These findings echo what we saw with the coffee mug. A meaningful relationship made people more attached to the property, and more likely to hold it dear. A poor relationship had the opposite effect, with participants more willing to quickly get rid of the house. Either way, these do not depict rational decisions based on pure financial logic. This behavior also extends beyond the "cognitive error" typically cited for the endowment effect. Instead, it highlights the significance of relational history in molding economic preferences and actions. Relationships are not only a source of emotional attachment or detachment but also a factor that influences how we perceive and evaluate our possessions and transactions.

EARMARKING SPACE: THE ROOM WHERE IT HAPPENS

We see that valuation judgments can change if a home is relationally earmarked. Our next question was whether a relational attachment to *just one room* inside the home could influence the decision to keep or sell an entire house. In this experiment, we earmarked a spare room that a mother-in-law occasionally occupies during occasional visits.

In this scenario, we asked a new set of respondents to imagine a friend who owns a two-bedroom home but faces some financial difficulties.[16] The mother-in-law, who lives a few hours away, sometimes visits during weekends and stays in the guest room. We asked our study participants what advice they would offer: either to sell the home and *downsize* to a smaller, more affordable one (which we indicated was the economically optimal course of action), or to *continue living* in the home by trying to reduce other expenses. This served as our baseline control scenario.

To layer relational context, we presented two alternate scenarios. In one, respondents were randomly assigned to read additional text that the mother-in-law and the home owner have a mutual, supportive, and close relationship. In the second, they frequently argue and it's evident that they don't get along well.[17]

Our data revealed that when the relationship with the mother-in-law was fraught, a striking 78% advised selling the

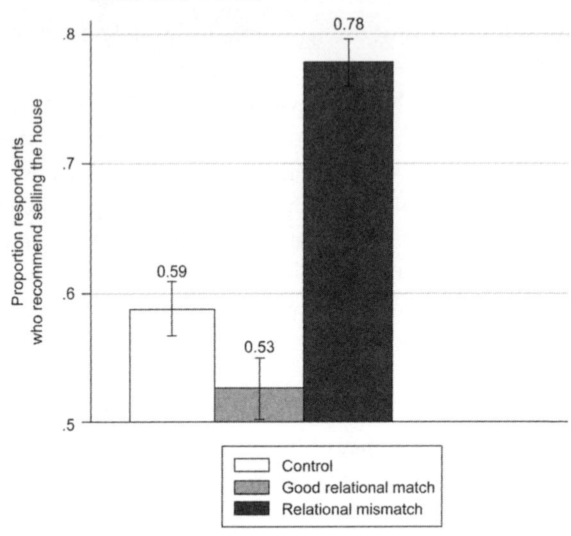

Figure 4.5: Percent of respondents that recommend selling vs. keeping a home with an earmarked spare room

house—significantly more than the 59% in the control group where no relational contexts were mentioned. Conversely, when the relationship was depicted as harmonious, only 53% suggested selling (fig. 4.5).[18] Here, the relational bond to the guest room seemed to override the more practical financial reasons for downsizing.

The implications are significant, especially when considering that for many, a home is their largest asset. If a relational connection to even one room in a home can tilt financial decisions around housing wealth, it could lead to potentially unwise or premature moves. Furthermore, the distribution and quantity of earmarked spaces in a home likely varies across households that have different family structures or domestic configurations, providing more or less exposure to these relational effects.

To understand why respondents made their decisions, we asked them to briefly reflect on their reasoning after completing the main survey task. We systematically topic-coded these responses and matched them with the experimental results we collected, allowing us to see how many respondents explicitly mentioned relational content in their explanation. In both this scenario and

Table 4.1: Summary of qualitative responses to earmarking (as percentages)

	Control		Good match		Mismatch	
	Economic	*Relational*	*Economic*	*Relational*	*Economic*	*Relational*
Rent	92.4	7.6	80.5	19.5	89.8	10.2
Sell	98.2	1.8	95.6	4.4	85.1	14.9
Total	96.0	4.0	88.7	11.3	86.4	13.6

Note: This table tabulates the frequency (%) of qualitative responses coded by whether they address economic or relational topics, separated by experimental condition. Columns indicate economic vs. relational codes. Rows tabulate across each condition for how many respondents recommended renting or selling as well as for the entire subsample for each condition. Note that if a respondent mentioned both economic and relational considerations, it was coded as relational.

the study where the entire home was earmarked, a great majority of respondents across all conditions mentioned only financial factors in determining their responses (see table 4.1).

That so many respondents refer only to *financial* considerations, even as our experiments reveal clear patterns of decision-making that vary based on *relational* manipulations, suggests that most of them were unaware of this sociological phenomenon, where it seems to operate below the level of individual consciousness.

Relational Investing, or Why Your Kids' College Savings Plan Is (Probably) Too Conservative

Our emotional connections to objects or assets don't just affect how much we value them; they also influence how we treat them and the kinds of risk decisions we make around them.

Let's say you've received a family heirloom, like your grandfather's watch. It's more than a timepiece; it carries the weight of memories and emotional bonds. Because of this, you're not just likely to value it more highly—you'd also be inclined to take extra steps to preserve and protect it. Perhaps you'll buy an insurance policy to cover it, or store it in a safe deposit box. This goes beyond insuring its monetary value; it's about safeguarding a relational connection.

Contrast this with an item that carries a negative relational association—say, the gift of an equivalent watch from a relationship that ended badly. You might find yourself treating it with less care, possibly relegating it to the back of a drawer or even giving it away, skewed by the underlying relational context.

These attitudes extend even to how we handle money. If we acquire money through questionable or dubious means, there's a greater chance we might treat it more casually, spending it freely or even recklessly. That money feels "tainted," and it can make us want to dispose of it quickly, perhaps through gambling or other high-risk activities.[19]

In this way, relational considerations can work on our risk preferences in addition to valuation. The presence of well-matched relational earmarks may make us more risk averse and cautious with our valued possessions or money, while mismatched earmarks may make us more prone to taking risks.

THE RISKS WE TAKE

Consider the following:

- Say that you have just finished saving for a "once-in-a-lifetime" vacation. Three weeks before you plan to leave, you lose your job. Do you cancel the vacation or go as scheduled? Perhaps you decide on a more modest vacation instead. Or maybe you choose to extend or upgrade your vacation, reasoning that this could be your last chance to travel first-class.
- You are on a TV game show and can choose one of the following. Which would you take? $5,000 in cash or wager a 50% chance to win $20,000 instead? What if the wager were a 20% chance to win $50,000? Or a 5% chance to win $200,000?
- When you think of the word "risk" which words come to mind first: Loss? Uncertainty? Opportunity? Thrill?

These items appear on a standardized financial risk tolerance questionnaire used extensively in the financial services industry to evaluate prospective clients.[20] If you've ever signed up for a retirement account like a 401(k) or 403(b), or have met with a financial planner, you probably filled out a form like this.

The purpose is to measure how willing you are to take risks in order to suggest suitable investments. If someone chooses to upgrade the vacation, take the longshot chance, and imagines a thrill, they would probably be advised to invest in growth stocks and other riskier assets. But someone who cancels the vacation, takes the sure money, and fears risk might be counseled to invest in more conservative blue-chip stocks and highly rated bonds. The idea is that everyone has their own risk tolerance, which can differ even among people with similar backgrounds.

We often think of risk tolerance as a deeply personal characteristic, something unique to each individual. But relational context can influence our willingness to take financial risks, especially when we're managing money on behalf of those we care about.

This question isn't purely academic. In today's world, where people increasingly manage their own investment portfolios—from 401(k)s to health savings accounts—we're also frequently making decisions that directly impact the well-being of loved ones. Whether it's saving for a child's college education through a 529 plan, handling an elderly parent's investment portfolio, or managing a spouse's retirement funds, many of our investment choices are inherently relational. Surprisingly, most research on everyday investors has glossed over how these relational dynamics could shape investment choices and risk-taking in those accounts.

This isn't a minor oversight; we're talking about significant amounts of money. For instance, as of 2024, 529 plans in the United States held over $471 billion across 16.4 million accounts.[21] And that's just one example. Couples often allocate the responsibility of joint financial decisions, including retirement investing, to one partner.[22] Considering the nearly $40 *trillion* currently held in retirement accounts, it's clear that many investment decisions are relationally motivated.[23]

The way that investors allocate their funds—that is, "portfolio choice"—is an important and ongoing question that bears directly on the economic security of individuals. As is often the case, mainstream economics assumes that when choosing portfolio allocations investors are rational beings who aim for the highest possible returns for their given risk tolerance. This view was crystallized over seventy years ago with the development of

Modern Portfolio Theory (MPT), a framework that's since garnered multiple Nobel Prizes in economics.[24] In particular, MPT models how to best diversify investments in order to maximize expected gains while minimizing risks.[25]

But real people don't invest like MPT assumes they should. Findings from behavioral finance often paint a picture where investors—both ordinary individuals and Wall Street professionals—frequently act in ways that defy MPT and the rational-actor model.[26] These "anomalies" have often been explained by way of cognitive psychology. One such concept from behavioral economics is *mental accounting*, which suggests that people compartmentalize their money into separate mental categories, each designated for a specific purpose. For example, an individual might have one mental account for paying bills or groceries, another for saving for a vacation, and yet another for retirement, even though it's all part of the same overall financial picture. As Richard Thaler points out, "Money in one mental account is not a perfect substitute for money in another."[27]

Using the idea of mental accounts, behavioral economists Hersh Shefrin and Meir Statman proposed a new way of looking at portfolio choice, called behavioral portfolio theory (BPT).[28] In this model, investors aren't solely driven by the mathematical balance of risk and return. Instead, they also factor in their own feelings and objectives. According to BPT, people categorize their investments into different mental risk buckets, ranging from safe to speculative, based on what those funds are intended for in the future. BPT better reflects how individuals actually invest for *themselves*, but it does not explain how they might invest for others.[29] If risk tolerance can differ between various accounts within one person's mind, it's not a stretch to consider that risk behavior could also differ when those accounts are relationally earmarked for loved ones.

This is where relational earmarking differs from mental accounting—it shifts the focus from individuals to social relations. From this perspective, we can actually think of mental accounts as a special instance of earmarking, but for one's own individual purposes. But when we make financial decisions that affect others, the stakes and implications are inherently different.

Let's return to the example of parents earmarking college savings. Zelizer makes the point that "when we earmark money for our child's college fund, . . . we are affirming our parental relationship to that child. On the other hand, by gambling the money away we would seriously undermine that connection."[30]

Think about the money that a parent has set aside for college. Barring some financial catastrophe, to spend those dollars on *anything but* tuition would be deemed inappropriate; however, the relational work does not stop there. It would be equally inappropriate to invest those monies with a risk profile that could put going to college in jeopardy—keeping that money safe is paramount to being a "good parent."

In their chapter on mental accounting, marketing professors Dilip Soman and Hee-Kyung Ahn relate the following story: "An acquaintance, an economist, . . . once borrowed a sum of money at very high interest rates to fund a home renovation when in fact he had that sum in a money market account earning a fairly small interest rate. The catch was that the money market account had been designated as his son's (who was 3 years old) education account."[31] In the end, this father could not come to terms with "breaking into" that account and opted for the high-interest loan—a seemingly irrational decision. While Soman and Ahn see this as an emotionally charged mental account, sociologists like Bandelj and her colleagues suggest that this actually showcases the symbolic value of relational earmarking.[32] However, there is another equally important (and also "irrational") detail of this story: the child's college fund—with at least fifteen years to go—was allocated to an incredibly low-risk, low-yield money market account!

There are, in fact, *two* social forces at work here: one is the direct parent-child relationship. The second is the fact that college and college savings are culturally salient financial goals in contemporary American society that coincide with an important life transition, or what sociologist Frederick Wherry would call an instance of "relational accounting."[33] Going to college is seen as a crucial life event, an avenue to personal and professional growth, and a rite of passage to middle-class membership. Failing to responsibly save for a child's college education is not just a financial misstep; in the eyes of many, it's a moral failure.[34]

Just as college savings are earmarked with a specific goal in mind, retirement represents another milestone event with investment accounts specially designated for it.[35] With the decline of company pensions, the onus is increasingly on individuals to build their own safety nets for retirement. A financial services industry survey underscores this point; more than two-thirds of Americans feel a "moral obligation to manage their investments responsibly."[36] But the report also concludes that this moral obligation is overwhelmingly focused on just one particular goal: securing a comfortable retirement.

The retirement account *itself* comes to symbolize aspirations for the future—a reward of leisure and freedom after a lifetime of work. The money reserved for retirement signifies the ability to achieve this goal.[37] Hence, saving for retirement is laden with both personal *and* broader social meaning: a share of stock in a 401(k) plan differs qualitatively from the same share held in another type of account. Indeed, people may be more conservative with their retirement accounts as opposed to other investments.[38]

Does our risk appetite really change when money is designated for a specific person or meaningful purpose? To explore this question, I teamed up with sociologist Rourke O'Brien and ran a set of new experiments.[39]

In the first, we asked study participants to imagine that they had $100 set aside to purchase a special gift.[40] This gift was randomly assigned to be earmarked for themselves or for someone they had a relationship with—either a spouse/partner, their child, or their nephew.[41] Next, these participants were presented with a hypothetical casino scenario, where they could gamble all or some of that $100 to potentially increase the gift fund. Respondents were given three options: bet on a single number in roulette (a high-risk, high-reward game), join a card game with a 50% chance of doubling their bet (a moderate-risk, moderate-reward game), or to not play at all (no risk, no reward). They were then asked to allocate the earmarked $100 across these three options. From this allocation, we constructed an index of overall riskiness.

Our findings revealed that people were far more willing to risk their own money than money intended for loved ones (fig. 4.6). Money saved for a child led to the least amount of risk-taking, highlighting a heightened sense of responsibility and caution

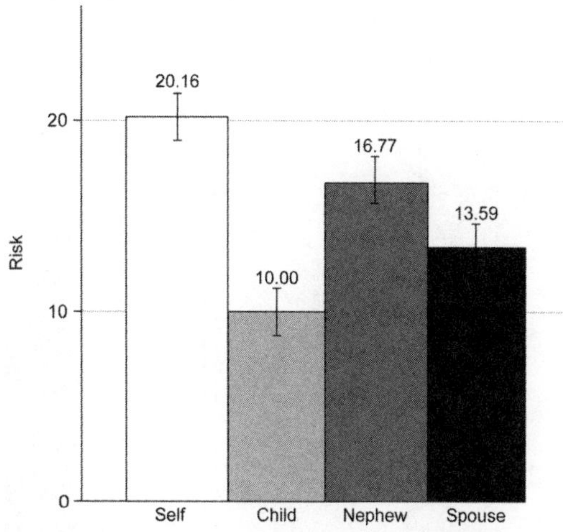

Figure 4.6: Risk-taking when gambling earmarked money

when the financial decision impacts someone they care deeply about. This demonstrates how relational context influences risk behavior, with individuals prioritizing the security and well-being of loved ones over their own.

But does this cautious relational approach also apply to more consequential and long-term investments like retirement or college funds? To find out, we designed a second experiment. This time, we asked respondents to imagine they were investing $5,000 over a ten-year period, with participants randomly assigned to one of eight experimental manipulations.[42] In four relational conditions, the money was to be invested generically for either themselves, their spouse/partner, their child, or their nephew. In the other four scenarios, the money was further earmarked for a specific purpose: retirement (for themselves or their spouse/partner) or college (for their child or their nephew). We fixed the time horizon at ten years so we could control for the influence of investment duration or tax treatment and focus solely on the relational context and purpose.

Participants then had to choose how to allocate the $5,000 among three investment options: a high-risk, high-reward stock fund; a moderate-risk, moderate-return bond fund; and a low-risk, low-yield savings account. Each option included detailed descriptions, ensuring participants were fully informed of the

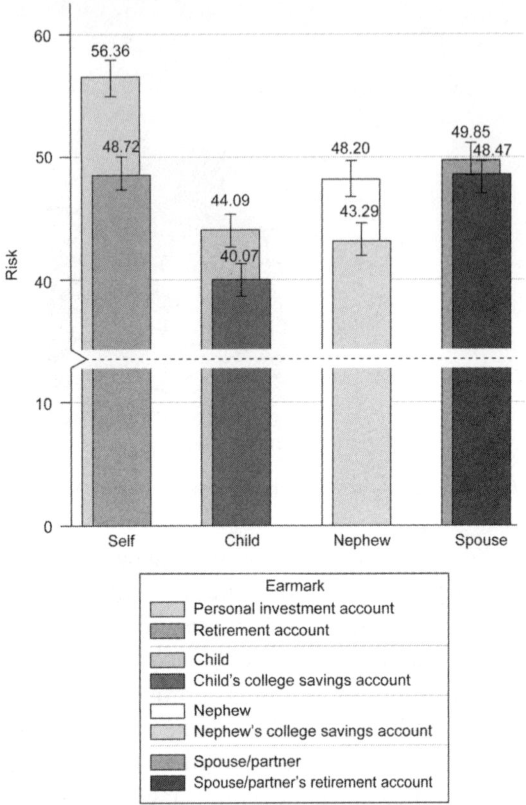

Figure 4.7: Risk-taking when investing earmarked money

possible outcomes. We then constructed a risk index based on their portfolio choices.

Figure 4.7 reveals the average portfolio risk for various earmarked relationships. Relational earmarks by themselves, such as those generically for self, child, nephew, and spouse/partner, appear to the left and slightly behind the corresponding labeled account conditions (i.e., retirement or college). Again, people are more willing to take risks with their own money not earmarked for a specific purpose. As earmarks become more relationally tied, those portfolios become more conservative, an effect that only intensifies with the addition of socially meaningful labels like college and retirement.[43]

*

Since the turn of the twentieth century, children have become almost universally recognized as "emotionally priceless" dependents.[44] When something is priceless, it is treasured, cherished, and safeguarded. And so the treatment of priceless things tends to be oriented toward preservation and security. Unsurprisingly, dollars earmarked for a child are invested with far less risk than those earmarked for oneself. Among these portfolios, the one dedicated to a child's college savings is the *most* conservative of all, carrying a third less risk than personal investments—and around 10% less risky than for a child generically. The commitment to fund a child's education underscores the intertwining of finance and family, often requiring significant sacrifices. As anthropologist Caitlin Zaloom affirms, parents believe their children are worth the price of paying for college.[45] As such, the "child" or "nephew" earmarks are enhanced by the added symbolic importance of the "college savings" label, translating into a more risk-averse investment approach that aligns with its moral connotation.

More conservative investment strategies may lead savers to believe that they are acting responsibly. However, their conservatism might inadvertently lead to an underinvestment in stocks. Given that these are long-term portfolios, both the capacity and willingness to bear risk should be higher to ensure adequate returns that compound over time and that prevent future financial shortfalls. Paradoxically, the social forces at work here may create a discrepancy between the objective chances of college attainment or retirement security and the subjective aspirations of 529 plan and 401(k) savers.

What might this mean for real-world savers? History shows that stocks have delivered higher average returns than bonds over any ten-year period since at least the 1920s.[46] This is due to stocks' inherently higher riskiness, which is compensated through greater expected returns—something known as the *equity risk premium*.[47] Using historical average annualized returns for stocks, bonds, and cash deposits, we can estimate that if a hypothetical $5,000 investment had been made to a personal investment account according to the average portfolio allocation of our study participants, it would have grown to approximately $10,175 over the following ten years. Had those funds instead been invested according to the portfolio allocation of the child's college savings account condition, the balance would have grown to just \$8,575 over the same timeframe—a disparity of nearly 20%. Over a twenty-five-year period and projecting the same historical returns into the future, the personal investment account would grow to be worth twice as much (see fig. 4.8).

In other words, relational investors—especially those caring and careful parents—are prone to lose out and leave money on the table due to earmarking. What's worse, it is a loss that compounds over the course of a child's entire childhood. These findings certainly suggest "value-rational" tendencies where people do not seek to maximize returns but instead prioritize conservation of funds that have been relationally earmarked. In Max Weber's terminology, value-rational action always involves "commands" or "demands" which, in the actor's opinion, are binding on them. It seems plain from this study that relational roles and meaningful labels each place binding demands on investors. But, as Weber also notes, and what is detrimental to relational investors in practice, "from the perspective of instrumental rationality, value-rationality is always irrational."[48]

PUTTING IT TOGETHER: EARMARKING SPACE AND RISK-TAKING

This chapter has explored how our relationships with others can shape our financial choices. It has shown that earmarking space in a home for a relative can affect how much people value their home and whether they will consider selling it or not. It has also

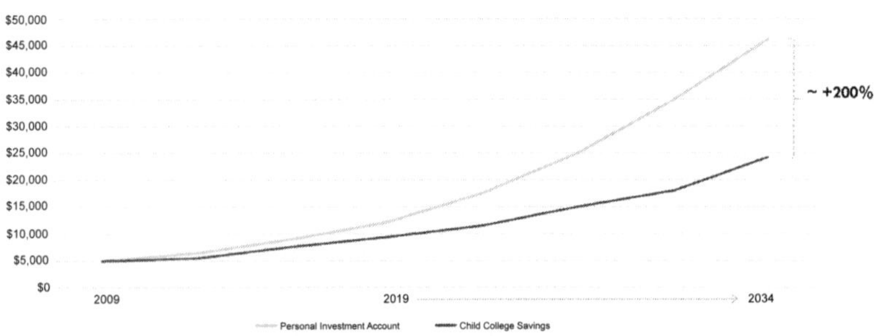

Figure 4.8: Comparison using experimental results

shown that earmarking investments can affect how much risk people are willing to take. But what happens if we combine these two aspects of earmarking—can earmarking space in a home affect risk preferences with regard to housing wealth?

To try and answer this question, let's return to my work with Max Besbris and the case of a home that's been relationally earmarked for a mother-in-law who occasionally stays in the spare bedroom. As with our previous study, we asked a group of respondents to read a vignette, but rather than describing a situation of financial hardship and asking whether to sell or keep the house, this study asked respondents to make a risk decision involving the home's equity.[49]

All study respondents saw the following:

> Your friend is happily married. S/he owns a two-bedroom house with her/his spouse. Her/his mother-in-law, who lives a few hours away, often comes and stays weekends in the second bedroom. **[condition]**
>
> Your friend has recently been offered the opportunity to invest in a new business venture that is highly risky, but which could also double her/his money quickly if things work out.
>
> However, in order to find the money to invest, your friend would have to take out a high-interest rate home equity loan on the house.
>
> Do you think your friend should take the home equity loan and invest? [Yes/No]

Participants were randomly divided into three groups with corresponding text shown where **[condition]** appears above: those with a harmonious relationship with the mother-in-law, those in a discordant relationship, and a neutral control group who saw no additional text.

The findings were eye-opening. People who read about a strained relationship between the home owner and the mother-in-law were more willing to endorse the risky investment—31% of them did, compared to 26% in the control group. Meanwhile, only 21% of respondents who saw the harmonious relationship scenario recommended taking out the loan (fig. 4.9).[50] These results suggest that relational earmarking can also have a significant impact on risk preferences with regard to housing wealth.

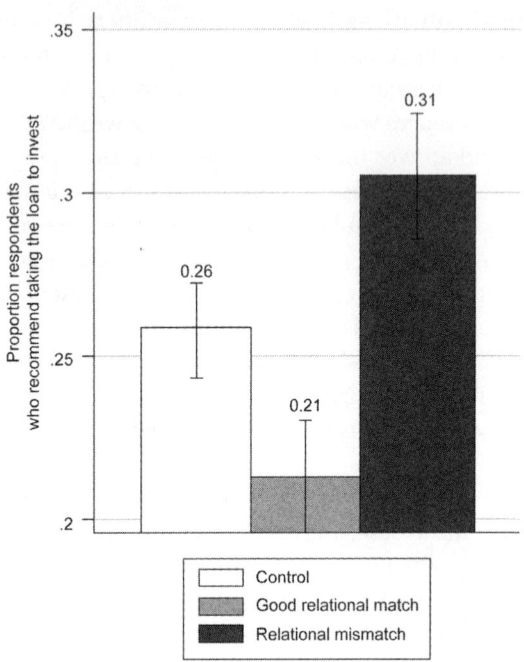

Figure 4.9: Proportion of respondents recommending using home equity to make a risky investment

When asked why they made their choices, most respondents again cited purely financial reasons. However, some did acknowledge the risk of losing their home if the investment failed. In the well-matched condition, respondents highlighted the potential harm to loved ones if the investment went wrong; as one respondent noted, "I do not believe she should take the loan as it is something that can cause issues for other people other than herself. It is highly possible to damage her relationship with her spouse and mother-in-law." Those who saw the poorly matched earmark and chose to speculate on the risky investment also linked that decision to both the home and the relevant earmark. One respondent remarked, "I know if my mother-in-law were visiting that often, I would think in a cavalier way that it would be great to lose the house so we wouldn't have to give her lodging anymore." Another wrote of the gamble, "It would all be worth it to get rid of the mother-in-law." Others framed the prospect in more positive terms: "Maybe the extra money could help buy the mother-in-law her own house in the future so she would not have to stay with him."

*

Navigating financial decisions, especially when they involve close others, complicates pure logic with the nature of our social bonds. The relationships we maintain, the commitments we honor, and the memories we cherish can steer our economic choices in meaningful ways. Rather than solely relying on data, spreadsheets, or market trends, considering the relational stakes can offer a more complete understanding of what's truly valuable to us. Who gave us this prized object? What hopes and dreams are invested in this account? Do vestiges of past relationships still cling to certain assets? By tuning into these subtle relational cues, we may uncover wiser courses than those dictated by cold logic or arithmetic alone.

The idea of relational earmarking helps us see this clearly. Money, assets, and other investments tied to significant relationships can carry extra weight in our decision-making process. A relational focus might not always maximize financial gains, but it fulfills a deeper obligation to protect and honor our social bonds. Sure, your returns may be smaller when prioritizing relationships, but the intangible benefits—peace of mind, fulfillment, and the preservation of important commitments—often make up for it.

Just as we might prioritize different outcomes in a casual game with friends compared to a serious competition, we make different economic choices depending on our relationships with the people involved. Imagine playing a friendly game of cards after work. You would probably prioritize having a good time and maintaining relationships over maximizing your winnings at the others' expense. You might let a friend take back a bet if they made it by mistake, or you might choose not to capitalize on another player's weakness if doing so would make them feel bad. Now imagine playing in a high-stakes poker tournament. In this context, you play to win. Exploiting your opponents' weaknesses and maximizing your own gains is not just accepted but expected. Making a "soft" play for the sake of being nice would be seen as irrational, even foolish. It's the same game, but the rules have somehow changed.

Similarly, in our economic interactions, we apply different rules and expectations depending on who we're dealing with and why. We might be more lenient and generous when dealing with family or friends, valuing the relationship over monetary gain. But in a professional or competitive setting, we might adopt a more strategic and profit-driven approach. Recognizing these different contexts and the relational dynamics at play allows us to navigate economic decisions with a nuanced understanding that goes beyond mere financial calculations. This approach recognizes that we align our economic behavior with our deeper values and social responsibilities, ensuring that our financial decisions support and strengthen the relationships that matter to us most.

5 * Rethinking Economic "Man": Gendered Dimensions of Economic Choice

Recall from the previous chapter these risk-profiling items:

- You are on a TV game show and can choose one of the following. Which would you take? $1,000 in cash, or wager a 50% chance to win $5,000 instead?
- When you think of the word "risk" which words come to mind first: Loss? Uncertainty? Opportunity? Thrill?

Which would you choose? Your decision is likely to be influenced by various factors, of course—but one of which is, perhaps surprisingly, your gender.[1]

Studies consistently reveal that women, on average, opt for safer choices—such as taking the guaranteed money rather than rolling the dice. On the flip side, men tend to be more inclined to take a gamble. This risk tendency goes beyond just money matters, showing up in various contexts, from skydiving and other adventures, to excessive drinking and drug use. Now, this isn't a hard-and-fast rule. Plenty of men are cautious, and many women are thrill-seekers. Still, it's a consistent pattern that holds true even after accounting for things like age, income, education, and other factors.[2]

Opinions vary on why these gender differences in risk-taking exist. Some point to biology, citing variations in brain structure or hormones like testosterone as the culprits behind men's riskier choices.[3] Sociologists instead argue that cultural cues, learning, and socialization come into play, shaping how men and women internalize and react to risk differently.

Boys might be encouraged to be adventurous, while girls might be implicitly taught to be more cautious and responsible.

Whatever the cause, this risk divide has real-world consequences, especially for women's financial wellness. For example, research indicates that women often end up with smaller retirement fund balances, despite living longer and thus needing that retirement money for a longer time. And although women generally contribute more of their income to retirement plans, their portfolios often underperform.[4] A study by Vanguard found that women are 14% more likely than men to take part in workplace retirement plans, yet still fall behind in long-term gains due to choosing more conservative investments.[5]

Financial literacy is another context where consequential gender differences regularly appear. Knowing how to budget, invest, and manage debt are essential skills in today's world where personal accountability is key, and especially when social safety nets are becoming less dependable. Falling behind in this area can lead to serious problems—skyrocketing debt, poor credit, or even bankruptcy.[6] Those who lack financial literacy often miss out on good opportunities to grow their wealth simply because they don't recognize or understand the opportunities in front of them. They're less likely to save and invest wisely or recognize hidden fees and costs, which puts them at a further financial disadvantage.[7] Facing this problem, many countries have invested heavily in financial education, with some programs beginning as early as elementary school, to arm citizens with the knowledge they need to navigate increasingly complex financial landscapes.[8]

Despite numerous efforts to increase awareness and education, however, financial illiteracy remains a widespread problem. More troubling, perhaps, is that there exists a persistent gender gap in financial literacy that appears time and again, in both developing and developed economies.[9] One recent finding from TIAA's 2020 survey of personal finances reveals that, on average, men answered 56% of the questions correctly, with women only 49%. A closer look at the data provides more insight: about 27% of men aced at least three-quarters of the questions, compared to only 12% of women; and only 15% of men scored in the bottom quartile compared to 21% of women.[10] Other research shows that these disparities hold even after controlling for various characteristics like age, race, educational attainment (regardless of major), marital status, and income.

These gender gaps are part of a larger conversation within feminist and gender studies of the economy. Research in these areas indicates that women are more financially vulnerable—they often have less in retirement savings, shy away from stock market investments, and when they do invest, they typically earn lower returns.[11] While issues like wage disparities and familial responsibilities can hinder women's financial opportunities, a lack of financial literacy also limits the choices they can make.[12] Although financial advisors can provide general guidance, their advice often fails to take into account the unique challenges and opportunities women face.[13]

And it's not as simple as being male vs. female. A review of over two hundred studies in behavioral economics found that while average risk tolerance indeed differs between genders, there are also considerable variations *within* the sexes—in fact, differences observed within each gender often surpass the differences between them.[14] In other words, while the average woman may have a lower risk tolerance than the average man, that does not mean that any particular woman will have such a risk tolerance; and even within a given person's life course, that individual may fluctuate between taking more risk and being more conservative with their finances depending on the immediate social context or broader shifts in cultural preferences.

Throughout this book, I have suggested that multiple levels of analysis are at play when it comes to understanding how people make economic decisions—the previous chapters have considered these levels starting with culture and social position, social networks and group membership, and interpersonal relationships and relational work. In this chapter, I will argue for the importance of accounting for gender differences in economic behavior and look at how gender intersects with those and other social forces. In particular, I will look at how gender socialization plays into economic decisions around (1) risk-taking and (2) financial advice and literacy.

Gender and Risk-Taking

When Lehman Brothers filed for bankruptcy in September 2008, it wasn't just another moment in financial history—it was a pivotal event that, many experts now believe, ushered in the global financial meltdown that sparked the Great Recession.[15] In the years leading up to its collapse, the firm had bet heavily on subprime mortgages and borrowed vast sums to make those bets—pursuing short-term profits at the expense of long-term stability. Excessive risk-taking by Lehman and other financial institutions continued as they ignored the warning signs of a looming crisis—only to then see it all unravel in a collapsing market. As things spiraled, efforts to save the company failed, and Lehman's insolvency reverberated around the globe. Lehman's bankruptcy exposed the fragility and interconnectedness of the global financial system, triggering a wave of panic and uncertainty that threatened to bring down the entire economy.

But did things have to turn out that way? Perhaps not. The so-called Lehman Sisters hypothesis is a thought-provoking alternative that was proposed in the wake of the Great Recession to better understand its cause and effect.[16] This hypothesis speculates that if Lehman Brothers had instead been run by women, the outcome of the crisis could have been very different. The idea draws from studies in the behavioral sciences that show women to be generally less likely to engage in the types of risky behaviors that are believed to have contributed to Lehman's collapse, such as excessive leverage and overconfidence. Supporters of this theory point to women's more collaborative, prudent, and long-term focused leadership styles as factors that could have led to wiser, more sustainable decision-making.

And there's data to back this up. Companies with higher levels of gender diversity, especially in leadership roles, not only perform better financially but also tend to be more resilient during economic downturns.[17] At the time of Lehman's collapse, though, only about 2% of top managers in the financial sector were women.[18] So, could more women in the executive ranks have softened the economic blow? It's a compelling thought.[19]

On an individual level, studies reveal that men, on average, are more likely than women to invest in higher-risk, higher-reward stocks and other speculative investments, are more willing to take out high-interest loans, and hold relatively larger amounts of debt.[20] Research also shows that men are more likely than women to start their own businesses and to take on the uncertainties associated with entrepreneurship.[21] Outside of finance, men more commonly participate in other risky activities, such as drug use, unprotected sex, reckless driving, or rock climbing.[22]

But these are broad trends, and they don't typically account for cultural, educational, or situational factors that can also shape our willingness to take risks, and in ways that could intersect with gender.[23] To address this, behavioral economists John List and Uri Gneezy revisited the perennial nature vs. nurture question, and their findings suggest that "nurture" (i.e., society and culture) has a lot more to do with risk preferences than just biology.[24] They challenged the long-held belief that women are innately risk averse and less competitive, and theorized that under the right conditions they can be just as competitive—and perhaps even more so—than men.

List and Gneezy ran several experiments to explore this idea. In one, they posted two similar online job listings for an administrative assistant in several American cities. One of the ads mentioned a position for a "Sports News Assistant" and the other for a "Community News Assistant." For each job, they also introduced two experimental conditions, one where the compensation was based on a fixed hourly rate, and another where the pay would depend on how the applicant performed compared to a coworker. The goal of the experiment was to see if the competitive aspect of the second condition influenced one gender more than the other. Unsurprisingly, they found that men were generally more interested in the sports-oriented position and women responded more to the community-oriented one. But when they described the compensation schemes, women were 70% *less likely* to apply for the competitive job, even when it was for the community news assistant—taking this as evidence that men are more receptive to risk-taking in competitive environments.

To pursue the nature vs. nurture question further, List and Gneezy traveled to India and visited one of the few matrilineal societies that still exists today, known as the Khasi, to see how that particular culture inculcates competitive inclinations between men and women.[25] Unlike much of the rest of the world today, in Khasi society, inheritance flows through mothers to their daughters; and when a woman marries, her husband moves into her home, making the matriarchal house the center of the family. As the holders of economic and household authority, Khasi women wield a lot of economic power. And, in a sort of role reversal, they found that Khasi women were indeed *more likely* to express competitiveness in experimental situations than Khasi men, revealing the significant role that culture plays.

This groundbreaking work provided hard evidence that the economic socialization found within specific cultural contexts can lead to differences in economic behavior and preferences. While it's easy to say "men are like this" and "women are like that," the truth is far more nuanced. Both biology and culture can play a part, and studies like this suggest that socialization processes might be far more potent than previously thought. Economic socialization is a by-product of playing the economic game and encompasses the acquisition of knowledge, skills, attitudes, and values related to various economic aspects, including money management, saving, spending, budgeting, and investing—all of which contribute to an individual's economic dispositions throughout life. Economic socialization, however, is not a neutral or homogenous process; it is subject to influences from factors such as culture, family, social context, and even religious upbringing.

Among these factors, gender socialization is particularly crucial. As individuals internalize gender norms and roles through interactions with key socializing agents like family, social networks, and institutions, they learn to "do" gender, including the adoption of gendered economic behaviors and attitudes.[26] Qualities like risk-taking and competitiveness tend to be cultivated as "masculine" virtues in boys, while girls are often socialized to be more cautious and cooperative.[27] This happens subtly and often without conscious effort, as societal norms and expectations quietly shape our worldviews. Common tropes still portray men as breadwinners who make financial decisions, while women are seen as caregivers and homemakers who focus on domestic duties.[28] Such gender stereotypes get reinforced through mechanisms like parental expectations, peer influences, classroom dynamics, and media messages. A young girl whose family only discusses finances with her brother while tasking her with household chores puts limits on her economic agency.[29] Parents have indeed been found to place greater emphasis on their sons developing financial acumen and independence at a young age, such as encouraging them to open bank accounts or paying them allowances—in contrast to daughters, who may receive more financial assistance but less hands-on education in money matters.[30]

Representations across television, movies, books, and advertising further entrench gendered economic roles. Even toy aisles divided between action figures and dolls propagate gendered ideals of economic behavior from an early age. It may seem like a small thing, but the toys children play with can speak volumes about the roles they're expected to assume in adult life.[31] Action figures and construction sets, often marketed to boys, come with implicit narratives of adventure, risk, and strategy, subtly encouraging qualities like leadership and entrepreneurship—attributes commonly associated with successful businesspeople or investors.[32] Dolls and play sets, on the other hand, often come complete with accessories like miniature houses and kitchens, subtly nudging girls toward domestic roles that emphasize care and nurturing.

Over time, the accretion of this messaging shapes girls' and boys' understanding of their own economic capacities and roles, ultimately guiding their financial behaviors later in life. This perspective prompts us to look beyond oversimplified biological explanations and consider the sociocultural scaffolding underlying observed variations in economic conduct.

Studying the effects of gender socialization within our own society presents challenges due to its deeply ingrained and often taken-for-granted nature. The overlap between cultural expectations, media portrayals, educational practices, and family dynamics, among others, further creates a complex web of influences, making it challenging to pinpoint the specific effects of gender socialization on economic behaviors. To better understand this phenomenon, we can look to cultures with unconventional gender roles. However, cultures like the Khasi, where conventional gender roles are reversed, are rare—which makes it hard to generalize List and Gneezy's findings. Intrigued, though, I sought out another cultural context where unique gender roles and expectations could help illuminate if and how socialization processes might exert surprising effects on individuals' economic behavior and preferences.

While teaching at the Hebrew University (incidentally, where Daniel Kahneman and Amos Tversky began their foray into behavioral economics in the 1970s), I learned that Ultra-Orthodox Jewish communities (known in Israel as Haredi) also exhibit distinct gender roles that depart from those typically found elsewhere. In these communities, devout men often forgo secular work entirely and engage solely with religious and spiritual learning. They spend long hours each day in seminaries known as *Yeshiva* (for boys) and *Kollel* (for married men), immersed in Torah study and Talmudic instruction, leaving Ultra-Orthodox women as the primary earners and managers of household finances. This unique division of labor leaves many of the men undersocialized in economic life and unaccustomed to basic financial practices.

But Haredi society, unlike the Khasi, is highly patriarchal, where men hold nearly all the authority in community and family matters. This creates an intriguing juxtaposition: while men enjoy higher social status in their communities, this status is not linked to their economic prowess or wealth accumulation in the conventional sense. Instead, their prestige stems from their devotion to religious study and spiritual leadership. Some Haredi men (roughly half) do work, but this is most often a reluctant concession to meet financial needs for large and growing households. Indeed, working men face significant social stigma and embarrassment for their families. Masculine role fulfillment in Haredi society is fundamentally tied to spiritual and religious devotion rather than economic success.[33] Still, these men gain exposure to the secular economy and are socialized to meet its demands.

Women, on the other hand, gain practical financial skills and experience through their roles as breadwinners and household financial managers—but, for many women, their economic agency and earning potential are often constrained by norms of modesty and the need to balance work with the demands of supporting large families as well as the expectation that they pursue occupations aligning with traditional gender roles, like teachers or caregivers.[34] As a result, despite shouldering the bulk of the economic responsibilities and gaining some financial skills, many Haredi women face structural and societal barriers that hinder their ability to fully leverage their economic potential and develop financial acumen.[35] Additionally, the demands of raising large families can further limit their ability to fully engage in financial matters beyond the household level, potentially leading to less rational and more intuitive financial decision-making.

These distinct gender roles with respect to economic life provide a unique opportunity to examine the impact of gender and socialization on financial risk-taking and economic decision-making. Working Haredi men ought to display the most "rational" economic behavior, as they have the greatest opportunity to learn and apply financial concepts in practice. Haredi women, and those men who study at Kollel, will at the same time face challenges in developing financial knowledge and skills—but for different reasons. Haredi women, while typically employed and the managers of household finances, may still demonstrate comparatively lower levels of risk-taking and financial competency due to the constraints on their economic agency and the limited scope of their financial possibilities. Meanwhile, Haredi men who study in Kollel, having the least exposure to economic life and free from financial responsibilities, may exhibit the lowest levels of financial literacy and rational decision-making among the three groups—despite being otherwise high-status men. Their lack of practical experience and immersion in religious studies give them few opportunities to develop and apply economic knowledge.

These hypotheses suggest that varying degrees of involvement in economic life and religious demands, as opposed to biological sex, may lead to different outcomes in terms of risk-taking, financial knowledge, skills, and decision-making. Testing these hypotheses could provide valuable insights into how gender roles and cultural norms shape financial behaviors not only within the Haredi community but also beyond.

To explore this, I collaborated with Yehudit Miletzki, a doctoral student in the sociology department at the Hebrew University, to design and field an original study that compared aspects of competitiveness, risk-taking behavior, and financial acumen between men and women in Haredi communities across Israel. Our sample included 143 women—of whom only six reported that they did not work.[36] (Israeli government labor statistics report that roughly 90% of Haredi women are employed.)[37] And, out of 280 men, fully 115 reported that they had never worked and only studied in religious seminaries (Israeli labor statistics report that upward of 50% of Haredi men do not work). Thus, we were able to construct three analytic categories: women; men with work experience; and men who have only studied. This grouping is important as it allowed us to investigate the differences in financial behavior not only between genders but also within the two groups of men to reveal the impact of socialization and enculturation with economic life.

First, we examined participants' financial risk-taking tendencies by asking a standardized question designed to gauge their willingness to engage in risky financial behaviors. We found that Haredi women were generally more risk averse than their working male counterparts; but interestingly, the *most* risk averse were the men in Kollel, pointing to the influence of practical economic experience on risk preferences (fig. 5.1).

Next, we looked at comfort levels with handling household finances like opening a bank account or writing checks. Men who worked felt more at ease than women did. However, men devoted

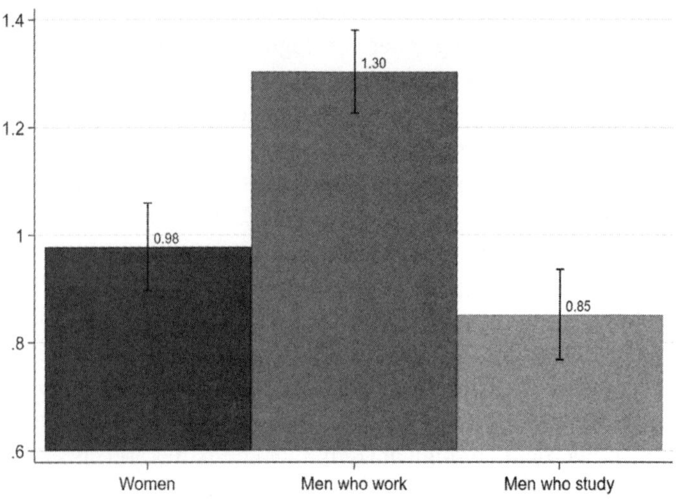

Figure 5.1: Financial risk preferences among Haredi men and women
Note: Error bars indicate standard errors. All reported differences are statistically significant at $p < 0.01$ or smaller.

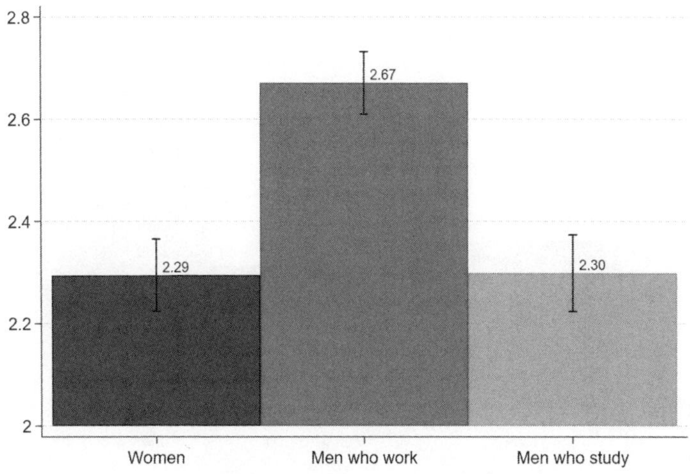

Figure 5.2: Self-reported financial literacy among Haredi men and women
Note: Error bars indicate standard errors. All reported differences are statistically significant at $p < 0.01$ or smaller.

to religious study were just as comfortable—or uncomfortable—with finances as women, bucking the typical gender gap in financial literacy observed elsewhere (fig. 5.2).[38]

We also wanted to gauge participants' loss aversion—recall from chapter 2, this is the irrational tendency to avoid financial losses compared to receiving equivalent gains. Due to religious prohibitions against gambling, we couldn't use a coin flip exercise, and so adapted the traditional Hanukkah game of dreidel (*sevivon* in Hebrew) to quantify this.[39] Our findings? Haredi women were somewhat more loss averse than the working men—but Kollel men were significantly more loss averse than either working men *or* women, suggesting an additional link between financial experience and attitudes toward loss (fig. 5.3).[40]

Last, in the spirit of Gneezy and List's experiments with the Khasi, we assessed general attitudes toward competitiveness.[41] Interestingly, men in both categories rated themselves as more competitive than women, but likely for different reasons.[42] While men who work may compete in a business setting, the men who study still engage in intense Talmudic debates and vie to be the most learned student, revealing a different form of competitiveness nurtured by their specific context (fig. 5.4).

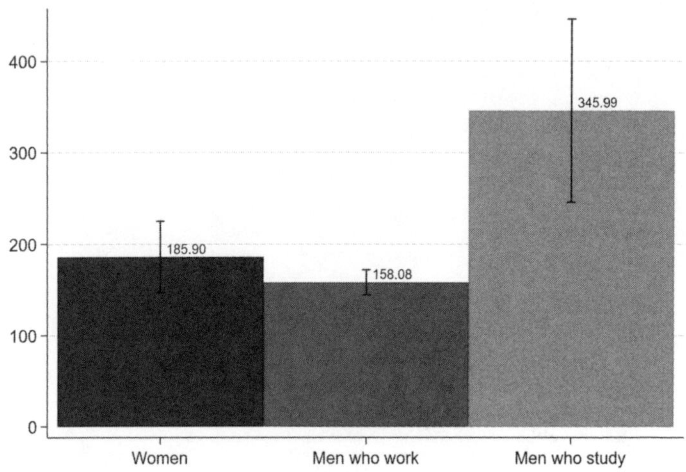

Figure 5.3: Loss aversion among Haredi men and women
Note: Error bars indicate standard errors. All reported differences are statistically significant at $p < 0.01$ or smaller.

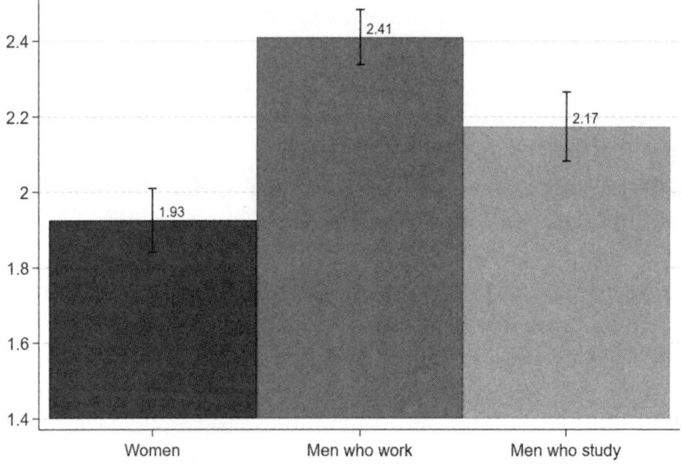

Figure 5.4: Competitiveness among Haredi men and women
Note: Error bars indicate standard errors. All reported differences are statistically significant at $p < 0.01$ or smaller.

In addition to differences between men and women, we were also interested in directly comparing the two subgroups of Haredi men, who should be nearly identical in every aspect except for their exposure to economic life. By directly comparing just these two groups, we can better isolate the effect of economic socialization from other factors, such as any potential biological or other gender differences, which would otherwise be difficult to control for.

We find that men in Kollel tend to be significantly more cautious with money, less financially savvy, and more averse to losses. They also show less appetite for competition. These differences hold even when we control for age, income, specific sect within the Haredi community, and city of residence—factors that could also shape one's attitude toward risk-taking and competition.

The Haredi case underscores the impact of nurture over nature in economic behavior. Indeed, Haredi men in Kollel not only refrain from participating in the economic sphere but actively avoid engaging in economic pursuits, viewing them as potential distractions from their spiritual goals and religious obligations.[43] This outright rejection of the "economic" further distances them from the practical aspects of money management and rational decision-making. While gender gaps in financial behavior observed elsewhere are still often attributed to biological differences, our study highlights economic socialization as a root cause. Social norms, cultural expectations, and exposure to economic environments play crucial roles in developing an economic mindset.

*

Like the Khasi, Haredi society assigns particular roles to people, which shape their attitudes toward money and how well they play the economic game. This happens alongside other deeply ingrained cultural and power dynamics, including patriarchy and religion. Traditional power structures remain intact, but the way individuals interact with money and finance seems to be molded particularly by economic socialization. In Western societies, economic socialization can encode gender norms that incentivize men to be the risk-takers and breadwinners and women the cautious savers and homemakers, thereby reinforcing those power dynamics. Haredi culture offers a different script. Here, men who prioritize religious studies over earning a livelihood are not only accepted but revered, even if their financial behavior skews "irrational." In doing so, the community turns the typical Western notion of gender-specific economic behavior on its head, reminding us that our financial habits and attitudes are not just individual choices but a reflection of broader social teachings and expectations.

Given the important role that economic socialization plays in shaping financial behavior, it's intriguing to reflect on how gender dynamics might surface in more "mainstream" settings: which invites us to revisit some of the research studies presented earlier in this book.

REVISITING THE FEEL FOR THE GAME

A key finding in chapter 2 was that composition of capital could influence loss aversion, following Bourdieu's theory of practice where individual-level rationality can be conferred through a "feel for the game" of economic life. In that study, people with relatively higher weightings of economic capital showed lower levels of loss aversion, and those with proportionally more cultural capital displayed greater loss aversion.

When the sample is subset by gender, something striking emerges. For starters, women in the sample were, on average, more loss averse than the men, which is consistent with other research.[44] But here's what stands out: the forms of capital that affect one's loss aversion differ markedly between the sexes.

Women, on average, appear to be highly sensitive to variations in their cultural capital, but men's loss aversion was instead tied to their economic capital. Specifically, women in the study who had higher levels of cultural capital exhibited a stronger tendency to avoid losses, regardless of their net worth. For men, the opposite pattern emerged: their degree of loss aversion correlated strongly with their financial standing, but their cultural capital didn't seem to matter (fig. 5.5).

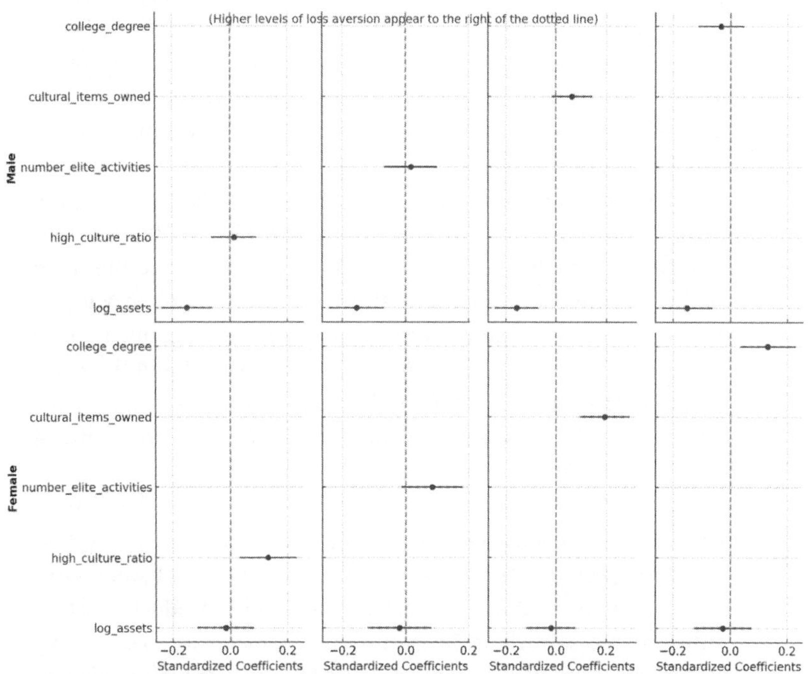

Figure 5.5: Individual loss aversion by sex, as it varies by economic capital and various measures of cultural capital (higher levels of loss aversion appear to the right of the dotted line)

These findings suggest that certain fundamental principles underlying economic decision-making may not be gender-neutral. Men appear to be more attuned to their financial circumstances, whereas women's choices might be guided more by their cultural qualifications.

And it's not just that men and women have generically different dispositions that might lead them to make different choices. It's that *among* different women and *among* different men, there are sociological factors related to composition of capital at work that shape their dispositions. Remarkably, as the figure indicates, the relative magnitude of the effect of cultural capital on women's loss aversion is comparable to that of economic capital on men's, but in the opposite direction. It suggests that the logics guiding the accumulation of these two forms of capital operate as parallel but inverse forces, subtly shaping economic decisions in gendered ways. This discovery challenges the assumption of universality in economic behavior and opens up a new avenue for exploring the roots of gender disparities in various other financial outcomes.

What explains these differences? The study does not provide definitive answers, but we can speculate. One thought is that traditional Western gender roles still haunt economic life: men as the breadwinners and so attuned to fluctuations in wealth, and women attuned more to family matters. Women, due to their historical exclusion from formal economic spheres and their traditional roles as caregivers and household managers, may have developed a more culturally informed approach to financial decision-making.

Another possibility is that these differences reflect the distinct ways in which men and women accumulate and deploy capital. Indeed money and finance are still often considered stereotypically more "masculine" domains, which could produce more of an economic sensitivity in men—with women more responsive to cultural capital, since activities like the arts are often viewed as more "feminine." Women, often tasked with the transmission of cultural values and practices within families and communities, may draw upon their cultural resources when navigating economic choices.[45] They may be more likely to consider the symbolic and cultural significance of their decisions, seeking to maintain or enhance their social standing and cultural legitimacy. Men, whose capital may be more closely tied to their economic achievements, may be less influenced by these cultural considerations in their financial decision-making.

Difference in engagement with cultural activities between men and women could offer another clue—as researchers have identified a gender gap in cultural participation favoring women.[46] To this point, sociologist Omar Lizardo has pointed out "the fact that women are more likely than men to participate in traditional high-status leisure activities constitutes one of the most consistent findings in the empirical study of cultural choice."[47]

Today's economic models don't account for culture. They still focus on economic resources and financial incentives as the primary drivers of individual behavior, sidelining nonmonetary forms of capital. Indeed, many economists may not even be aware of these more sociological concepts, or may consider them to be completely irrelevant to economic behavior. And, even if some economists might find the notion of cultural capital interesting, they rarely integrate it into their models—let alone account for how its effects may differ by gender. This leaves us with an incomplete, even male-biased, understanding of economic decision-making.

RELATIONALITY AND RELATIONAL MATCHING

Chapter 4 tapped into Viviana Zelizer's ideas about how our relationships affect our money choices. We found that when people were investing money intended for someone they care deeply about—or for a significant life event like college or retirement—they generally chose less risky investment options. But what happens when we consider the gender of the investor?

Figure 5.6 shows the gender breakdown of this tendency. Interestingly, while both men and women showed similar patterns of caution with earmarked funds, women consistently picked more conservative portfolios.

This raises important considerations for long-term wealth accumulation. If you invest too conservatively, especially for long-term goals like retirement or college tuition, the end result can be significantly lower returns. Imagine a single mom and a single dad both saving for their child's education. The data suggest that moms would, on average, be more conservative with their investment choices. Even if both parents contribute the same amount each year, the mom would likely accumulate a smaller amount by the time her child turns eighteen, owing to her lower-risk approach. According to our study, she's likely to choose a portfolio that is 25% less risky than a dad in a similar situation—which could mean a significantly smaller nest egg in the long run.

Regarding the studies in the previous chapter where space was earmarked in a home, respondent gender did not make a difference when it came to selling vs. renting an inherited home or whether to downsize the home with a visiting mother-in-law. However, men were 60% more likely to suggest taking out a high-interest home equity loan and investing in a risky venture,

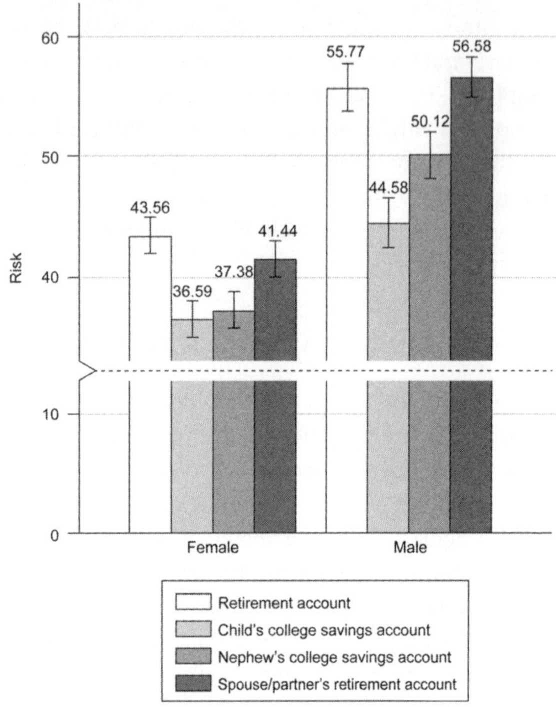

Figure 5.6: Portfolio riskiness of earmarked accounts, segmented by respondent gender

even after we controlled for the experimental manipulations and respondent demographics.

Gender, Financial Literacy, and Financial Advice

Can you make sense of retirement savings? Diversify investments? Pick the right credit card or bank account? Calculate compound interest? These questions all center around *financial literacy*—a term that sums up how well people understand money matters and how to make smart financial decisions. Good financial literacy is not just about having the right knowledge; it's about using that knowledge to steer clear of financial troubles. People with higher levels of financial knowledge and skills are better equipped to make informed decisions about saving, investing, and managing debt. They are more likely to plan for retirement, build an emergency fund, and avoid costly mistakes like high-interest loans or excessive credit card debt. Conversely, those with lower financial literacy may struggle to navigate the complex financial landscape, leading to suboptimal choices and potential financial hardship. Improving financial literacy, therefore, is not just an academic exercise—it has real-world implications for people's financial well-being and long-term security.

Despite progress toward equality in recent decades, there remain noticeable disparities in how men and women engage with and benefit from financial guidance. Research consistently shows a gender gap in both financial literacy and confidence with financial matters, even when controlling for things like income, educational attainment, and marital status.[48] These disparities start early, with high school and university-aged girls already exhibiting lower financial literacy scores than their male peers.[49] Scholars point to wide-ranging cultural conditioning into traditional roles that shape economic behaviors and attitudes in gendered ways, similar to what we saw with risk-taking above.[50]

Gender disparities in financial literacy and confidence also appear to extend into financial advice-seeking contexts. Women report greater satisfaction when receiving financial advice from women advisors, perceiving them as more understanding and relatable—while women who obtain their advice from male advisors report feeling less knowledgeable, take fewer risks, and are more anxious about their investments.[51] Having access to female financial advisors could provide women with relatable perspectives and shared experiences that inform better financial decision-making. Yet the financial advisory field remains heavily male-dominated. Recent industry demographics disclose that less than one-quarter of certified financial planners worldwide are women, as are only 17% of all financial advisors registered in the United Kingdom—a low level that has not budged since 2005.[52] This lack of diversity may limit the narratives and financial subjectivities available to women seeking guidance.[53]

To be sure, traditional financial advice has long endorsed masculine subjects and subjectivities, dating back centuries. A group of literary historians recently completed a comprehensive analysis of financial advice texts dating back to their earliest days, and they found that framing finance as a means to masculine empowerment has been a persistent undercurrent throughout its history. Despite doubts about its practical usefulness, the rhetoric of financial advice used from the seventeenth century through today has naturalized financial participation as a domain largely of maleness and whiteness. As the authors explain, "It is not simply significant that such texts are overwhelmingly written by white men, but also that they typically project an implied reader who is likewise white and male. . . . [T]o be invested (both financially and emotionally) in the stock market is simultaneously to be invested in a particular conception of subjectivity—in this case, a subjectivity that is forcefully and decidedly male."[54] This cultural conditioning over the past centuries has tacitly shaped prevailing norms and assumptions about who constitutes a financial subject, along with the type and content of advice they should receive.

The language used in contemporary financial advice and promotional materials may further reinforce these gendered notions. Linguist Cecilia Boggio and her team analyzed marketing materials from major financial institutions in several countries and discovered that they often use terms and metaphors tied to traditionally masculine domains—such as war, sports, or farming. This language may inadvertently make men feel more included but leave women feeling alienated.[55]

And yet, both public perception and the finance profession's self-image largely paint a different picture. They perceive and promote financial literacy and the advice they give as being neutral, unbiased, and objective. This discrepancy is significant, as it suggests a practical disconnect between the implicitly gendered nature of financial advice—as identified by the above research—and the prevailing societal and professional belief in its neutrality.

Outwardly, men and women still often perceive the domain of financial advice to be impartial, in part due to the accepted narrative that financial decisions ought to be rational—that is, based on coherent analysis and mathematical evaluation of figures and tables—seemingly devoid of social or cultural influences. Even behavioral finance, which acknowledges the psychological faults in economic decision-making, often frames these deviations from rationality as universally human, rather than varying by gender.[56] Taken together, this approach promotes the belief of finance being a field governed by universal principles, equally relevant to everyone. However, this broad perspective inadvertently conceals the historical and present-day gender (and other) biases that permeate the field. For instance, a 2022 survey by Hartford Financial found that a majority of both male and female respondents, across all ages, preferred financial advice that was deemed neutral and not tailored to any specific gender.[57] They desired such impartiality even while acknowledging that men and women might very well have different financial needs. This paradoxical stance exemplifies the conflict between what people say they want (stated preferences) and what their actions suggest they actually value (revealed preferences) in the context of financial advice and decision-making.

A large body of research informs us that implicit biases are powerful drivers of behaviors and decisions, even when explicit views appear egalitarian.[58] These biases reflect associations outside conscious awareness that develop from repeated cultural exposure and social experience—and can diverge markedly from stated attitudes. For instance, while overt racism has declined markedly in the United States, experiments using implicit association tests consistently uncover enduring racial prejudices that influence an array of interpersonal behaviors and judgments about others. As an example, most individuals today report that race should not factor into evaluating political candidates. Yet experiments demonstrate that when a candidate's race is made salient, both white and black participants exhibit implicit biases in favor of their own racial group.[59]

Gender biases similarly permeate tacit judgments and actions in a range of contexts.[60] Studies find that stereotypes associating men with science and women with the arts still shape academic interest and performances, even when controlling for ability.[61] Hiring experiments also reveal persistent pro-male undercurrents among both male and female evaluators, influencing employment and compensation decisions.[62] This body of work demonstrates how unintentional but implicit attitudes and stereotypes develop through ongoing exposure to cultural messaging and social dynamics.

A similar phenomenon may also shape financial advice contexts: While surveys find both men and women state a preference for gender-neutral financial guidance, unconscious biases likely still permeate the judgments people make and the receptivity of the advice that is received. And this can reinforce gender gaps in literacy and confidence as financial advice is consumed and acted upon. Consequently, a critical next step is to investigate whether implicit biases factor into the production, consumption, and interpretation of financial advice, even among those professing a desire for neutrality.

ENTER THE "FINFLUENCERS"

Recognizing the potential gender bias in financial advice, two doctoral students, Ambreen Ben-Shmuel, Vanessa Drach, and I decided to undertake a study to investigate alternative sources of financial information and their impact on financial decision-making.[63] Because traditional advice has already been identified as implicitly "male," we directed our focus toward a new trend in financial advice: social media's financial influencers, or "finfluencers." These modern-day advisors are growing in popularity, especially among younger generations. A recent survey shows that over a quarter of Gen-Z and a fifth of Millennials get their financial advice primarily from social media. Additionally, 60% of Americans, including a significant chunk of Gen-Z and Millennials, have acted on the financial tips they find online.[64]

Over the past several years, finfluencers have amassed large online followings by sharing a wide array of financial insights, from trending stock picks to long-term investment strategies. They occupy platforms such as TikTok, Instagram, and X/Twitter, making financial know-how more accessible to the public. While some finfluencers have formal financial backgrounds, most are everyday individuals who've acquired financial acumen through personal experience, and they share this wisdom freely online.[65] However, this easy access to advice comes with a caveat: the quality and applicability of their tips can vary widely. This often prompts the use of disclaimers like "this is not financial advice" to what is, ostensibly, financial advice.

Importantly, finfluencers tend to be far more diverse than the licensed professionals. Indeed, the social media influencer space is predominantly female. One marketing report found that more than three-quarters of online influencers are female, with more women than men also following influencers across all age groups.[66] This trend is reflected in the world of finfluencers too—Dasha Kennedy (@thebrokeblackgirl) and Delyanne Barros (@delyannethemoneycoach), for instance, are women of color with large followings. Moreover, seven of the "Top 10 Personal Finance Influencers to Follow in 2022" were women.[67] For the first time, financial advice from a diverse array of voices and personalities, not just those endorsed by the financial services sector, is being widely distributed. By analyzing content posted by male and female finfluencers, we can dig into the ways gender impacts financial advice and its delivery.

Our research adopted a phased approach to analyze the gender dynamics in finfluencer content. First, we conducted a qualitative analysis, combing through hundreds of individual posts from prominent male and female finfluencers on platforms like Instagram and TikTok, which allowed us to spot themes and patterns that differed based on the gender of the finfluencer. This laid the groundwork for a quantitative phase, where we aimed to discover if men and women respond differently to financial advice that has gender-coded elements (i.e., do people prefer like-gendered financial advice), even when the identity of the finfluencer is concealed.

STUDY 1: IS FINANCIAL ADVICE GENDERED ONLINE?

Ambreen and Vanessa began with a digital ethnographic approach by consuming, interacting with, and documenting a range of finfluencer content, engaging daily with content from 40 popular finfluencers—20 men and 20 women—on social media platforms like Instagram and TikTok. From this, we selected several posts from each influencer. Half of these were taken from random dates, while the other half coincided with significant events in the financial markets, such as the market turmoil in March 2020 due to the COVID-19 pandemic or the Russian invasion of Ukraine in 2022. In all, we examined more than 620 posts to explore how finfluencers offer financial advice and the varying strategies they employ.

What caught our eye was how male and female finfluencers employ different communication styles, sometimes reinforcing existing stereotypes. For example, posts by male finfluencers often featured bold fonts and primary colors, whereas female finfluencers favored pastels and varied, decorative fonts and styles. More specific to financial content, the topic of empowerment through financial inclusion and economic independence was seen exclusively among women's posts. As a pointed example, one post declared "A Man Is Not a Financial Plan!" (@investdiva). Female finfluencers also appeared to be more likely to discuss the emotional and mental health aspects of financial planning. As another example, one female finfluencer posted "Money and mental health go hand in hand. . . . Get the help you need. Don't be ashamed to reach out. And know that your mental health is the ultimate investment" (@clobaremoneycoach). By using social media as a platform to address feminist issues specifically related to financial literacy and finance, female finfluencers are able to position themselves as both experts and advocates.

Men and women finfluencers often took different stances on the same subject matter. Men looked at real estate more as an investment opportunity, while women connected it with the dream of owning a home. Male finfluencers framed "the market" to emphasize specific investment vehicles such as cryptocurrency, stocks, and other financial instruments. In contrast, female finfluencers generally portrayed "the market" in a more abstract manner, highlighting its capacity to preserve and grow wealth. Likewise, both men and women described market volatility as an exciting experience, yet different emotions were invoked when discussing these market fluctuations. Whereas men described volatility as a "thrill" or "adrenaline rush"—as a potential opportunity—women tended to describe volatility more as "stressful" or "anxiety-inducing" and something that one should patiently ride out.

Our analysis further revealed several nuanced themes that varied depending on the finfluencer's gender, despite appearing superficially neutral. While subtle, such differences could potentially shape the attitudes and actions of their followers. Male finfluencers, for example, frequently presented numerical data, such as returns, prices, and percentages, which are integral to conventional financial advice. Women focused more on the consequences of overspending or not budgeting—and were therefore much more likely to encourage their followers to focus on saving money rather than spending it. References to individual stocks, ETFs, mutual funds, and cryptocurrency were predominantly linked to men, whereas topics like retirement plans, emergency savings accounts, and student debt were more often associated with advice from women.

In addition to presenting specific strategies or information, many finfluencers made more general statements in their content. For instance, a male finfluencer might urge followers to "get in the game" by sharing his investment experiences, while a female finfluencer might advise followers to "take it slow," citing her own personal financial journey. Importantly, we identified differences in the emotional framing of advice: men often appealed to emotions like fear and greed, promoting opportunities to get rich quick. In contrast, women tended to appeal to anti-shame and empathy, sharing personal anecdotes that emphasized debt reduction alongside wealth accumulation. The ways in which these generalized statements are phrased could also have an impact on how audiences perceive the advice given—particularly in the case of investing—and how they are motivated to act on it.

Table 5.1 offers a snapshot of some of the recurring themes in our sample, broken down by the frequency of various topics by gender. The final column presents the net difference between "masculine" and "feminine" coded themes, serving as a lens through which to view gender-specific trends. For example, while "budgeting and saving" was a talking point in 32% of posts by female finfluencers, it appeared in only 7% of posts from their male counterparts—resulting in a 25-point net difference in favor of women. Likewise, men were significantly more likely to include "numbers and graphs," appearing in over 53% of their posts, as opposed to just 17% for women, leading to a net difference of 36 points leaning toward men.

Armed with this understanding, we were able to identify the most distinctly "masculine" and "feminine" coded topics, which serve

Table 5.1: Top topic codes from finfluencer posts on social media

Main Code	Subcode	Women ♀	Men ♂	Difference
Personal finance	Budgeting and saving	32.33%	7.27%	♀ 25.06
	Finance 101 (how to . . .)	23.87%	4.24%	♀ 19.62
	Job and career advice	15.70%	5.16%	♀ 10.54
	Personal debt	13.29%	3.94%	♀ 9.35
	Emergency savings	4.23%	0.30%	♀ 3.93
Type of assets/ financial accounts	Individual stocks	2.42%	16.06%	♂ 13.64
	Cryptocurrency	0.91%	10.30%	♂ 9.39
	NFTs	0.00%	8.18%	♂ 8.18
	Index funds/ETFs	5.44%	10.30%	♂ 4.86
	Retirement plans	12.39%	8.18%	♀ 4.21
Approach to investing	General investing	17.52%	28.48%	♂ 10.96
	Tactical (short-term buy or sell)	1.81%	12.42%	♂ 10.61
	Strategic (long-term buy or sell)	1.81%	11.52%	♂ 9.71
Relation to current events and issues	Reacts to social justice events and issues	38.98%	11.22%	♀ 27.76
	Reacts to economic/ financial headlines and issues	6.04%	33.03%	♂ 26.99
Content style/ approach	Numbers and graphs	17.52%	53.64%	♂ 36.12

Main Code	Subcode	Women ♀	Men ♂	Difference
	Secrets revealed	5.74%	34.24%	♂ 28.50
	Sharing their own financial decisions	3.32%	13.33%	♂ 10.01
	Off-topic (not finance related)	7.25%	0.00%	♀ 7.25
	Pop-culture reference	7.55%	1.52%	♀ 6.03
Emotional framing	Empathy	22.96%	10.30%	♀ 12.66
	Fear	9.37%	19.70%	♂ 10.33
	Greed	5.74%	15.45%	♂ 9.71
	Shame (and anti-shaming)	8.46%	0.91%	♀ 7.55

as a framework for our quantitative study that follows. But first, here is a glimpse into the most prevalent qualitative topics:

Numbers and Graphs

Numbers, figures, charts, and graphs showed up much more frequently in men's posts than in women's. One recurring trope was to depict a price chart of some stock or investment going up or down over time, along with some commentary. Other common examples included numerical examples or specific figures in the form of dollar amounts, timeframes, interest rates, or rates of return (among others):

> Becoming a millionaire is a simple math equation. . . . Invest $100/m for 55 years, Invest $200/m for 46 years, Invest $500/m for 35 years, Invest $1,000/m for 27 years, Invest $2,500/m for 17 years. There is no "luck" involved. You either invest the amount you need to or you don't (@budgetdog)

> $100,000 in your bank with a 3% annual inflation leaves you with around $40,100 of buying power in 30 years. $100,000 in stock market with a 7–12% annual return gives you around $1,700,000 of buying power in 30 years. Your salary alone isn't going to make you wealthy. Invest early and often as possible (@calltoleap)

Secrets Revealed

Some posts were framed as letting people in on a little-known secret, often touted as a way to profit from exploiting that secret. This tactic was more prevalent among male finfluencers:

> So you want to know how to make money during a stock market crash/pullback? Trust me, I'm not making anything up. You can do this with a little thing called SPREADS . . . That's right a lot of retail investors actually don't know how to do this. (@calltoleap)

> Here's what they don't want you to know about your retirement: you can go from insecured account to a secured account. In an insecured account you can actually lose money—the market goes down, you lose money. A secured account you can't lose AT ALL. So if you have a 401(k), TSP, or 403(b), you better make sure you go from that insecured account to a secured account before you lose. (@rorykdouglas)

Reacting to Short-Term Swings and Headlines

Male finfluencers were more likely to identify headlines or market events as short-term trading opportunities, with specific recommendations made for their followers. For instance, in March of 2020, as the effects of the COVID-19 pandemic began to become more obvious, the following post was made by @ wall_street_trapper:

> Through every crisis there's always an opportunity. Now isn't the time to panic, it's time to research: ZOOM & VISA are 2 great

> businesses to have during these times. In lockdown, people will work from home and use video communications to still be able to meet with colleagues. Zoom has just donated its services to in-home schools for this time. People won't be going in public and order everything online on credit cards. While people sit home, Visa is the most used card of all financial services.

Men were also more likely to respond to company-specific news headlines like earnings calls:

> Chipotle stock is up almost 13% today because they crushed their earnings, guided to higher growth, and just bought back $200M of their stock. And some analysts are calling for a $2,800 price target. (@austinhankwitz)

Individual Stocks or Tickers

Men, much more than women, posted about individual stocks or tickers. This theme already appears in some of the examples above, with ticker symbols on social media posts often denoted by the "$" for easier searching online.

> I feel like a kid in a candy store . . . over the next few weeks, we have a window of opportunity to buy investments at a discounted price . . . in February, Tesla ($TSLA) stock was trading at $835, the stock is now worth $445 . . . now is the time to buy. (@theinvestingtutor)

> Things aren't so bad when you zoom out: Return Over the Last Year
>
> - NVIDIA (NVDA): +70% 🤖
> - Alphabet (GOOGL): +38% 🔎
> - Microsoft (MSFT): +31% 🎮
> - Berkshire Hathaway (BRK.B): +30% 👴
> - Apple (AAPL): +16% 📱
> - S&P 500 (SPY): +14% 📈
> - Meta Platforms (FB/META): +13% 🤳 (@tickstocks)

Job and Career Advice

Women finfluencers were much more likely to give advice on career management and the job search. For example,

> PSA: Recruiters can see when you apply to a bunch of different roles at their company. Do your research and apply to 1–3 roles that best fit your skills and career objectives—not 100 different roles just because. (@babeonabudgetblog)

She continues in the caption, "Tailor your resume to the job(s) you're applying to, and make sure to use keywords from the actual job description(s). Once you've done that, try to find the recruiter on LinkedIn and let them know you've applied! I promise you, this approach will be more fruitful."

Other advice focused more on salary negotiation or how to ask for a raise. For instance:

> I know there's a voice in your head that whispers "am I really worthy enough to negotiate? Am I deserving enough?" Yes, yes you are. Companies EXPECT you to negotiate, and they're purposefully offering you LESS than what you're worth and what they're willing to offer with the expectation that you will negotiate. So, take this as your sign. . . . (@herfirst100k)

Empathy and (Anti-)Shame

Empathy is frequently used by both men and women, but women in particular use it to demonstrate that they, too, have been in challenging situations. This allows them to relate with their followers and encourage them by making suggestions for how to move forward. Nearly one-quarter of posts by female finfluencers were framed using empathy for their audience, supporting their financial challenges and recognizing potential shame surrounding past practices. Encouraging advice was often illustrated by personal, authentic examples where shame is openly addressed rather than implied. This approach often challenged followers to acknowledge their lack of financial literacy as an opportunity to learn and grow rather than be chastened. Some examples include:

> . . . don't be scared to admit you're wrong & change your mind. It's actually quite liberating once you start. Putting up a facade that you know everything is actually quite exhausting. Try saying "Oh I didn't know that. Can you tell me more?" You'll learn so much! (@delyannethemoneycoach)

> Remember, it's ok to make money mistakes. It's ok to make mistakes in general. The key is to learn from them, and hopefully you can learn from mine. (@your.richbff)

> If you keep telling yourself you're bad with money—that's the reality you'll keep living. See, your brain is really freaking smart, and once it believes something to be true, it will try and find more and more evidence to support that truth. . . . But the irony of all of this is that you're not actually bad at money. You just haven't been given the tools to really succeed. Imagine what it would feel like to believe you're GOOD with money. (@ellyce.fulmore)

Budgeting and Saving

These two closely related pieces of financial advice are a focus of one-third of female finfluencer posts compared to only 7% of the male posts we analyzed. This advice often took the form of straightforward tips coupled with words of encouragement to stick with a budget or savings plan once in place. Others offer more detailed advice, even going line by line through followers' budgets on occasion in order to show weak spots and recommend corrections.

> Plan out your weekly spending & saving goals and review your past week spending/saving habits. This may be difficult at first but it will help in the long run and build your financial confidence. (@myfabfinance)

> There are three reasons I see budgets fail: 1) They aren't rooted in purpose, 2) They were unrealistic from the jump 3) They don't account for the unpredictable. (@moneywithkatie)

Personal Debt

In addition to student loans, which prominently featured in the posts of female finfluencers, personal debt was a broad topic that they addressed (as opposed to just 3% of the male creators). This advice ranged from taking advantage of student loan relief programs to prioritizing paying off high-interest debts and refinancing loans. The most common theme, however, was to motivate oneself to begin repaying personal debt with the goal of eventually eliminating it altogether.

> 3 years ago I had $222,000 worth of student loan debt and no idea how I was going to pay it off. 3 years later I'm almost debt free and own a small business. A lot can change in a short amount of your time—you just need to start. . . . Seriously though, just start. (@babeonabudgetblog)

STUDY 2: DO MEN AND WOMEN PREFER TO CONSUME GENDERED FINANCIAL ADVICE?

Our qualitative analysis shows that financial advice is gendered online by male and female finfluencers in both subtle and overt ways. While significant in their own right, these findings tell us little about whether and how consumers of financial advice respond to this gender-coded content. After all, it could be that finfluencers gender their content because they believe it will attract more followers, or it could simply be a matter of their personal taste. Perhaps finfluencers are not even fully aware of the gendering they perform when circulating financial advice. Regardless of their motivations, it is important to know if men prefer masculine-coded financial advice and women prefer feminine-coded financial advice.

First, we wanted to see if we could confirm what industry surveys report, that both men and women say they prefer gender-neutral advice. So we ran a brief survey that asked respondents: "When it comes to the content of financial advice, would you prefer it to be": (A) "Gender-specific: Tailored advice considering gender-specific financial challenges and opportunities"; or (B) "Gender-neutral: Universal advice applicable to all, regardless of gender."[68]

Seventy-five percent of all responses selected "gender-neutral," a significant majority. When segmented by respondent sex, there was a bit of a difference, with men showing a stronger preference for neutral advice. While a significant 65% of women still selected "gender-neutral," more than 88% of men did.

Next, to see how men and women respond to the financial advice online, we selected the most masculine and feminine codes identified above and identified exemplar posts from our sample that incorporated those codes.[69] We first anonymized these posts by placing their content in a generic Instagram frame, effectively hiding the influencer's identity and gender, and then presented them to respondents who were asked to carefully consider each post and assess their favorability.[70] We finally segmented our analysis to separate those posts that most strongly exemplified female-prevalent vs. male-prevalent codes to isolate the influence of gendered messaging on audience reactions.

Here, we found clear evidence of implicit gender biases in the assessment of financial advice posts. The men in our sample rated finfluencer posts exhibiting more masculine themes and codes much more favorably than women did. At the same time, female respondents viewed posts containing feminine content or rhetorical patterns significantly more positively than men. Remember, we removed all identifying features of the finfluencer, so respondents knew nothing about the content creator's identity. If reactions to financial advice were truly neutral, we would expect the respondent gender to be nonsignificant in both models.

These gender preferences persist even when controlling for various demographic factors as well as social media usage and influencer following habits—which implies that the tacit gender coding within the content of the financial advice itself is likely driving the differences in reception by men and women rather than familiarity with online content. Irrespective of platform familiarity or general engagement with influencers, the subtle integration of masculine versus feminine themes, assumptions, figures of speech, and messaging frames appears to resonate differently across gender lines.

When we asked participants afterward about the study's objective, almost all participants thought it was about financial advice and social media, but not one suggested that gender was a key element. People, therefore, seem to be unaware of their gender-based preferences in financial advice. To confirm this, we conducted a follow-up study asking a new set of participants to explicitly rate each anonymized post's gender orientation as either masculine, feminine, or gender-neutral.[71] Despite viewing the same images as in the study above, the majority of responses for each post was gender-neutral, from both male and female respondents. This reiterates the fact that people don't typically recognize the gendered nature of financial advice, even as our quantitative study demonstrates clear patterns of gendered preference for consuming it.

These findings add nuance to the research on financial literacy. While traditional financial advice is often seen as impartial, our research suggests that it may inadvertently favor men's perspectives and preferences. In other words, men and women may receive exactly the same advice, but interpret it differently or make different decisions based on that same information. This could be one of the hidden factors contributing to the gender gap in financial literacy.

This is not to say that one type of advice is better than the other. Or that the solution is simply to create separate, gender-specific financial advice. However, traditional advice might not be as effective in helping women feel confident about their financial decisions. This is important, as research has shown that women often report lower levels of confidence in their financial knowledge, a factor that could account for up to a third of the gender gap in financial literacy.[72]

As social media and other digital platforms become the go-to sources for financial advice, our study gains added relevance. Online spaces often feature a more diverse range of voices, making it easier for women to find relatable advice. And research shows that women feel more confident and take greater financial risks when advised by women, which could make the online world a game-changer in closing the gender gap in financial literacy.[73]

*

Traditional economic theories have long operated under the assumption that all individuals, regardless of gender, strive to make the same rational choices. But gender does matter. Evidence shows that women, on average, exhibit more caution taking financial risks, are less competitive, and have lower confidence in financial matters compared to men. Such findings expose the limitations of economic models that ignore or diminish the role of gender, and they raise doubts about their ability to accurately predict economic behavior across diverse populations. By failing to account for such differences, these models risk offering a skewed or incomplete picture of economic realities. This not only reduces the predictive power of their models but also hampers the development of policies and interventions that could foster greater economic equality and empowerment.

In sports and gaming, gender differences manifest in both preferences and strategies. Research shows that men tend to be drawn more toward contact sports like football or first-person shooter video games, showcasing aggressive tactics; while women prefer sports emphasizing precision and strategy, such as volleyball, and more commonly opt for puzzle or simulation games.[74] Within the same activity, strategies can diverge too, with men potentially adopting a more assertive or competitive play style, and women focusing on teamwork and strategic positioning. These variations reflect not only physical differences but also how societal norms and expectations shape behavior in competitive environments. We can think of playing the economic game similarly—where men and women employ different strategies and preferences that reflect their social conditioning in their approaches to risk, competition, and financial decision-making.

In recent years, feminist economics has made some good progress by questioning gender-neutral assumptions and advocating for more gender-sensitive approaches. However, as a field, economics still grapples with how to fully account for the complex social and cultural influences that shape gendered economic behavior.[75] Behavioral economics comes closer, by acknowledging that humans don't always act rationally—but still often treats gender differences as innate and fixed personal traits, rather than fluid characteristics dynamically constructed by society. While recognizing cognitive biases, behavioral economics may look for differences in the brains of men vs. women, but overlook how asymmetric gender socialization fundamentally molds the very preferences, confidence levels, and risk calculations that drive economic decisions.

Sociologists are uniquely positioned to explore gender roles and relations—they have been studying gender for decades. Unlike the abstract rationality assumptions of traditional economics, sociological perspectives contextualize decision-making within the sociocultural narratives, institutional arrangements, power relations, and structural inequalities that make some economic choices more viable or desirable than others based on one's socially ascribed identities.

While this chapter zeroes in on gender's role in economic behavior, it's important to acknowledge that other ascribed characteristics, such as race and ethnicity, also weigh in. Although these factors didn't influence the outcomes of the specific studies presented here, they're far from irrelevant. Researchers note glaring racial and ethnic disparities in financial literacy among young American adults.[76] Furthermore, persistent income and wealth gaps affecting minority groups suggest that systemic barriers and historical discrimination continue to shape unequal economic outcomes.[77] An intersectional approach is key for analyzing how gender works with and alongside with other identities like race, class, and sexuality in configuring economic experiences.

6 * Rationality by Design: Opportunities and Dilemmas in Realizing *Homo Economicus*

Homo economicus is not behind us, he is ahead of us: like the moral and dutiful person; like the person of science and of reason. Man has been something else for a very long time; and it is not long ago that he became a machine, complicated by a calculator.

Marcel Mauss (1960)

Yes, Homo economicus does exist, but [he] is not an a-historical reality; he does not describe the hidden nature of the human being. He is the result of a process of configuration. . . . He is formatted, framed and equipped with prostheses which help him in his calculations, and which are, for the most part, produced by economics.

Michel Callon (1998)

In early 2020, the global economy suddenly ground to a halt. The COVID-19 virus was rapidly spreading and governments around the world were scrambling to keep the disease at bay. Country after country began to impose emergency measures such as quarantines, work and school closures, and stay-at-home orders. At the same time, governments and health experts urged public mask-wearing to slow down the spread of airborne droplets, and later vaccinations to boost immunity and promote better health outcomes. Officials, however, soon became frustrated at the relatively slow uptake—and even fierce resistance—directed by some at these measures. In order to boost adoption, policymakers turned to behavioral economics and the use of normative "nudges" to encourage people to behave more "rationally" concerning their own well-being and public health.[1] Yet it turned out these nudges did not often have the desired effect in the context of the coronavirus pandemic, much to the dismay of behavioral economists.[2]

A nudge is a subtle psychological intervention designed to influence people's behavior in a particular direction without using explicit incentives or penalties. Nudges are designed to correct decisions that are not in people's own best interests, or which deviate from rational choice theory due to cognitive biases, heuristics, or other psychological issues. By recognizing and addressing these biases, it is widely believed that nudges can improve both individual choice and public welfare—and they have been implemented in several real-world contexts. A well-known example proposed by Richard Thaler and his colleagues was to automatically enroll employees into their company retirement plans with the option to opt-out, rather than having to initially opt-in.[3] The change from opting-in to opting-out greatly increased 401(k) plan participation, and, they argue in turn, should lead to greater retirement security in years to come. Another real-world nudge has involved repositioning more natural and nutritious food products to be more accessible for shoppers (e.g., at eye level or at the checkout aisle) in order to increase healthy eating habits while keeping junk foods farther out of reach.[4]

In their popular book, *Nudge: Improving Decisions about Health, Wealth, and Happiness,* Thaler and coauthor Cass Sunstein outline how various other environments or situations can be deliberately designed with a choice architecture that subtly guides individuals in the right direction.[5] In doing so, they promote a spirit of "libertarian paternalism," whereby nudges can put you on course to make a normatively better decision (the paternalistic part), but are lenient enough that you aren't actually coerced into doing anything against your will (the libertarian part). Thus, a nudge can supposedly work on the subconscious mind while at the same time respecting one's autonomy and freedom to choose. The allure of nudging has since been adopted by many organizations and policymakers around the world, where some national governments have even implemented dedicated "nudge units" (officially called "behavioral insights teams") to proactively push the public toward socially desirable outcomes.[6]

So, when the COVID-19 pandemic hit, it seemed like an obvious choice to deploy nudging strategies to encourage people to think or act in desired ways for the purposes of public health. These included targeted messaging, information campaigns, and various other subtle cues aimed at encouraging mask-wearing in public, social distancing, vaccination, and the voluntary adoption of lockdowns or quarantines. But nudging largely failed to get certain people to wear masks or get vaccinated, especially among those who became ideologically aligned with the "anti-mask, anti-vax" camp. Indeed, Richard Thaler himself lamented in a 2021 *New York Times* op-ed that "persuading vaccine holdouts to get shots will require increasingly forceful interventions," concluding that behavioral nudges were unfortunately not enough to convince them.[7]

Why did nudges fail? Well, to begin with, new research that has retrospectively analyzed reams of both academic publications and government statistics on nudges more broadly concludes that there is actually no good evidence that nudges work at scale in the first place, and in some cases they have even backfired. Scholars from University College London and the University of Amsterdam conducted a large meta-analysis of nudging research and were able to calculate the true effect across more than two hundred published studies—which was essentially *zero*.[8] Moreover, nudges are usually crafted as generic one-size-fits-all solutions; and indeed, the studies that have found nudging to work tend to sample from a relatively homogenous population (e.g., white, highly educated, employed, middle-class). Another recent study by a Wharton Business School researcher examined the accuracy of predictions made by hundreds of behavioral scientists—who are the supposed experts in the field of human behavior and decision-making, and the ones who craft and deploy policy interventions like nudges.[9] The study asked over six hundred of them to predict the results of a series of behavioral science experiments. When these forecasts were pitted against random chance, basic linear models, and null hypotheses like "behavioral interventions don't affect outcomes," the results were eye-opening. Simple models often matched or even outperformed the predictions made by the behavioral scientists. In some cases, the "experts" fared worse than if one had assumed no behavioral effect at all! These insights cast doubt on the reliability of behavioral predictions and raise questions about the effectiveness of policy interventions, such as nudges, which are grounded in behavioral science.

Even without questioning the efficacy of nudges, it's important to note that, like much of economics, they are generally designed as cognitive triggers that tend to overlook the social fabric in which human behavior occurs. By not accounting for social influences—like the cultural norms, group identity, interpersonal relationships, political beliefs, and religious values (among others) discussed in this book—these nudges essentially decontextualize human behavior. For instance, a nudge promoting savings by placing a money jar in a conspicuous location might not work if the person is part of a social circle that prioritizes lavish spending over saving. Similarly, placing trash cans in public areas to encourage proper waste disposal may miss the mark since certain cultural attitudes prioritize personal convenience over environmental stewardship. And forcing employees who may be in a precarious financial position to opt-out of a retirement plan rather than opt-in might inadvertently cause stress or resentment. Moreover, nudges often assume a universal set of preferences or values, which may not hold true across diverse populations. A nudge designed to encourage healthy eating by prominently displaying nutritional information might be less effective in communities where traditional foods hold significant cultural importance, regardless of their nutritional content. Similarly, a nudge to promote energy conservation by showing comparative usage among neighbors might backfire in societies where resource consumption is viewed as a status symbol.

Some behavioral economists claim they're already taking into account factors like social norms, but their efforts often fall short of capturing their true essence. Take an example from Thaler and Sunstein's *Nudge*. In the book, they argue that simply informing people that most of their fellow citizens pay their taxes can successfully "nudge" them to do the same. They back this up with a Minnesota study that tested various messages in letters mailed out to taxpayers: some were told about the public benefits of taxes; some were threatened with punishment for noncompliance; some were offered help with filling out their tax forms; and some were simply told that more than 90% of Minnesotans already complied with their obligations under tax law.[10] They report that only the last intervention had a statistically significant effect on tax compliance, and they conclude that this is because of norms.

But there are some holes in this story.[11] First, what the letter called a "social norm" doesn't actually qualify as one. A true social norm is a shared expectation or unwritten rule of behavior that is based on mutual agreement and enforced by social pressure.[12] Indeed, we've seen that people frequently follow norms without fully agreeing with them or consciously choosing to adhere to them—socialization and the fear of sanction often lead people to abide even if they privately disagree or feel ambivalent. Consequently, this taxpayer intervention operates less on the principles of social norms and more like a form of statistical persuasion. Genuine social norms are not just about what most people are doing; they involve a level of social endorsement or moral imperative that a mere statistic cannot convey. The letter does not tell the taxpayers what their peers think or do, or why; but what the government wants them to think or do. For example, consider the difference between wearing seatbelts and tipping in restaurants. Both have high compliance rates, but they exist on different ends of the social norm spectrum. Seatbelt-wearing, like paying your taxes, is legally mandated and is more a matter of law than a social expectation. Tipping, on the other hand, isn't legally required but remains a common practice in many places. It's an expectation, based on a collective understanding. Simply saying that 90% of people comply doesn't reveal why they comply.

The authors also claim that only the one letter that said most people paid their taxes is a nudge, because it uses behavioral economics principles. But the other letters could also be seen as based on behavioral economics. For example, the letter that says "pay your taxes because it supports public services" is using framing to make tax compliance seem more altruistic. Framing is a well-known technique that influences people's decisions by presenting the information in deliberate ways. And, the letters that say "pay your taxes or we will audit you" vs. "pay your taxes and we will assist you" could be construed as invoking loss aversion to motivate people to avoid negative outcomes. It seems that the authors are arbitrarily calling the one letter a "nudge" because it worked, and the letters that did not work something else.

Importantly, their claim ignores the sociological insight that different groups of people will probably respond differently to different messaging, depending on their values, beliefs, motivations, and identities. For example, a newer study reanalyzed the data from the Minnesota experiment and found that the effect size of the social norm letter was actually very small (the difference between the people who got this letter and the control group was $12—that is, they paid, on average, $12 more in taxes) and this amount varied across different professions and tax histories.[13] They found that some taxpayers, such as those who needed an adjustment the previous year or those who worked in cash-intensive occupations, were more influenced by threats of audits; while others, such as those who worked in public service or education, were more responsive to information about public services or tax assistance. They also found that some taxpayers were more likely to increase their charitable contributions—thus lowering their taxes—rather than pay more tax when they received the "social norm" letter.

Bringing in sociological concepts could be one way to improve nudging.[14] By understanding the cultural, social, and ideological contexts in which people operate, we can design interventions that are not just psychological tricks but rather tailored to the heart of the community's values. If we look at conservative Republicans in the United States, for example, antivaccination could be seen as part of a larger group identity that has adopted a worldview internalizing beliefs about individual rights and freedom, and a concern that government mandates and regulations could encroach upon these rights. A resistance to vaccination, therefore, isn't just a stand-alone opinion but part of a broader ideology. This same group identity that embodies a sense of individualism and self-determination could, at the same time, promote skepticism of institutions thought to align with liberal or progressive agendas, such as government officials or public health authorities.

Sociologists Andrew Whitehead and Samuel Perry explored the anti-vax phenomenon using a broad sample of American adults.[15] Their research uncovered a shared ideology among conservatives—what they term "Christian nationalism"—as being a stronger predictor of vaccine hesitancy than either political or religious affiliations by themselves. Part of this shared ideology casts scientific expertise as a possible threat to traditional values and a source of moral corruption. Those adhering to Christian nationalism were more likely not only to express anti-vax views but also to doubt medical consensus more broadly and believe conspiracy theories about elites withholding cures or trying to implant microchips via vaccines.[16] This reveals how even matters of personal health can become entangled with group identity and perceptions of social change. Adherence to a particular worldview within one's cultural milieu can override considerations of personal or scientific rationality. Ideology is a powerful force. We also see evidence of a feedback loop at work, where the influence of charismatic leaders and media personalities who publicly rejected vaccines and downplayed the severity of the virus further solidified anti-vax beliefs among some conservatives. Their public stance not only validated existing skepticism but also amplified it, reinforcing the notion that vaccines—and by extension, government and scientific authority—are not to be trusted.

A traditional psychological nudge is ill-equipped to change behavior in such a context. Nudges operate on the principle of altering the immediate environment to make certain choices more salient or accessible, assuming that people will want to act in their rational self-interest and just need some help getting there. However, in the case of these individuals, their skepticism toward vaccination isn't just a matter of misinformation or lack of awareness—it's tied to a broader worldview that is deeply suspicious. A nudge that simply presents facts about the efficacy of vaccines, for example, not only would fall on deaf ears but could even backfire, as it could be perceived as a manipulation or coercion. Similarly, a nudge that tries to leverage social proof by saying "most people are getting vaccinated" may be counterproductive, as it could be interpreted as further evidence of a society moving away from the group's traditional values.

For behavioral nudges to work in real-world settings and with real people, it's essential to address social context.[17] This would entail crafting nudges as appeals not just to rational self-interest but to a greater sense of self, core values, and the broader culture. Research on attitudes toward environmentalism, for instance, shows that people are more likely to engage in sustainable behavior if they perceive that it aligns with their identity or that of their community. In general, many Americans view the "green" movement and concerns about climate change as a decidedly progressive or left-leaning agenda.[18] However, researchers also find that reframing pro-environmental rhetoric in terms of protecting the purity of the "wilderness," a moral value that resonates primarily among conservatives, largely eliminated the reported difference between liberals' and conservatives' environmental attitudes.[19] Just as reframing environmental concerns in terms of wilderness conservation clicked better with conservative values, similarly informed nudges aimed at promoting vaccination could be reframed in ways that not only appeal to rational self-interest but align more as an act of personal responsibility, a patriotic duty, or a religious and moral obligation.[20]

While an individual's psychology should not be ignored, the importance of sociological concepts should not either. By integrating these ideas into the design and implementation of nudges, we can create more effective, context-sensitive interventions that not only inform but also inspire and motivate diverse populations to change their behaviors.

Automating Rationality: Meet the Roboadvisors

If doubt has been cast on the effectiveness of nudges for socially engineering more rational outcomes on a large scale, technology is already stepping in to fill the gap. Over the past decade, advances in computing have made algorithms a ubiquitous part of our daily lives. We rely on GPS to guide us along the quickest route, we heed the suggestions of Netflix or Spotify to decide what to watch or listen to next, we use search engines and AI chatbots, and we scroll through social media feeds curated by advanced software. Increasingly, algorithms are also taking charge of our finances. Financial technologies, or *fintech*, are introducing more and more people to new forms of financial convenience and inclusion. These include peer-to-peer payments, online borrowing and lending, the use of alternative digital currencies, automated investment platforms, and more.

Technology, and especially fintech, is changing the way we think and act economically. To understand its impact, we ought to adopt a sociological perspective that examines how technology and society interact. This perspective does not simply assume that technology is a neutral tool that enhances efficiency and productivity. It goes beyond this assumption and critically investigates how it shapes our behaviors, influences our decisions, and restructures societal norms. Take social media, for example. It's not just about connecting with friends more effectively to share photos or updates. It's changed how we see ourselves, how we value "likes" and "shares," and how we view privacy. Or look at online shopping. It's not just about buying stuff from the comfort of your couch. It's changed our expectations for convenience, customer service, and product selection. And think about how a fitness tracker doesn't just count your steps; it motivates you to walk more and compare progress with friends. Similarly, a budgeting app doesn't just track your expenses; it induces you to spend more wisely.

Fintech, therefore, does a lot more than make it easier to transfer money or pay bills from your phone. It can manipulate and compel us to make certain decisions that can have us appear more rational. In this way, fintech has the capacity to transform us into "pseudo-rational" actors who appear to be making optimal decisions, but who are in fact being guided by the underlying algorithms and design choices of these platforms. Moreover, with the ease and speed of technology today, many economic decisions can be delegated completely to algorithmic platforms to achieve what appear to be rational outcomes—but at the same time these platforms reduce our agency and control over our financial lives. This raises important ethical and societal questions about the role and responsibility of fintech in shaping our economic futures. In this way, fintech brings the idea of *Homo economicus* closer to reality, but it also prompts us to question if this is the reality we really want.

In the remainder of this chapter, I will demonstrate how financial technologies that are available and accessible today can already transfigure ordinary individuals into such pseudo-rational actors, using the case of "roboadvisors." These are automated investment apps that use algorithms to manage and allocate portfolios, based on a user's risk tolerance and investment goals. They offer a seemingly efficient solution to personal investment, eliminating the need for human intervention and the potential for emotional or biased decision-making. However, as we look into the workings of roboadvisors, I will show that they are not just neutral tools to automate investing. They actively shape users, guiding them toward what the algorithms (and those who created them) determine to be the rational thing. At the same time, these platforms use the principles of behavioral economics as a kind of disciplinary system, employing everything from subtle corrective nudges to overt reprimands to keep us from tinkering with our portfolios and interfering with the cold logic of the algorithm. In this way, roboadvisors not only automate investing but also condition investors, transforming them into compliant (but rational!) subjects who allow the algorithms to take charge.

STUDYING THE ROBOADVISORS

Let's begin with a little background. Wall Street has already been dominated by algorithmic trading for more than a decade: by 2010, a majority of all trades executed on US stock exchanges were done by algorithms, and in 2022 more than three-quarters of overall stock market volume was generated by algorithmic trading.[21] Until recently, however, these algorithms mainly served Wall Street professionals or benefited the affluent who could afford them. With the introduction of roboadvisors over the past few years, however, ordinary individuals can now plug in to the same financial technoculture. In 2010, a technology start-up called Betterment launched as the world's first roboadvisor, with the aim of disrupting the traditional mode of financial planning. By embodying a classical model of financial economics into their platforms (i.e., MPT), roboadvisors like Betterment hope to achieve optimal outcomes for their clients and at the same time make those outcomes accessible for nearly all. Since then, the number of roboadvisors has grown to several hundred worldwide, created by numerous start-ups as well as large incumbents like Vanguard, Schwab, and TIAA. Far larger than some niche or fad, "robos" collectively managed over $2 *trillion* of client money for tens of millions of users worldwide in 2024. According to industry forecasts, by the year 2034 this amount will almost double, making up an impressive 15% or more of all retail investment in just a few short years.[22]

In the past, somebody looking to become an investor really had just two options: "do-it-yourself" using a self-directed online brokerage platform like E-Trade or TD Ameritrade; or hire a professional financial advisor to manage assets and make expert recommendations. The problem is that do-it-yourselfers very often employ suboptimal investment strategies where they fall victim to cognitive and emotional errors such as those identified by behavioral economics (e.g., loss aversion, overconfidence, and so on). Self-directed investors also tend to trade too much, fail to diversify, and chase trendy stocks without undertaking due diligence.[23] Hiring a financial advisor, on the other hand, may (or may not) produce better results, but this comes at a cost—typically, 1% or more in annual fees based on the amount of assets managed. Financial advisors, moreover, typically require opening account balances of at least five or six figures, effectively barring a large percentage of potential investors who lack the minimum amount of liquid assets, and so have little choice but to become a do-it-yourselfer if they want market exposure. These end up being the credulous and unskilled investors who, in turn, generate the market "noise" that feeds profits to professional trading desks and high-frequency trading algorithms.[24]

The roboadvisors were created to solve both these problems simultaneously, by offering state-of-the-art asset management but with very low starting balances and inexpensive fee structures. In fact, some roboadvisors today charge close to zero in annual fees (the usual fee structure is something like 0.25% of assets managed annually) and have very low account minimums, so you can literally start investing with just a few dollars, where every cent is allocated to an optimally diversified portfolio.

To be profitable, roboadvisors must attract a large number of small accounts, which necessitates aggressively courting people in the realm of "low finance" for the first time. Through my own interviews with several roboadvisor executives, I identified an intentional reorientation of advising toward "low net-worth investors"; as the founder and CEO of one roboadvisor explained to me,

> The traditional advisors and to some extent the hedge funds have had decades of time spent to figure out how to get a $1 million or a $100 million client. And now for the first time, everybody is focused on how to get the $10,000 client, the $1,000 client. And if you're that $1,000 client, there's a whole new litany of companies trying to earn your business.[25]

According to data collected by FINRA (a major financial regulator in the United States), roboadvisors do tend to attract clients that are lower income, younger, and more ethnically diverse than the typical investor.[26] The clients' median age at the roboadvisors I followed was reported to be between twenty-five and thirty years old, whereas the FINRA data indicate the median American investor is fifty-five to sixty years of age. It is telling that Millennials and Gen-Z'ers are specifically targeted in roboadvisors' advertising and marketing campaigns, which are carried out mainly via social media and digital channels. The vice president of growth and strategy at one medium-sized roboadvisor related, "We have for example, a lot of Uber and Lyft drivers as customers so they can start saving, and they feel comfortable already with digital platforms. With just $5 you can become an investor. It's very low barriers to entry."[27]

ENACTING A RATIONAL ACTOR

Let's examine how well this technology aligns with rational financial decision-making by comparing its outcomes to that of an idealized rational investor.

In the introduction, we met the classical sociologist Max Weber through his insightful analysis of different forms of "rationality" that motivate human behavior and social interaction. One of his most influential and enduring contributions to sociology is the analytic concept of "ideal types"—pure, abstract models that capture the essential features of some social phenomenon. For example, the ideal-type "voter" would have complete information about every candidate and policy, carefully weigh costs and benefits, and vote based solely on maximizing their own well-being. Or the ideal-type "student" would be purely motivated by learning, always engaged in class, and thriving in an academic environment. While no example perfectly embodies an ideal type, these conceptual tools allow us to better understand and analyze complex social realities by comparing subjects in the real world (e.g., actual voters or actual students) against this hypothetical ideal.

Take instrumental rationality, which Weber defined as the calculated pursuit of clearly defined goals using the most efficient means available. An ideal type of instrumental rationality oriented to the economy would describe *Homo economicus*, who single-mindedly optimizes actions to achieve objectives. We know that economic behavior is shaped by a multitude of factors beyond pure instrumental rationality. Yet the ideal type serves as a valuable yardstick to assess how closely real-world decision-making approximates this abstract model.

As technology advances, especially in the realm of high-speed computing and sophisticated algorithms, Weber's ideal types might actually come to life—not just as models for understanding human behavior but existing in their own right. While humans continue to be flawed and often irrational, technology could potentially elevate ideal types like rational actors from theoretical constructs to practical, operational realities.

To get an inside look at how roboadvisors use algorithms to optimize financial choices for everyday people, I undertook three complementary approaches:

1. I became an actual user on multiple roboadvisor platforms to experience firsthand how they operate.
2. I dug into the official documents that these platforms have submitted to the Securities and Exchange Commission (SEC) and other regulatory bodies.
3. I sat down for comprehensive interviews with key players at several roboadvisor companies.

Through this study, I was able to scrutinize the investment choices made on my behalf and see how rational decisions are born out of the interplay between human input, algorithmic programming, and well-established economic models. This doesn't mean that using a roboadvisor magically turned me—or any other of its users—into a financially sophisticated, rational decision-maker. Far from it. If I had to select my own investments or crunch the numbers myself, I'd undoubtedly fail. What's fascinating is that I could remain blissfully unaware of the finer points of finance and still come out ahead with ostensibly rational outcomes, thanks to these platforms' rigorous adherence to Modern Portfolio Theory (MPT), the canonical model in financial economics we saw back in chapter 4.[28]

MODERN PORTFOLIO THEORY AND THE IDEAL-TYPE RATIONAL INVESTOR

Modern Portfolio Theory is like a recipe for cooking up the perfect investment mix. Conceived by economist Harry Markowitz in the 1950s, the theory operates on the assumption that investors are both rational and risk averse, meaning they are willing to accept more risk but only for potentially greater returns. Using some clever math, MPT helps you figure out the best combination of investments—like stocks and bonds—to maximize expected returns for the level of risk you're comfortable with.

Markowitz would go on to earn a Nobel Prize for this groundbreaking work, which he first laid out in a paper unassumingly titled "Portfolio Selection." At its core, the paper addressed a key problem facing investors: it's about picking not just which investments to hold but also how much of each to own. MPT takes the guessing out of the game by telling you exactly how to divvy up your investment dollars among different assets.

Markowitz's model allowed him to distinguish between "efficient" and "inefficient" investment portfolios. An "efficient" portfolio according to MPT is one that has been mathematically optimized so that there exists no other possible mix of assets that would offer higher expected returns for the same level of risk.[29] In doing so, MPT lays out a road map called the *efficient frontier*, which identifies the most rational investment combinations across various risk tolerances.

If all of this seems a bit heavy, a simple visual can help. Imagine the efficient frontier represented by the curve drawn in figure

6.1. This curve plots out the best possible investment mixes for different levels of risk. Initially, the curve rises steeply, indicating that a little extra risk (say, more growth stocks and fewer bonds) can potentially yield higher rewards. But as it extends, it starts to flatten. That signifies a diminishing return on risk—the more you're willing to risk at that point, the less additional return you can expect. Portfolio mixes that fall below this curve are "inefficient" because there's a better asset mix out there that would offer either less risk for the same returns or higher returns for the same risk. Conversely, you won't find any portfolio combinations that exist above this curve—they're the stuff of investment fantasy.

So, if you're investing according to MPT, you're essentially mimicking what a perfectly rational investor would do. This hypothetical ideal investor knows their math, understands all the investment options available, and uses this information to pinpoint the exact blend of stocks, bonds, and other assets that will give them the best possible returns for their risk tolerance. Simply put, if you're following MPT, you're acting like a rational investor.

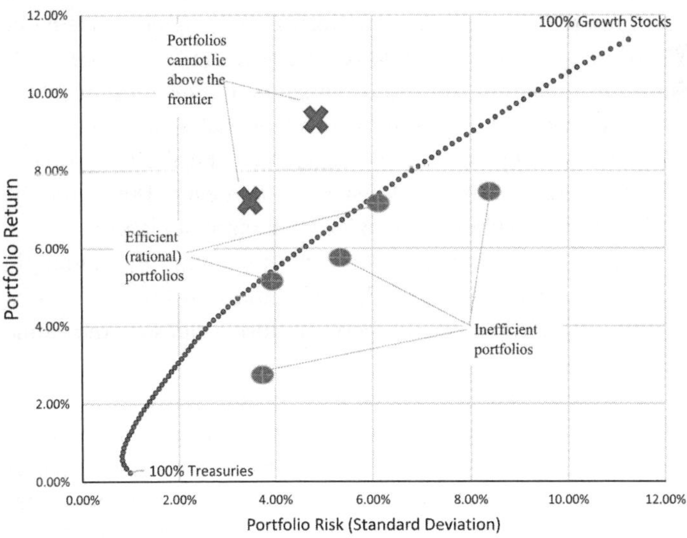

Figure 6.1: Efficient frontier January 1, 2015–December 31, 2017

As with any ideal type, the MPT investor described by Markowitz and his colleagues was never intended to actually exist. And, although he makes no mention of sociological theory, Markowitz had, in fact, specified the Weberian ideal typical investor. To be sure, Markowitz himself underscored the fact that MPT "applies to an *idealized rational decision maker* with limited information but unlimited computing powers and is not necessarily a hypothesis about actual human behavior." Moreover, he described MPT's objective as "to provide a theoretical foundation for portfolio analysis as a practical way to approximately maximize the derived utility function of a rational investor."[30] James Tobin, a contemporary of Markowitz also working on portfolio choice at the time, too, acknowledged that MPT's "main interest is prescription of rules of rational behavior for investors."[31]

Even if we could somehow push aside our cognitive biases and psychological errors—along with any sociological factors that intervene—the sheer mathematical complexity of crafting and maintaining the perfect investment mix with MPT is beyond daunting. Imagine coping with all the various asset types, identifying the very best securities from each, and then orienting that to your own risk tolerance—all without any mistakes. Plus, markets aren't static. Maintaining this perfectly balanced portfolio requires ongoing monitoring and frequent adjustments. Even the most adept investor would struggle to manage all this single-handedly. In a detailed evaluation of how investments are selected in real-world retirement plans, behavioral economists have found that people simply do not have the ability to solve the necessary optimization problems; and that even if they did, they lack sufficient willpower to execute an optimal plan.[32]

This is where roboadvisors come into play. By automating investment choices and sticking faithfully to the principles of Modern Portfolio Theory, these platforms sidestep the human pitfalls in investing.[33]

At its core, MPT serves as a blueprint for what's known as *passive investing*. Unlike active traders, who try to outsmart the market by picking specific stocks or timing their trades, passive investors aim to mirror the market's overall performance. This is often done by investing in broad benchmark indexes that represent various asset classes, like the S&P 500 for large US stocks.

Why should the "ideal" investor consider a passive strategy like MPT? For starters, it's cheaper and easier. Many platforms today even offer commission-free trades and use low-cost index funds to build portfolios.[34] Second, passive investing operates on the assumption that markets are more or less efficient, meaning that stock prices should fairly reflect all available information. If that's true, then searching for under- or overvalued stocks is a fool's errand; and even if such opportunities did exist, professional traders would quickly swoop in and neutralize them.

Skeptical? Well, the data back up the benefits of passive investing. If active investing—that is, timing the market or hand-picking stocks—really worked, we should see a fair number of fund managers consistently outperforming the market. But the numbers tell a different story. In fact, studies show that most fund managers fail to beat the market in any given year. Extend that to a fifteen-year timeline, and a mere 8% of managers come out as winners—and that dwindles to just 2% once you account for taxes, fees, and trading costs.[35] Another eye-opening study looked at the actual portfolios of some 70,000 ordinary investors who picked their own stocks without a fund manager—the average person underperformed the S&P 500 index by more than seven percentage points per year.[36] In an interview with the head of investments and strategy at one prominent roboadvisor, the influence of Markowitz's MPT equations on producing rational outcomes becomes clear:

> I think you can say roboadvisors' use of Modern Portfolio Theory, mean-variance optimization, . . . that we're making the argument that that's how you should be investing. That that is the model you should be using and it's the rational way to go about it.

DID ROBOADVISORS GIVE ME RATIONAL OUTCOMES?

To find out how closely roboadvisors actually follow the idealized "rational investor" model central to Modern Portfolio Theory, I decided to become my own test subject and signed up with twenty leading North American roboadvisors. These platforms represented around 90% of the market share at the time and included both start-ups and those offered by established financial institutions.

Posing as both a hypothetical fifty-five-year-old and a thirty-five-year-old, each with moderate risk tolerance, I opened and funded accounts to see what portfolio each service would generate for me.[37]

But before looking at the data, I needed to ensure these roboadvisors were actually investing my money based on MPT principles.[38] After closely reviewing their official websites and combing through regulatory filings, I was able to confirm that MPT was indeed the cornerstone of their investment strategies, either directly or augmented with other optimization techniques (see table 6.1).[39]

Table 6.1: Roboadvisors' use of Modern Portfolio Theory (MPT)

Roboadvisor	Uses MPT?	Excerpt
Acorns	Yes	"Acorns manages client portfolios in the Program with strategies based on Modern Portfolio Theory."
Ally Invest	Yes	"Services are based on Modern Portfolio Theory ("MPT")."
Betterment	Yes, w/ Black-Litterman	"Betterment's asset allocation is based on a theory by economist Harry Markowitz called Modern Portfolio Theory."
Covestor (Interactive Brokers)	Yes, w/ Black-Litterman	"We use an approach that is guided by the Black-Litterman approach to portfolio construction."
Ellevest	Yes	"The asset allocations are based upon tenets of modern portfolio theory."
E*TRADE Core Portfolios	Yes	"E*TRADE Capital Management follows a disciplined investment strategy based on principles of modern portfolio theory."
FidelityGO	Yes	"The model portfolio construction process . . . [is] designed to be similar to [that] of an appropriate asset allocation strategy for a particular risk profile of an investor."

Roboadvisor	Uses MPT?	Excerpt
Future Advisor (Blackrock)	Yes	"Our asset allocation strategy incorporates Modern Portfolio Theory, which suggests that investors should build portfolios that are as well diversified as possible among assets expected to provide positive long-term return."
Honest Dollar (Goldman Sachs)	Probably	"The investment recommendation relies entirely on the responses you provide regarding your time horizon and risk tolerance."
Merrill Lynch Guided Investing	Yes, w/ Black-Litterman	"We forecast long-term expected return, risk, and correlation assumptions for each asset class."
Schwab Intelligent Portfolios	Yes, w/Full-Scale Optimization	"The optimized portfolio is equal to the average weights of the results from the mean variance optimization and full-scale optimization."
SigFig	Yes	"SigFig creates portfolios matched to a range of risk tolerances through the Modern Portfolio Theory ("MPT") techniques."
SoFi	Yes	"We use mean-variance optimization . . . rooted in the modern portfolio theory work of Harry Markowitz and others."
TD Essential Portfolios	Yes	"The asset allocation tactical asset allocation tool [is] based on modern portfolio theory."
TIAA Personal Portfolio	Probably	"The model portfolios are based on the portfolio management team's judgment of how different combinations of Funds can achieve exposure to each asset class targeted for a strategic asset allocation, while also limiting the correlation among the investments."

Table 6.1 (continued)

Roboadvisor	Uses MPT?	Excerpt
Vanguard Personal Advisor	Probably	"[Our] methodology uses a strategic approach by first focusing on the mix of asset classes (i.e., stocks, bonds, cash) that align with your willingness and ability to take risk."
Wealthfront	Yes	"Wealthfront Advisers offers an automated investment advisory service based on Modern Portfolio Theory."
WealthSimple	Yes	"Using proprietary models and research based on Modern Portfolio Theory (MPT), WealthSimple manages individually tailored Client portfolios through primarily a passive investment strategy."
WiseBanyan	Yes	"WiseBanyan's focuses on building fully diversified model portfolios while minimizing fees and tax consequences. This strategy is based upon Modern Portfolio Theory."
Zack's Advantage	Yes	"Zacks Investment Management developed our own strategic approach for allocating assets within investment portfolios. The first step in the process is to apply the MVO (Mean Variance Optimization) within a portfolio based upon the Modern Portfolio Theory (MPT) of investing."

Note: Refer to the SEC's Investment Adviser Public Disclosure website (https://adviserinfo.sec.gov/) for latest information.

Based on the asset weightings I received, I reverse-engineered the portfolios that each roboadvisor created for me, providing me with their risk and return profiles. This allowed me to see how closely these portfolios hug the efficient frontier—the closer a portfolio is to this frontier, the more "rational" it is, according to MPT.

How did they do? Surprisingly well. Both the portfolios for the hypothetical fifty-five-year-old and thirty-five-year-old landed quite close to the efficient frontier.[40] Even after accounting for the typical 0.25% fee roboadvisors charge, the portfolios remained quite efficient (see open and closed circles plotted on fig. 6.2). Roboadvisors do a commendable job emulating rational investment choices.

But how do they stack up against other typical investment methods? I first compared the roboadvised portfolios to so-called lazy portfolios—simple, buy-and-hold strategies often recommended by financial gurus and self-help investment guides. They are "lazy" in that an investor can buy a small number of low-cost index funds and hold them for an extended period of time. Although these had a similar risk profile to the fifty-five-year-old roboadvised portfolio, the lazy portfolios lagged in returns (as shown by the square in fig. 6.2).[41]

Next, I looked at self-managed portfolios. According to data from the American Association of Individual Investors, these do-it-yourself portfolios, too, had comparable risk levels over the study period but, once again, substantially lower returns than their roboadvised counterparts.[42] After adding transaction costs and fees into the equation, their performance was even less impressive (depicted by the diamonds in fig. 6.2).[43]

Finally, I looked at the performance of portfolios managed by human financial advisors.[44] These were noticeably more conservative and also quite a bit farther away from the efficient frontier than any other option, particularly after considering the typical 1% fee charged annually by these advisors (marked by the triangles in fig. 6.2). While human advisors bring personalization and human judgment to the table, their portfolios cannot match the efficiency achieved by roboadvisors that leverage an algorithmic devotion to Modern Portfolio Theory (MPT). Indeed, the efficiency of roboadvisors stands out, particularly when compared to the less-than-stellar performance of their human counterparts—the technological option appears to offer a near-rational investment strategy at a fraction of the cost.

THE ACTIVE CONSTRUCTION OF PASSIVE INVESTORS: MAINTAINING RATIONALITY THROUGH DISCIPLINE

Automating financial models is core to constructing rational outcomes, but human beings still tend to "get in the way." One of

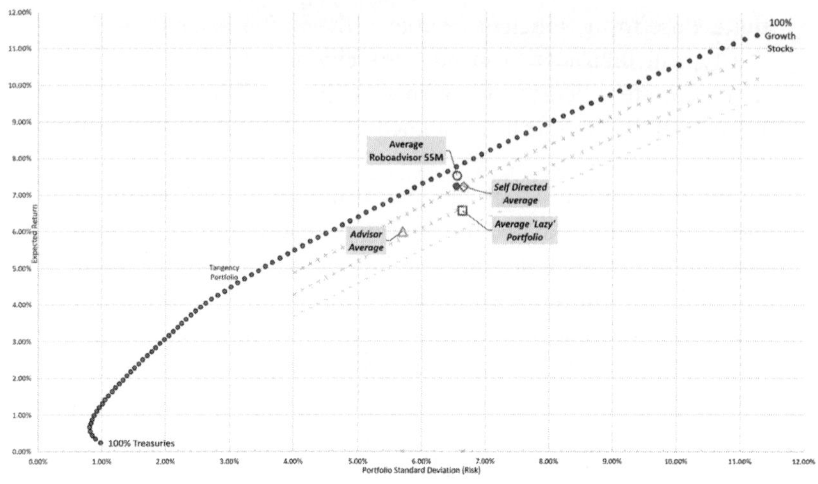

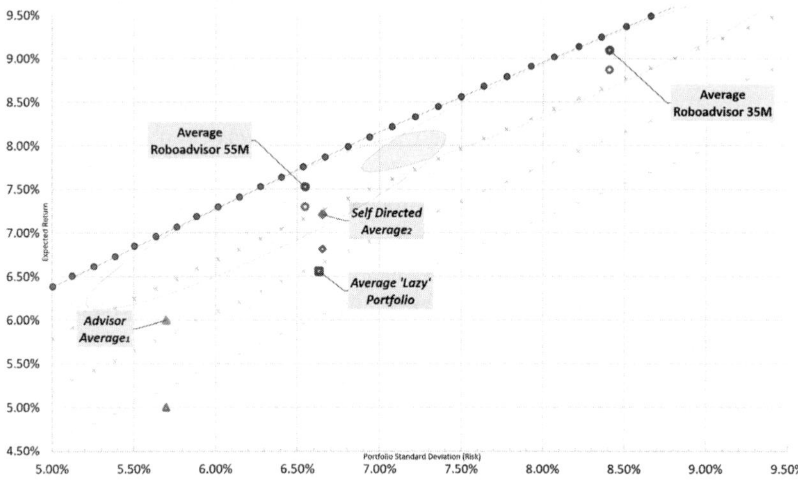

Figure 6.2: Efficient frontier January 2015–December 2017

Notes:

1. Advisor average source: Research Affiliates, LLC 3-year historical average (2015–2017). "Portfolio represents the average asset allocation of many financial advisors. The portfolio is heavily invested in U.S. stocks and bonds with smaller allocations across a number of other higher expected return asset classes."
2. Self-directed average source: American Association of Individual Investors (AAII), Asset Allocation Survey (average of monthly survey results, January 2015–December 2017).

the most striking themes that emerged from this research project is that roboadvisors construct passive investors in not one but two ways: first, by building and automating portfolios that follow MPT and, second, by imposing measures that keep users at a distance from their investments.

A former head of analytics described this "doubly passive" orientation to me:

> It's kind of more passive than self-directed passive investing, that, you know, you're not managing your own taxes and the tax implications of buying and selling. . . . you don't have to reinvest your dividends, you don't have to—really if you don't want to you don't have to know anything about investing. . . . I really see it as an extension of passive investing and kind of a more passive version of passive . . .

Financial algorithms hold the potential to generate impressive outcomes, provided their users are willing to hand over control to the algorithm—a process of intentional non-engagement. To make sure this happens, roboadvisors also combine their technology with principles of behavioral economics in order to *discipline* their users.

Most of the informants I spoke with acknowledged the detrimental impact emotions can have on investor success and viewed it as their responsibility to eliminate such irrational influences from their users.[45] Among the various people I interviewed, a strong belief emerged that roboadvisors have a "duty" to enforce restraint, as average investors often lack self-discipline and market knowledge. "I don't think people can stay the course," remarked one roboadvisor executive. "They don't have the time or the discipline—and you need a certain level of mathematical competence too. A lot of people just don't have those skills." "The data show time and time again that left to our own devices people make bad decisions," said another, "I mean, not everyone obviously, but most people are not going to have the necessary discipline."

The first layer of discipline is imposed at account creation, where the amount of financial risk an investor can assume is limited. Clients provide their time horizon and financial goals, and once the algorithm determines an optimal allocation, many roboadvisors lock you into that risk setting—they won't let you dial up the volatility, even if you feel you can handle it. Some may allow minor adjustments to your risk score (e.g., a notch or two lower, but not any higher) or restrict you to updating your risk assessment to only once a month. While these constraints can frustrate some users who think they can shoulder more risk, the idea is to keep them from straying into potentially harmful territory.

I encountered this roadblock myself when, based on my level of income and reported age, the algorithms at some of the roboadvisors I studied assigned me to a moderate portfolio, even when I thought I was willing to take more risk. When I expressed my frustration about being limited, the head of business development at one roboadvisor explained:

> You know, we won't let them—if they say, "you put me in moderate, but I want to be in aggressive." We allow them to be more conservative than our suggestion, so if they're aggressive we allow them to invest in moderate or conservative portfolios. But if you're conservative that is all you can invest in—we don't want to encourage our users to take more risk than what we think is optimal for them.

Once your portfolio is up and running, the core financial algorithms that will drive performance embody a model built on mainstream financial theory (i.e., MPT). The algorithms that discipline, however, are built on concepts from behavioral economics. Rather than operating under the belief that the standard models of economics are flawed, the corrective use of behavioral economics by roboadvisors insinuates that the models are fine—it is the human users who are in need of fixing. Accordingly, measures to control emotion and govern behavior are incorporated into the user experience. A crucial aspect of the design strategy that fosters "better behavior" involves either redirecting or redefining a user's motivation, often by initiating targeted nudges to modify specific reactions. As one of my interviewees admitted, "It's our job to sort of help manage the psychological side of things so that you can do the rational thing."

Consider how roboadvisors try to counteract loss aversion and availability (recency) bias, two psychological tendencies that we saw in chapter 3, and which can undermine self-control. Behavioral economics shows that individuals tend to overweight the present and make impulsive decisions based on recent events, to the detriment of their future welfare. So, unlike traditional brokerage platforms that provide clients with a wealth of historical data, charts, and tools to stimulate buying and selling (such as in E-Trade or Robinhood), roboadvisors aim to keep clients from trading altogether. The result is a design that accentuates the individual's future self while de-emphasizing past or current alternatives.[46]

Those I interviewed acknowledged that while the technology is increasingly user-friendly and reliable, many people still have reservations about fully entrusting their finances to software.[47] To counter this, a common feature offered by roboadvisors is the availability of basic financial tools or calculators for users to interact with. But these tools are only there to maintain investor compliance and distract them from the algorithmic processes that govern their portfolios day to day. For instance, some roboadvisors offer retirement calculators that produce pretty charts and graphs, but have no impact whatsoever on a user's investment strategy. "If you give them some perceived agency over the platform, they're much more likely to go ahead with it," one informant remarked. This is reminiscent of so-called placebo-buttons found in places like pedestrian crosswalks or elevators.[48] These are buttons that we commonly encounter that we think do things but actually do nothing; the changing of traffic lights or closing of elevator doors are in fact usually determined by timers or sensors. Roboadvisors design their platforms with this sort of concept in mind to "empower" people with a sense of agency, letting them toggle the meaningless levers and dials of inert financial tools so that they trust the platform and are more likely to work well with the algorithms rather than view them as a limitation (fig. 6.3a and fig. 6.3b).

Another interesting capability of roboadvisors is their ability to leverage large amounts of data to identify patterns of behavior among their users and respond accordingly. For instance, during a market downturn, only those apprehensive users who

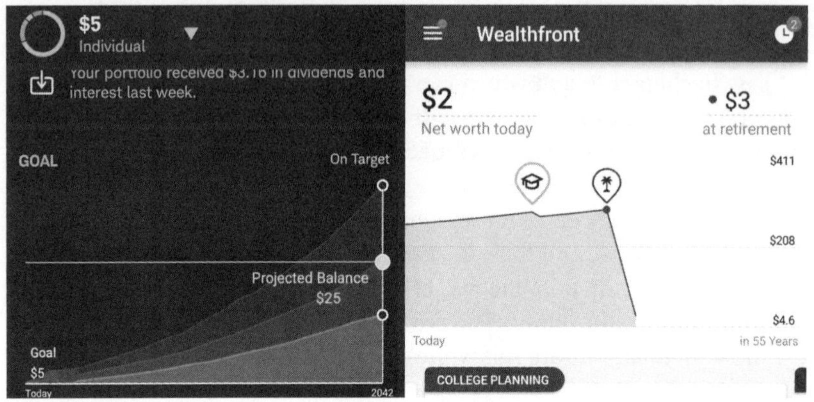

Figure 6.3a: Examples of self-directed investment apps

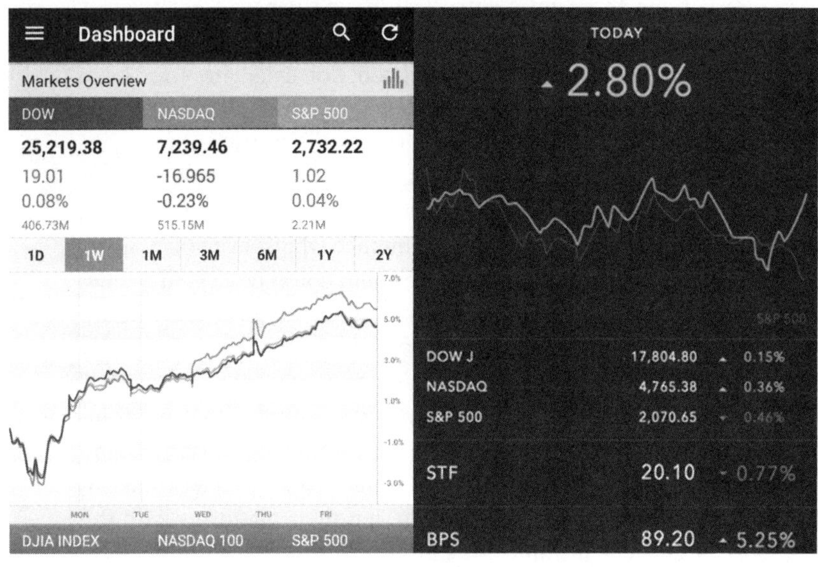

Figure 6.3b: Examples of roboadvisor apps

frequently log onto the platform to check their account balances are proactively messaged to "stay the course," while those messages are not sent to "calmer" users, which could create unnecessary anxiety among them.

Perhaps the most surprising corrective element that I found among several of the roboadvisors I surveyed was the reintroduction of human financial advisors. However, their roles and duties are entirely redefined compared to what we expect from traditional financial advisors. Instead, they serve as "counselors" or "coaches" to alleviate users' tendencies to micromanage their portfolios and to keep their emotions, particularly fear and greed, in check. As one executive told me, "Our advisors are not there to decide what strategy somebody should be in or to build a portfolio *or anything like that*, they are there to help make sure the client feels comfortable and sticks with it." When I reached out by email to one of my human advisors at a roboadvisor account to ask him to change something for me, he replied:

> Our role as advisors is to answer questions around our investment strategies/methodologies, portfolios, our services. . . . We as advisors are not able change portfolio allocations. This is done through our questionnaire and the corresponding recommendation made by our algorithm.

The human advisor is only there to help keep users adhering to MPT. Their presence creates a familiar social relation between the end-user and the unfamiliar calculative equipment at their disposal, which helps to keep the experience manageable—much like having a human pilot and copilot present during a flight that is largely controlled by autopilot. A manager at one roboadvisor explained that users sometimes just want to have a "cathartic experience," to speak to a human being who can provide a sense of reassurance, even if the facts and concepts of investing remain the same.

For the most part, these measures collectively do seem to result in "better behavior." According to several informants, approximately 80–90% of users comply with the algorithms' direction at any point in time: "By far, the vast majority take our advice, on allocations and transactions and things of that nature."

The Tragedy of Rationality

What happens when the ideal of rational action, long considered a gross oversimplification, starts becoming our lived reality? Roboadvisors appear to be turning ordinary investors—often regarded as unskilled and irrational—into extraordinarily rational players in the market. My analysis shows that portfolios managed by roboadvisors generally align closely with the efficient frontier, outperforming alternatives like self-directed investing or relying on human advisors. Surprisingly, a robo-managed account with just a $5 investment seems to fare better in terms of efficiency than a multimillion dollar portfolio overseen by a high-priced professional. This can level the playing field between the wealthy and the average Jane or Joe investor.

But, if we were to look a roboadvised user in the eye, we would not see *Homo economicus* staring back—just an ordinary human being. This rational investor is a chimera, like Frankenstein's monster: stitched together with formal mathematical procedures and brought to life by algorithmic systems. It is a creature made from human parts but lacking any human qualities. It does not feel, think, or care about anything or anyone. It simply operates with a cold, mechanical precision, devoid of the emotional, psychological, and social features that shape (and some economists would say, distort) the decisions of actual human beings.

It is a double-edged sword: delegating financial decision-making to rational algorithms can free up time and emotional energy, allowing us to focus on other important matters. As the mathematician and philosopher Alfred North Whitehead once remarked, "Civilization advances by extending the number of important operations which we can perform without thinking about them."[49] And granting unthinking financial calculation to the masses could be a positive and egalitarian achievement for society, especially since economic outcomes of individuals are increasingly tied to how well they navigate the markets.

However, this can also create a perilous disconnect between users and the technology they depend on. Without understanding the principles or assumptions behind these tools, users may be exposed to hidden risks or unintended consequences. This not only disempowers users but exposes them to model risks that even experts struggle to grasp.[50] Moreover, if technological systems fail, a lack of financial literacy, skills, and knowledge leave us ill prepared. This highlights a disjuncture between knowledge and agency: Is rational action rooted in calculating risk and return when choosing investments, or is it simply in choosing to use an optimizing tool like a roboadvisor? If it's the latter, then rational choice is no longer essentially tied to one's own competence for calculation. Instead, a different set of skills are favored that can discriminate between which algorithm to choose or the best possible platform.

This, in effect, leaves end-users detached from their economic lives. As portfolios are built, optimized, monitored, and rebalanced, the human user can remain blissfully unaware of Modern Portfolio Theory, or even the fundamentals of financial literacy, yet still achieve seemingly rational results. This can reduce human beings to "rational idiots"—optimal investors who know nothing about finance; optimal drivers who know nothing about navigation; optimal diagnosticians who know nothing about medicine; or any other optimal role that no longer requires particular expertise, skill, or knowledge to achieve that optimality. The rational use of tools should not preclude us from also cultivating the knowledge needed to direct our own paths.

One interesting property of roboadvisors is that they draw on theories of rational *and* irrational human behavior to achieve their goals. On the one hand, they use MPT to construct optimal portfolios that portray investors as rational and risk averse. On the other, they use behavioral economics to nudge and direct investors away from cognitive biases and emotional impulses that could undermine that rationality. By doing so, roboadvisors create a hybrid form of investor agency that is neither fully rational nor fully irrational, but rather a mediated mixture of both. Through combining behavioral economics and MPT, roboadvisors mobilize a conceptual basket in which their joint use, in effect, functions as a *counterperformative* invalidation of the former. Counterperformativity is a sociological concept that suggests that certain models or theories can undermine their own effectiveness when widely adopted in practice. In this way, roboadvisors recognize the irrational aspects of investors but minimize their influence by strategically deploying behavioral elements as checks. In other words, it's almost as if they're using irrationality to cancel out irrationality, thereby manufacturing a semblance of rationality.

*

But what does this all mean for the individual investor? Initial discussions with platform users suggest that the practical aspects of roboadvisors, like their low cost and set-it-and-forget-it ease of use, attract far more people than the prospect of becoming a rational investor. It's as if the roboadvisors, with a nod from regulators, are gently coaxing people to adhere to MPT. Yet, embracing MPT's principles comes with a catch—it requires giving up on the dream of outperforming the market or becoming an extraordinary investor. It requires people to accept the reality that matching the market's returns is the hallmark of rational investment.

In a society that celebrates individual excellence and aspires for above-average achievements, this can be a troublesome message. It challenges narratives that often equate rationality with exceptionalism, instead arguing that being "rational" sometimes means accepting the wisdom of being "average." This hints at a conflict between what economic models deem rational and the broader cultural values that push us to strive for exceptional performance.

While roboadvisors might bring the concept of the rational investor to life, they also show us that even if *Homo economicus* can exist, he might not always want to. But the idea of widespread rationality has broader implications than just its impact on individual decisions. As Donald MacKenzie, sociologist of markets and technology, cautions, economically rational action may not always promote stability.[51] Increasing reliance on roboadvisors and other optimizing financial technologies could unintentionally destabilize market systems.

"Market failure" is a concept that interests economists and other social scientists. It's the idea that markets, under certain conditions, don't deliver the most efficient outcomes. For instance, when they crash. This can happen for various reasons, such as too much asymmetric information where some players know more about what's going on than others—but irrational behavior is also thought to be a major contributor. When individuals and firms don't act accordingly in their own self-interest, the invisible hand of the market can fail to match supply with demand. Consequently, we end up with a less optimal distribution of resources, sometimes prompting intervention from governmental or regulatory bodies to correct the imbalance. This is why we see policies like consumer protection laws or regulations aimed at providing more transparent information, so that the market can function more efficiently.

Economists argue that if everyone just acted rationally and had equal access to information, market failures could be avoided. And, as I have shown, some aspects of fintech have the real potential to simulate *Homo economicus*, unburdened by information gaps, emotions, calculative errors, and other human deficiencies. The intuitive conclusion could be that if everyone were to use algorithms that perfectly followed economic models and made optimal decisions, then there would no longer be price bubbles, crashes, or other market failures. If only everyone were rational, everything would improve.

But what if there's a tipping point for rationality in markets? Exceed this, and they actually become unstable—not because of irrationality but because of an overabundance of apparent rationality. When more investors follow MPT, there is less "noise" in the market and more uniformity in the "signal," as the less informed, less skilled, lay investors opt for optimizing algorithms. When something unexpected happens—say, interest rates take a sudden turn or a company reports lower earnings than anticipated—it could trigger a synchronized reaction from these algorithmically "rational" investors. With similar models and assumptions driving their decisions, the reaction tends to be quicker and more extreme. Additionally, these highly informed "investors" will foresee how other similar investors will likely react, creating a dangerous feedback loop of piling on. If you expect others to panic sell, you panic sell faster. It turns into a self-fulfilling prophecy that can snowball into market extremes that models did not anticipate. Essentially, hyperrationality sows the seeds for irrational market outcomes. Too many investors basing decisions on the same "right" data and models make markets fragile rather than resilient.

Perhaps more nefarious, Modern Portfolio Theory is inherently price-insensitive—which means the model doesn't actually analyze if the stocks or assets it recommends are overpriced or not—it just says how much of your portfolio should be allocated to each asset class based on past statistical relationships rather than current valuation or expected future earnings. An exaggerated scenario illustrates this more esoteric point: Imagine *everyone* does the seemingly rational thing and uses MPT through roboadvisors, resulting in a complete cessation of all active trading. In this case, the roboadvisors would continue passively pouring money into index funds and ETFs even if constituent stocks become wildly overvalued and create a bubble (because nobody is left to actually trade those indices' component stocks). With no active valuation or price discovery, there is no self-correcting mechanism as bubbles emerge unchecked. Like an engine without a thermostat, temperatures can keep rising past safe levels before crisis hits.

In this sense, MPT on a mass scale structurally disarms markets of their stabilizing elements: differences in opinion and human scrutiny no longer provide grounding friction or the insight to detect unstable detachments from value. Pure rationality creates brittle markets optimized to an illusion—one that is exposed once anomalies inevitably reconcile. A market completely purged of its "irrational" elements isn't necessarily a better market.

*

Thought experiments aside, it's important to recognize that even in our hypothetical market, populated entirely by model-following algorithms, the "rationality" of those models and algorithms is itself a product of human culture and history—created by people, run on servers maintained by people, and regulated by rules and laws made by people. In other words, the market is never just "the market." It's a complex social institution, affected by a multitude of rational and irrational behaviors and motivations. When we talk about the limitations or dangers of an "overly rational" market, what we're really talking about is the danger of forgetting that markets are social constructs, embedded in complex webs of human relations, politics, and collective values. In short, our quest for rationality, whether individual or collective, is always going to be a social endeavor, bounded not just by the limitations of human cognition but by the societies we live in.

In essence, the pursuit of individual rationality, when scaled to the collective, can sometimes end up undermining the very systems it aims to optimize—and the market is just one such case. Researchers have similarly shown that if too many drivers on the road use route-optimizing algorithms with GPS, traffic congestion could actually worsen due to bottlenecks on smaller streets. Even autonomous vehicles, which are sometimes hailed as a silver bullet for solving traffic congestion, could ironically make the problem worse if we don't consider the broader systemic implications.[52]

Let's take another example from finance: imagine a new fintech app that automatically shifts your deposits from bank to bank to ensure you are always earning the highest interest rate, and for very low cost thanks to the use of advanced algorithms and seamless integration with banks' APIs.[53] While this seems individually rational, if everyone used this app, it could set off a chain of unintended consequences. Banks offering lower interest rates would suddenly find themselves hemorrhaging deposits, causing financial instability and raising concerns about bank runs and long-term viability.[54] Meanwhile, those banks offering higher interest rates will be flooded with new deposits, putting unexpected pressure on their cash management—forcing them to recalibrate their loan-to-deposit ratios and potentially turning to risky lending practices just to make use of the sudden capital influx. This constant shifting of funds could erode the very stability that a banking system requires to function effectively. It might even lead to a chilling scenario where banks, wary of the consequences, become reluctant to offer competitive interest rates at all. That would be a lose-lose situation: persistent and low interest rates would make savers worse off; and banks concerned about their deposit bases might be more cautious about lending, making loans harder to come by for borrowers.[55]

These kinds of examples resemble the "tragedy of the commons," a situation where people acting in their own self-interest end up harming everybody, including themselves.[56] Take the classic case, where a group of shepherds all share the same public grassland for their sheep to graze. Each shepherd wants to make a little more money, so they add more and more animals to their herds to eat from the field. But if every shepherd keeps doing this, the field will soon run out of grass and none of the animals will have any food. This hurts all of the shepherds even though they were each just trying to do what was best for themselves. Or imagine a village with a shared fishing pond. If everyone fishes just enough to feed their families, the pond thrives. But when one person decides to take more, thinking, "If I don't, someone else will?" Before you know it, the pond is empty. Be it a fishing pond, grazing land, or the Earth's atmosphere, when everyone has access and acts out of individual self-interest, we risk depleting that resource for everyone.

However, there is a critical difference when it comes to examples like Modern Portfolio Theory, GPS driving, and automated banking apps. Unlike grasslands, fish, or other physical assets, what's being depleted here is not material but *social*—it's the system or network's capacity to cope with so many rational actors.

This "tragedy of rationality" was never a concern in the past, because human behavior has always been naturally punctuated by elements of irrationality, unpredictability, and emotion. It is only in the past few years that algorithms have begun optimizing our choices to an extent that risks eroding the natural equilibrium. The presence of "irrational actors," is, in fact, a feature, not a bug. These actors contribute to dynamic social systems that are able to maintain a certain balance. Their actions, while not always maximizing their own self-interest, can indirectly promote stability by acting as shock absorbers in the system, preventing it from tipping into dangerous territory. Take, for example, the perspective of the sociologist Alex Preda, who has studied financial markets in depth. Preda argues that the presence of uninformed, unskilled "noise traders" is actually stabilizing for markets because they create trading opportunities that add to the market's liquidity and efficiency.[57] Noise traders tend to act on whims, rumors, or misconceptions, rather than making informed decisions based on fundamental analyses. This behavior, while seemingly erratic or irrational, provides the market with a constant stream of buy and sell orders that reflect much-needed variety of opinion. Far from being nuisances, these players are crucial to the market's overall health.

Similarly, drivers who ignore or turn off their GPS and take a route based on intuition or past experience often contribute to a smoother flow of traffic. These drivers create more diversity and randomness in the traffic network, which can alleviate congestion and gridlock.[58] Examples like these demonstrate that so-called irrational actors can have a positive net impact on social systems by countering the effects of rational actors.

With the rise of algorithmic rationality, the balance created by having some irrational actors in the system could be disrupted, setting the stage for a challenging question: How do we allocate rationality in society? There may come a time when some individuals or companies will need to sacrifice their own best interests for the sake of overall stability. This dynamic would create new forms of social inequality, as there will invariably be "winners" and "losers" in the distribution of rational outcomes.

Consider the investor who is allocated a suboptimal portfolio yielding smaller returns, or the driver who is directed along a less efficient route, resulting in a longer journey. Over time, these seemingly minor discrepancies can lead to significant disparities in economic and social outcomes. To prevent this, we may need to safeguard the shared social resource of rationality, ensuring that the algorithms and technologies we use are cognizant of the systemic limits and consequences of individual actions.

How do we determine who receives the most rational outcome and who must settle for a less optimal one? This is a complex issue requiring thoughtful deliberation. Should rationality be assigned randomly, or on a rotational basis? Should it be allocated based on urgency, and if so, who says what is urgent? Should it be a democratic decision—or based on skill, merit, or financial capacity?

Each option comes with its own set of challenges and drawbacks that could generate inequalities and unfair outcomes. Random or rotational distribution may seem fair at first glance, but it could result in the uneven distribution of benefits where some end up with more than they need, while others get less. Basing it on urgency could open the door for manipulation, as people could exaggerate their needs. A democratic approach is tempting, but it risks descending into majority rule at the expense of minority interests. And if we allocate based on skill, merit, or financial status, we risk deepening existing inequalities, giving the advantaged even more of an upper hand.

No matter which path we choose, we have to be aware that no solution is perfect. Inequalities and unfairness will inevitably arise. But acknowledging these challenges is the first step toward creating algorithms that are as fair and equitable as possible. By carefully considering the potential pitfalls of each approach, we can aim to develop systems that do more than optimize—they can also strive to be just.

*

Is a world overrun by rational economic actors really what we want? Peter Fleming's provocative book, *The Death of Homo Economicus*, serves as an ominous warning.[59] Fleming not only questions the feasibility of a society driven by rational actors but also highlights the damage such a mindset inflicts. He argues that this pursuit of self-interest has helped fuel widespread societal issues like rising inequality, environmental degradation, and increased feelings of social isolation.[60]

If we program our world with algorithms designed to amplify this kind of rationality, we risk making worse these already significant problems. In this context, we may need to rethink Adam Smith's famous "invisible hand"—the notion that individual self-interest naturally promotes societal benefits of its own accord—and replace it with a more visible hand of responsible stewardship. We will need to remember that self-interest is not the only or the best motive for economic action; that equitable societal benefits are not the inevitable result of market interaction; and that rationality is not a static or universal concept that can be applied or imposed on everyone in the same way.

The potential dangers of hyperrational algorithms in the economic game can be understood by comparing the role of an individual player to that of the game designer. A game's designer needs to consider the health of the system as a whole, not just the perspective of players trying to maximize their own score. So too should policymakers consider the systemic effects of automatically optimized strategies, not just the benefits to individual firms or investors.[61]

Imagine a popular multiplayer game where the designers have inadvertently made one particular strategy or character much more powerful than any other options. Players who discover this optimal strategy will start to use it more and more, and as knowledge of the strategy spreads, soon everyone is using it. From the perspective of an individual player, using the optimal strategy is the rational choice. If you've ever played a game that becomes overrun by bots (players using automated scripts), you've seen how quickly it can become unplayable for human participants. If you don't use it, you'll be at a disadvantage compared to everyone else and you'll score fewer points. The dominance of one strategy makes the game less diverse, less interesting, and less fun. If every match plays out the same way, the game becomes stale and predictable. Moreover, if the optimal strategy is too powerful, it can actually break the game entirely. Players might start to quit in frustration, or the game might become unbalanced to the point of collapse.

The same dynamics can play out in the game of the real economy. If powerful algorithms allow firms or investors to discover and exploit hyperoptimized strategies, it can spark a kind of arms race where everyone is forced to adopt similar strategies to stay competitive. We've already seen a glimpse of this with high-frequency trading, where algorithms execute large volumes of trades in fractions of a second, amplifying market volatility and creating unfair advantages.[62] This can lead to a loss of diversity and resilience in the economic system. And if the hyperoptimized strategies are too "good," they can paradoxically lead to market instability and fragility, like the flash crashes that have been caused by high-frequency trading algorithms.

But it's not all doom and gloom. The rise of algorithmic rationality also presents exciting opportunities for innovation and progress. We can harness algorithms' incredible optimization capabilities to tackle major challenges like developing renewable energy solutions, designing more efficient supply chains, and optimizing resource allocation. By crunching vast data sets and exploring wide possibility spaces, rational algorithms can identify nonobvious insights and innovative solutions that were previously impossible with limited human cognition. With robust oversight and the proper societal guardrails, rationality-enhancing algorithms could help solve complex logistical puzzles and overcome human cognitive biases in ways that raise living standards equitably.

But we should not, in this pursuit, dismiss aspects of human behavior that often defy the logic of rationality and self-interest, as seen in examples of altruism, sacrifice, cooperation, and creativity. These traits, which are inherently human, add a valuable dimension to our societies and to our lives—bestowing collective benefits that surpass what could be achieved through self-interest alone. Moreover, these traits act as a needed counterbalance to the potential overreliance on cold, calculated algorithmic judgment. They remind us that while rationality can be a powerful tool for decision-making and problem-solving, it is not the only tool at our disposal. Our ability to empathize, collaborate, and harness imagination are not just touching embellishments—they are vital evolutionary advantages.

In the end, it's not about wholly abandoning or defending rationality, but rather being more rational about our rationality.

*

As we close the pages on this exploration, let's reflect on the questions that spurred this journey and on the themes that emerged along the way. This book was born from a desire to dig deeper into the well-worn paths of behavioral economics and to illuminate some of its blind spots. While behavioral economics has brilliantly shown how humans deviate from the textbook model of rationality, it's not without its own limitations—in particular, its adherence to cognitive psychology. In response, I have presented sociology as an underutilized but powerful lens through which to better understand the complexities of economic behavior.

But this book was never just about economics or sociology; it's been a quest to understand what really drives us—the social beings behind every swipe of a credit card, every click on a "Buy Now" button, and every contemplative glance at a financial statement. What I hope has become clear is that we can't view individual choices in isolation; they are intrinsically tied to the social contexts we inhabit.

We often think we're making our own choices, but even our innermost sense of identity is a social construct. The choices we make are influenced by immediate family and friends, as well as by the broader circles we are part of—our communities, our workplaces, our virtual social networks. These circles shape our very sense of self and belonging. We aren't solitary figures navigating a calculable economic landscape; we are nodes in a vast, interconnected network, seeking meaning, status, and human connection. Our choices reflect an amalgam of motivations beyond cold logic.

We've seen how the quality of our relationships can profoundly affect the value and meaning of economic transactions in the moment. Whether negotiating a business deal or discussing household finances, the terms are not just dictated by market forces or individual preferences but negotiated in a social context, replete with its own set of unwritten rules and expectations.

As we moved through these themes, we also confronted the issue of gender—which serves as a compelling case for how social categories and cultural beliefs shape behaviors, opportunities, and outcomes. The impact of gender on economics isn't just a "women's issue" or a "diversity issue." It's a human issue that permeates our economic systems, influencing everything from wage gaps to investment decisions and consumer behavior. When we talk about gender, we're also talking about power dynamics, social expectations, and historical legacies that have profound economic consequences.

We find ourselves entangled in webs of social norms, cultural narratives, and complex relationships that defy simplistic models. If behavioral economics has taught us that we're not as rational as classical economic theories would like to believe, then our journey through the sociological landscape has shown us why that's not only okay but fundamentally human. It's a humbling realization but also an empowering one. It opens up new possibilities for understanding and shaping economic behavior in ways that are not just efficient but also equitable, meaningful, and aligned with our collective values. So when academics or policymakers "nudge" us toward making "better" choices by subtly altering the environment in which those choices are made, we should ask what exactly constitutes a "better" choice: Is it the most rational one according to some economic model? Or is it the choice that aligns with our deepest values, identities, and the meanings of our human lives?

And what happens when we introduce financial technology into this already complex landscape? Do instruments like roboadvisors resolve complexities or introduce new ones? In a world that's increasingly driven by data and algorithms, it's tempting to believe that we can engineer our way to a more rational society. But as this book has hopefully shown, there's a depth to human behavior that resists simple quantification. On the one hand, algorithms promise to optimize our lives, making our decisions more rational and our systems more efficient than ever before. On the other hand, optimizing technologies, when used all at once, can also inadvertently amplify systemic risks, pushing our delicately balanced systems toward unforeseen tipping points.

And herein lies the crux of the matter: economic rationality, whether algorithmic or human, doesn't exist in isolation. It's part and parcel of our contemporary culture and society, influenced by a host of factors that stretch beyond the individual. Our pursuit of rationality, for better or worse, therefore, isn't just a cognitive endeavor but a profoundly social one.

NOTES

Chapter One

1. Given that she was able to service the existing debt, there was no chance that a smaller monthly payment would have put her at risk of default and losing the house. Indeed, in some states without homestead exemptions, credit card companies can petition a court to put a lien on a property in addition to seizing bank accounts, assets, and garnishing wages.

2. *Curb Your Enthusiasm*, season 7, episode 3, "The Reunion."

3. R. H. Frank, "Shrewdly Irrational," *Sociological Forum* 2, no. 1 (1987): 21–41.

4. Ö. B. Bodvarsson and W. A. Gibson, "Economics and Restaurant Gratuities: Determining Tip Rates," *American Journal of Economics and Sociology* 56, no. 2 (1997): 187–203.

5. See J. Waldfogel, "The Deadweight Loss of Christmas," *American Economic Review* 83, no. 5 (1993): 1328–36; Mauss Marcel, *The Gift: The Form and Reason for Exchange in Archaic Societies*, trans. W. D. Halls (1925; London: Routledge, 1990).

6. The original "invisible hand," introduced by Adam Smith, describes how individuals pursuing self-interest unintentionally benefit society, creating an efficient economic order. In contrast, the second "invisible hand" refers to social forces—cultural norms, expectations, and relationships—that guide our economic behaviors beyond pure self-interest. These two concepts complement each other, illustrating how both market dynamics and social frameworks shape our economic world.

7. Cognitive psychology is the study of mental processes such as perception, memory, decision-making, and problem-solving. It investigates how people process and use information by considering individuals' behavior, mental state, brain structure, and genetic makeup.

8. A. Swidler, "Culture in Action: Symbols and Strategies," *American Sociological Review* (1986): 273–86.

9. N. J. Smelser and R. Swedberg, eds., "Introducing Economic Sociology," *Handbook of Economic Sociology* 2 (2005): 3–25.

10. M. Weber, *The Protestant Ethic and the Spirit of Capitalism: And Other Writings* (1905; Penguin, 2002).

11. H. R. Bowles, L. Babcock, and L. Lai, "Social Incentives for Gender Differences in the Propensity to Initiate Negotiations: Sometimes It Does Hurt to Ask," *Organizational Behavior and Human Decision Processes* 103, no. 1 (2007): 84–103; E. T. Amanatullah and M. W. Morris, "Negotiating Gender Roles: Gender Differences in Assertive Negotiating Are Mediated by Women's Fear of Backlash and Attenuated When Negotiating on Behalf of Others," *Journal of Personality and Social Psychology* 98, no. 2 (2010): 256.

12. R. H. Thaler and C. R. Sunstein, *Nudge: Improving Decisions about Health, Wealth, and Happiness* (London: Penguin, 2009).

13. A. S. Hayes, "The Active Construction of Passive Investors: Roboadvisors and Algorithmic 'Low-Finance,'" *Socio-Economic Review* 19, no. 1 (2021): 83–110.

14. N. Ocean and R. Woodman, "When Nudges Backfire: How Not to Improve Attitudes towards Shared E-Scooters" (2020), available at SSRN 4040090. https://papers.ssrn.com/sol3/papers.cfm?abstract_id=4040090.

15. See F. Pasquale, *The Black Box Society: The Secret Algorithms That Control Money and Information* (Cambridge, MA: Harvard University Press, 2015).

16. For example: theft, extortion, bribery, insider trading, money laundering, fraud, counterfeiting, etc.

17. D. Ariely and S. Jones, *Predictably Irrational* (New York: HarperCollins, 2008).

18. R. J. Shiller, "Narrative Economics," *American Economic Review* 107, no. 4 (2017): 967–1004.

19. Some economists in the early and mid-twentieth century also conceived of the economy as a game and went on to create "game theory" to describe how rational actors would behave strategically within it.

20. R. H. Thaler and L. J. Ganser, *Misbehaving: The Making of Behavioral Economics* (New York: W. W. Norton, 2015).

21. *Behavioral* economics as a distinct subdiscipline, however, has been somewhat resistant to incorporating sociological theory. Instead, it has increasingly turned to neuroscience to examine how the brain makes economic decisions. This emerging field of neuroeconomics uses devices like fMRI machines to measure how neurons fire in response to different options. However, this approach risks overlooking the broader social context in which these decisions take place.

22. The "Nobel Prize" in economics is not an official Nobel Prize. Rather, it is properly known as the Sveriges Riksbank Prize in Economic Sciences in Memory of Alfred Nobel.

23. H. A. Simon, "A Comment on 'The Science of Public Administration,'" *Public Administration Review* 7, no. 3 (1947): 200–203.

24. As opposed to *risk*-aversion that appears in mainstream economics, where a gain and an equivalent loss are treated symmetrically.

25. D. Kahneman, *Thinking, Fast and Slow* (London: Macmillan, 2011). (0.50)(−100) + (0.50)(150) = 25.

26. R. Thaler, "Some Empirical Evidence on Dynamic Inconsistency," *Economics Letters* 8, no. 3 (1981): 201–7.

27. Sometimes referred to as *present bias.*

28. S. DellaVigna, "Psychology and Economics: Evidence from the Field," *Journal of Economic Literature* 47, no. 2 (2009): 315–72.

29. "Normative" economics is used to describe value judgments and prescriptive statements about how things ought to be in the world, as opposed to "positive economics," which describes and explains economic phenomena as they are. See D. W. Hands, "The Positive-Normative Dichotomy and Economics," *Handbook of the Philosophy of Science* 13 (2012): 219–39.

30. H. Rachlin, "Altruism and Selfishness," *Behavioral and Brain Sciences* 25, no. 2 (2002): 239–50; M. R. Bennett and C. J. Einolf, "Religion, Altruism, and Helping Strangers: A Multilevel Analysis of 126 Countries," *Journal for the Scientific Study of Religion* 56, no. 2 (2017): 323–41.

31. R. J. King, *Lobster* (London: Reaktion Books, 2012).

32. A. K. Sen, "Rational Fools: A Critique of the Behavioral Foundations of Economic Theory," *Philosophy and Public Affairs* (1977): 317–44.

33. The persistence of this narrow economic view can be attributed to several factors. First, the mathematical elegance and predictive power of rational choice models make them appealing to economists and policymakers alike, even if they don't always reflect real-world behavior. Second, the individualistic ethos of Western societies, particularly in the United States, resonates with the idea of the self-interested, utility-maximizing actor. Finally, the disciplinary boundaries between economics and sociology have hindered the integration of more contextual and relational approaches to understanding economic behavior.

34. W. Streeck, "Does 'Behavioural Economics' Offer an Alternative to the Neoclassical Paradigm? (Discussion Forum II: Behavioural Economics)," *Socio-Economic Review* 8, no. 2 (2010): 387–97.

Chapter Two

1. Some studies in educational psychology have actually found that supposedly left-brained students score better on logic and math evaluations, while more right-dominant students are among the low achievers. The stronger the left-brain preference, the greater a student's aptitude in problem-solving tasks. See R. Lusiana et al., "The Influence of Right and Left Brain Intelligence on Mathematics Learning Achievement," *Journal of Physics: Conference Series* 1321, no. 3 (2019); S. C. Lee, *Cognitive Style Preferences among Adolescent Mathematics Achievers: Perception, Processing and Hemisphericity* (PhD diss., Nanyang Technical University, Singapore, 1995); D. L. Roubinek, M. L. Bell, and L. A. Cates, "Brain Hemispheric Preference of Intellectually Gifted Children," *Roeper Review* 10, no. 2

(1987): 120–22; and S. E. Taber, *A Study to Determine the Effect of Hemispheric Preference on Mathematical Problem-Solving Activity* (MS thesis, Missouri State University, 1986).

2. See J. A. Nielsen, B. A. Zielinski, M. A. Ferguson, J. E. Lainhart, and J. S. Anderson, "An Evaluation of the Left-Brain vs. Right-Brain Hypothesis with Resting State Functional Connectivity Magnetic Resonance Imaging," *PloS One* 8, no. 8 (2013): e71275; and J. Marcus, *The Left- and Right-Brain Myth* (unpublished research paper, Lynn University, 2017).

3. A less metaphorical definition of social structure is the patterned and stable arrangement of individuals, institutions, and interactions in a society comprised of both hierarchies and horizontal relations.

4. P. Bourdieu, *Algeria 1960: The Kabyle House or the World Reversed* (Cambridge: Cambridge University Press, 1979), 42.

5. Bourdieu's concept of fields describes the structured spaces of social life, such as politics, culture, and economics, each with its own rules, resources (capitals), and power dynamics. Individuals who accumulate and hold onto the specific capitals valued in a particular field come to occupy dominant positions within that social structure. A person's habitus, shaped by their social position and experiences, influences their thoughts and actions in congruous ways, like a set of lenses coloring their encounters with the world. Although Bourdieu acknowledges that individuals have some agency within these constraints, the habitus tends to guide people toward behaviors and attitudes that are consistent with their social position.

6. When he spoke of "culture," Bourdieu included not just artistic pursuits like art, literature, and music but also expertise in areas like science, law, and religion. Similar to how money confers real advantages, these cultural resources can help people gain or maintain their social standing and can be handed down through generations.

7. T. Veblen, *The Theory of the Leisure Class* (1899; Oxford: Oxford University Press, 2009).

8. This hard distinction between cultural and economic spheres is made here to lend analytic clarity—doing so spotlights how individuals rich in one type of capital but not the other can find themselves lacking intuitive mastery of "the other game." This lends insight into behaviors in the economic sphere seemingly at odds with strict rationality. But we should be careful not to overstate their true separation. In reality, there is far more complexity between the two poles of "economic" vs. "cultural." Cultural and economic capital can intersect, with prestige and profits sometimes flowing between the two realms through avenues like sponsorship of the arts, cultural tourism, infrastructure investment, and more. For instance, business elites often engage in cultural signaling through status displays. See, e.g., A. Offer, "Between the Gift and the Market: The Economy of Regard," *Economic History Review* 50, no. 3 (1997): 450–76. Power dynamics further link cultural influence to economic advantage. This sort of blending underscores

the constant interplay between the economic and cultural realms—which is a larger point I want to acknowledge.

9. For some cultural sociologists and Bourdieu scholars, my treatment and use of his theory of practice here may come across as cursory or incomplete, ignoring several important points like class fractions (e.g., the "dominated dominant"), social trajectory, and a richer description of habitus as bound up with personal history. The passage suggests that Bourdieu sees the economic and cultural fields as fundamentally opposed, which is not entirely accurate—but useful for my analysis. Bourdieu indeed argues that these two fields can be interconnected and that one form of capital can be converted into another, though it's true that they often follow different logics. For my purposes, and to speak to a broader audience, I purposefully pick and choose the pieces of Bourdieu's theory of practice as it relates to individual economic dispositions in its application to behavioral economics.

10. Fortunately, a successful artist with a poor head for numbers can still hire a financial advisor or accountant to deal with mundane numerical tasks.

11. As Bourdieu noted, the art world, from an economic perspective, is a "loser takes all" game.

12. In Bourdieu's own words, "The artist cannot triumph on the symbolic terrain except by losing on the economic terrain, and vice-versa."

13. See, e.g., O. Lizardo and S. Skiles, "Cultural Consumption in the Fine and Popular Arts Realms," *Sociology Compass* 2, no. 2 (2008): 485–502; T. Katz-Gerro, "Highbrow Cultural Consumption and Class Distinction in Italy, Israel, West Germany, Sweden, and the United States," *Social Forces* 81, no. 1 (2002): 207–29.

14. See, e.g., S. Mullainathan and E. Shafir, *Scarcity: Why Having Too Little Means So Much* (London: Macmillan, 2013).

15. Here N = 583 respondents (55% female; 79% white; 60% w/4-yr college degree or higher; 51% married; median age 42; median income $50,000/yr; median assets $50,000). Respondents were sourced from Amazon's "Mechanical Turk" (mTurk) tool, an online labor pool that allows individuals and businesses to outsource various tasks to a large network of workers on demand, who are paid approximately the pro-rata U.S. federal minimum wage. For academic research purposes such as this and other studies that will appear in this book, mTurk provides reliable access to a diverse subject pool who can complete questionnaires and survey instruments online. While relying on mTurk samples has been debated on dimensions of attention, fairness, and representativeness, many studies have found mTurk subjects to be just as good as or better than, and more demographically varied while exhibiting fewer behavioral biases, than typical undergraduate student samples. Many findings in the social sciences have furthermore been repeatedly replicated using mTurk samples. Furthermore, in this and other studies featured in this book, mTurk respondents were prescreened for quality and then through the use of attention checks. Nevertheless, findings should be interpreted with the limitations

of nonrepresentative online samples in mind. See, e.g., K. B. Sheehan and M. Pittman, *Amazon's Mechanical Turk for Academics: The HIT Handbook for Social Science Research* (Irvine, CA: Melvin & Leigh, 2016); D. Hauser, G. Paolacci, and J. Chandler, "Common Concerns with MTurk as a Participant Pool: Evidence and Solutions," in *Handbook of Research Methods in Consumer Psychology* (New York: Routledge, 2019), 319–37; M. D. Buhrmester, S. Talaifar, and S. D. Gosling, "An Evaluation of Amazon's Mechanical Turk, Its Rapid Rise, and Its Effective Use," *Perspectives on Psychological Science* 13, no. 2 (2018): 149–54.

16. For the optimal blackjack strategy, see R. N. Werthamer, "Optimal Betting in Casino Blackjack," *International Gambling Studies* 5, no. 2 (2005): 253–70; but note that respondents were not instructed on this or any other type of strategy.

17. The order of the task was presented randomly to respondents.

18. In a sense, this is like predicting that "left-brained" people will perform better at logic puzzles.

19. B. I. Carlin and D. T. Robinson, "Fear and Loathing in Las Vegas: Evidence from Blackjack Tables," *Judgment and Decision Making* 4, no. 5 (2009): 395. See also K. Yu and H. Wang, "Economic Analysis of Blackjack: An Application of Prospect Theory," in *Canadian Economic Association 43rd Annual Conference*, vol. 2931 (2009).

20. B. Mezrich, *21: Bringing Down the House–Movie Tie-In: The Inside Story of Six MIT Students Who Took Vegas for Millions* (New York: Simon and Schuster, 2008).

21. P. Bourdieu, *Distinction*, trans. Richard Nice (Cambridge, MA: Harvard University Press, 1987), 1–63.

22. It is true that Pierre Bourdieu's research on cultural capital and taste, as presented in his book *Distinction*, focused on France in the 1960s. However, this does not automatically mean that his findings and methods are not applicable or useful today. While social and cultural contexts have certainly changed since the time of Bourdieu's research, many of the underlying principles and social dynamics that he analyzed continue to be relevant and observable in contemporary society.

23. Bourdieu wrote of this, "social subjects, classified by their classifications, distinguish themselves by the distinctions they make, between the beautiful and the ugly, the distinguished and the vulgar, in which their position in the objective classifications is expressed or betrayed" (*Distinction*, 6).

24. See K. Kontiza, A. Liapis, and C. E. Jones, "Reliving the Experience of Visiting a Gallery: Methods for Evaluating Informal Learning in Games for Cultural Heritage," in *Proceedings of the 15th International Conference on the Foundations of Digital Games* (2020), 1–11.

25. R. Barthes, "The Photographic Message," in *Theorizing Communication: Readings across Traditions*, ed. Robert T. Craig and Heidi L. Muller (2000), 191–99.

26. Using net wealth as a measure of economic capital is often preferred to income because it provides a more comprehensive and long-term view of an individual's financial well-being. It takes into account accumulated assets and liabilities, offering insight into financial flexibility, intergenerational comparisons, and the capacity to mitigate income volatility. Unlike income, which can be offset by expenses, net wealth reflects what remains after accounting for all financial factors, offering a more stable indicator of overall economic resources.

27. Embodied cultural capital is measured using a count variable of elite or highbrow activities, following O. Lizardo and S. Skiles, "Highbrow Omnivorousness on the Small Screen? Cultural Industry Systems and Patterns of Cultural Choice in Europe," *Poetics* 37, no. 1 (2009): 1–23; and B. Matthes and A. Trahms, "Working and Learning in a Changing World. Part II: Codebook," FDZ data report (2010) (https://www.researchgate.net/profile/Britta-Matthes/publication/256645437_Working_and_Learning_in_a_Changing_World_Part_II_-_Codebook/links/0deec52386789ae6bf000000/Working-and-Learning-in-a-Changing-World-Part-II-Codebook.pdf), where respondents are asked whether they had in the past three years (1) attended a dance or ballet performance, (2) attended a classical music or opera performance, (3) attended a live theater or drama performance, (4) visited a domestic or foreign gallery or museum, or (5) read a book for pleasure (see also DiMaggio and Useem, 1978; Katz-Gerro, "Highbrow Cultural Consumption"; van Rees et al., 1999). A similar set of items appears in the German National Educational Panel Study (NEPS) (see https://www.neps-data.de/Mainpage), and aims to measure socially distinctive highbrow activities.

28. But merely possessing cultural capital isn't always sufficient. Access to resources such as education, cultural institutions, financial means for cultural participation, and the right social networks are equally vital to success. Hence, the interplay between economic and cultural capital, and the games associated with each, interact with one another in both cultural and economic life.

Objectified cultural capital is measured by an adapted item battery from the questionnaire of the Programme for International Student Attainment (PISA) 2003 survey (https://nces.ed.gov/surveys/pisa/pdf/2007048.pdf) which also appears in the German National Educational Panel Study (NEPS); see F. Goßmann, "Measuring Cultural Capital in the NEPS," NEPS Survey Paper (2018), 48. It consists of questions on cultural possessions (e.g., "At home, do you have classic literature, books with poems, works of art?").

The items on the number of books is adapted from C. Paulus, "Die 'Bücheraufgabe' zur Bestimmung des kulturellen Kapitals bei Grundschülern" (2009), https://www.cpaulus.de/files/BA_Artikel.pdf; and S. Sieben and C. M. Lechner, "Measuring Cultural Capital through the Number of Books in the Household," *Measurement Instruments for the Social Sciences* 1, no. 1 (2019): 1–6, which shows that book count can serve as a valid benchmark for one's level of objectified cultural capital.

29. Syngjoo Choi, Shachar Kariv, Wieland Müller, and Dan Silverman, "Who Is (More) Rational?," *American Economic Review* 104, no. 6 (2014): 1518–550.

30. Bourdieu, *Distinction*.

31. Respondents identifying as Latino/Hispanic overwhelmingly scored highest on recognition compared to other races; race was not significant in any other model. This is likely because Kahlo was of Mexican and Spanish descent.

32. This finding contrasts, for example, with 1960s France which Bourdieu studied.

33. D. Kahneman and A. Tversky, "Prospect Theory: An Analysis of Decision under Risk," in *Handbook of the Fundamentals of Financial Decision Making*, pt. 1, ed. Leonard C. MacLean and William T. Ziemba (World Scientific, 2013), 99–127.

34. Loss aversion in the context of investing is known as the *disposition effect*. It is also thought to be responsible for the so-called endowment effect, where individuals place greater value on an object they already own than the same object not in their possession.

35. A. Tversky and D. Kahneman, "The Framing of Decisions and the Psychology of Choice," *Science* 211, no. 4481 (1981): 453–58.

36. D. Kahneman, *Thinking, Fast and Slow* (London: Macmillan, 2011), 284.

37. Although the practical usefulness of loss aversion has come under recent criticism (see, e.g., D. Gal and D. D. Rucker, "The Loss of Loss Aversion: Will It Loom Larger Than Its Gain?," *Journal of Consumer Psychology* 28, no. 3 [2018]: 497–516), it is still quite influential and is consistently observed among respondents in hypothetical survey choices as well as in real-world experimental or observational studies.

38. A. Bruhin, H. Fehr-Duda, and T. Epper, "Risk and Rationality: Uncovering Heterogeneity in Probability Distortion," *Econometrica* 78, no. 4 (2010): 1375–412.

39. J. D. Hey and C. Orme, "Investigating Generalizations of Expected Utility Theory Using Experimental Data," *Econometrica* 62, no. 6 (1994): 1291–326.

40. Kahneman, *Thinking, Fast and Slow*, 284.

41. Sample: N = 1,387. 53% male; 77% white; 59% w/4-yr college degree or higher; 54% married; median age 39; median income $50,000/yr; median assets $50,000.

42. The ordering of all questions was randomized.

43. D. Blake, E. Cannon, and D. Wright, "Quantifying Loss Aversion: Evidence from a UK Population Survey," *Journal of Risk and Uncertainty* 63, no. 1 (2021): 27–57; L. Walasek, T. L. Mullett, and N. Stewart, "A Meta-Analysis of Loss Aversion in Risky Contexts," *Journal of Economic Psychology* 103 (2024): 102740.

44. Note that a very small subset of respondents in the behavioral economics literature, as well as in our own study, report $\lambda < 1.0$, indicating

these respondents are in fact *risk-seeking*. While some attribute this to innate predispositions, sociological factors such as peer and family influences, challenging environments, gender socialization, and access to resources or social safety nets may contribute to risk-seeking behavior. The nature of risks may also vary across social positions, with those possessing high economic and cultural capital engaging in more calculated and strategic risks, while those with lower levels of capital face more existential and immediate risks driven by the need to survive and overcome daily challenges.

45. Respondent net wealth was my measure for economic capital. Cultural capital is again measured in three forms: embodied in the cultural activities one participates in, objectified as cultural objects owned, and institutionalized through one's education. For this study, I also utilize an additional, more sophisticated measure of embodied cultural capital that constructs a ratio of the number of highbrow interests or activities respondents enjoy or partake in (such as classical music, poetry, fine dining, wine tasting, and so on).

I use a more sophisticated measure of cultural capital based on the ratio of highbrow to lowbrow activities that people enjoy or do. I asked another group of respondents (not from the main survey) to rate different activities from very lowbrow to very highbrow. I selected the top 32 activities that were either very lowbrow or very highbrow and balanced them by category and cost. I asked the main survey respondents which of these activities they enjoy or do a lot. I calculated the ratio of highbrow/(highbrow + lowbrow) activities for each respondent. This ratio reflects the idea that cultural elites consume both highbrow and lowbrow culture, while lower-status people consume mostly lowbrow culture. A higher ratio means more cultural capital and vice versa. O. Lizardo, "Why 'Cultural Matters' Matter: Culture Talk as the Mobilization of Cultural Capital in Interaction," *Poetics* 58 (2016): 1–17; Lizardo and Skiles, "Highbrow Omnivorousness"; R. Peterson and R. Kern, "Changing Highbrow Taste: From Snob to Omnivore," *American Sociological Review* 61, no. 5 (1996): 900–907.

46. In a series of supplemental analyses, I test models' sensitivity to respondents' race/ethnicity, geographic region, whether they have children, and self-reported assessments of competitiveness, financial literacy, and math abilities; I have found no substantive deviations from our main findings (results available upon request). Age and age-squared are statistically significant in all models.

I measured risk tolerance by asking how willing people are to take financial risks on a scale from "I am not willing to take any risks even though that greatly reduces my expected returns" to "I am willing to take a substantial amount of risk, in the hopes of earning substantial returns." See, e.g., M. Rabin, *Diminishing Marginal Utility of Wealth Cannot Explain Risk Aversion* (Munich: University Library of Munich, 2000); M. O. Rieger, M. Wang, and T. Hens, "Risk Preferences around the World," *Management Science* 61, no. 3 (2015): 637–48.

47. Michael Lee Wood, Dustin S. Stoltz, Justin Van Ness, and Marshall A. Taylor, "Schemas and Frames," *Sociological Theory* 36, no. 3 (2018): 244–61.

48. Max Besbris, "Romancing the Home: Emotions and the Interactional Creation of Demand in the Housing Market," *Socio-Economic Review* 14, no. 3 (2016): 461–82.

49. See, e.g., A. S. Booij, B. M. Van Praag, and G. Van De Kuilen, "A Parametric Analysis of Prospect Theory's Functionals for the General Population," *Theory and Decision* 68 (2010): 115–48; T. Schonberg, C. R. Fox, and R. A. Poldrack, "Mind the Gap: Bridging Economic and Naturalistic Risk-Taking with Cognitive Neuroscience," *Trends in Cognitive Sciences* 15, no. 1 (2011): 11–19; L. Walasek and N. Stewart, "How to Make Loss Aversion Disappear and Reverse: Tests of the Decision by Sampling Origin of Loss Aversion," *Journal of Experimental Psychology: General* 144, no. 1 (2015): 7; H. M. Von Gaudecker, A. Van Soest, and E. Wengström, "Heterogeneity in Risky Choice Behavior in a Broad Population," *American Economic Review* 101, no. 2 (2011): 664–94; Walasek, Mullett, and Stewart, "Meta-Analysis of Loss Aversion."

50. See M. Arora and S. Kumari, "Risk Taking in Financial Decisions as a Function of Age, Gender: Mediating Role of Loss Aversion and Regret," *International Journal of Applied Psychology* 5, no. 4 (2015): 83–89. See also chap. 5 of this book on the role of gender in economic behavior.

51. P. R. Locke and S. C. Mann, "Professional Trader Discipline and Trade Disposition," *Journal of Financial Economics* 76, no. 2 (2005): 401–44; R. H. Frank, T. Gilovich, and D. T. Regan, "Does Studying Economics Inhibit Cooperation?," *Journal of Economic Perspectives* 7, no. 2 (1993): 159–71. Does working with economic matters create economic dispositions and wealth? Or do people with economic mindsets choose such work or studies? I do not aim to explain causality here; I think there is a mutual and interdependent relationship. Habitus is the mental reflection of social structure but also its source: "Social reality exists, so to speak, twice, in things and in minds, in fields and in habitus, outside and inside social agents" (P. Bourdieu and L. J. Wacquant, *An Invitation to Reflexive Sociology* [Chicago: University of Chicago Press, 1992], 127). The result is a dialectic that both shapes dispositions based on social position and also reinforces the objective structure of social space through actions and beliefs.

52. M. Wang, M. O. Rieger, and T. Hens, "The Impact of Culture on Loss Aversion," *Journal of Behavioral Decision Making* 30, no. 2 (2017): 270–81.

53. Pierre Bourdieu, *Algeria 1960: The Kabyle House or the World Reversed* (Cambridge: Cambridge University Press, 1979), 9.

54. Economist Frank Knight distinguished between measurable "risks" and unmeasurable "uncertainties." The Kabyle people, in their rhythmic and cyclical approach to life and the future, inherently recognized what many modern economic models overlook: that the future holds

uncertainties which cannot be neatly quantified or predicted. Their practices reflect an understanding that, while we may try to forecast and prepare, the future's true nature is often beyond the realm of calculable risk.

55. E.g., E. Zerubavel, "The Language of Time: Toward a Semiotics of Temporality," *Sociological Quarterly* 28, no. 3 (1987): 343–56.

56. Eviatar Zerubavel, *The Seven Day Circle: The History and Meaning of the Week* (Chicago: University of Chicago Press, 1989).

57. T. T. Campbell, "The Four-Day Work Week: A Chronological, Systematic Review of the Academic Literature," *Management Review Quarterly* (2023); https://doi.org/10.1007/s11301-023-00347-3.

58. J. Beckert, *Imagined Futures: Fictional Expectations and Capitalist Dynamics* (Cambridge, MA: Harvard University Press, 2016).

59. M. D. Bea, "Relational Foundations of an Unequal Consumer Credit Market: Symbiotic Ties between Banks and Payday Lenders," *Journal of Consumer Affairs* 57, no. 1 (2023): 320–45.

60. L. Green, J. Myerson, D. Lichtman, S. Rosen, and A. Fry, "Temporal Discounting in Choice between Delayed Rewards: The Role of Age and Income," *Psychology and Aging* 11, no. 1 (1996): 79; B. D. Bernheim, D. Ray, and Ş. Yeltekin, "Poverty and Self-Control," *Econometrica* 83, no. 5 (2015): 1877–911.

61. N. Fligstein and A. Goldstein, "The Emergence of a Finance Culture in American Households, 1989–2007," *Socio-Economic Review* 13, no. 3 (2015): 575–601.

62. Bourdieu, *Algeria 1960*, 164.

63. SoFi, "17 Ways to Save Money on Coffee Expenses," https://www.sofi.com/learn/content/save-money-on-coffee/.

Chapter Three

1. While one's "social networks" can certainly be facilitated or extended via online social media platforms, they are not to be confused with sites like Facebook or Twitter; indeed, social networks analysis existed long before the advent of the internet.

2. "Social identity" and "group identity" are related concepts that have slightly different meanings (although they are sometimes used interchangeably). Social identity is the part of our self that comes from belonging to social groups. These groups can be based on various characteristics, such as race, ethnicity, gender, religion, nationality, or even shared interests or hobbies. Social identity is often formed through a process of social comparison, where we evaluate ourselves in relation to others and use group membership as a way to define ourselves. Group identity, on the other hand, is the sense of belonging and connection that members of a group have. These feelings are often shared among members of a group and distinguish them from other groups. Group identity can be based on various factors, including shared experiences, values, and goals. So, social identity is a more personal construct that is based on membership

in social groups, and group identity is more of a collective construct that reflects the shared characteristics and experiences held by the group members.

3. See, e.g., A. K. Zinn, A. Lavric, M. Levine, and M. Koschate, "Social Identity Switching: How Effective Is It?," *Journal of Experimental Social Psychology* 101 (2022): 104309.

4. S. Bindra, D. Sharma, N. Parameswar, S. Dhir, and J. Paul, "Bandwagon Effect Revisited: A Systematic Review to Develop Future Research Agenda," *Journal of Business Research* 143 (2022): 305–17.

5. M. Granovetter, "Economic Action and Social Structure: The Problem of Embeddedness," *American Journal of Sociology* 91, no. 3 (1985): 481–510. Granovetter's concept of embeddedness using a social networks approach was adapted from Karl Polanyi's earlier development of institutional embeddedness, or the idea that economic systems and markets are not autonomous entities but instead bound up historically and situated within broader social, political, legal, and cultural institutions. Polanyi challenged the idea that the development of market economies is natural or inevitable; he challenged the idea that markets are self-regulating, instead positing that they must be constructed and maintained.

6. B. Uzzi, "Social Structure and Competition in Interfirm Networks: The Paradox of Embeddedness," *Administrative Science Quarterly* (1997): 35–67.

7. P. DiMaggio and H. Louch, "Socially Embedded Consumer Transactions: For What Kinds of Purchases Do People Most Often Use Networks?," *American Sociological Review* (1998): 619–37.

8. F. Kramarz and O. N. Skans, "When Strong Ties Are Strong: Networks and Youth Labour Market Entry," *Review of Economic Studies* 81, no. 3 (2014): 1164–200.

9. M. Granovetter, *Getting a Job: A Study of Contacts and Careers* (Chicago: University of Chicago Press, 1995).

10. See, e.g., S. Utz, "Is LinkedIn Making You More Successful? The Informational Benefits Derived from Public Social Media," *New Media and Society* 18, no. 11 (2016): 2685–702.

11. P. Bourdieu and L. J. Wacquant, *An Invitation to Reflexive Sociology* (Chicago: University of Chicago Press, 1992), 126.

12. G. Mead, "The Case of Kabylia: Explaining Elective Affinities in Bourdieu's Mediterranean," *Postcolonial Studies* 19, no. 3 (2016): 325–41.

13. P. Bourdieu, *Algeria 1960: The Kabyle House or the World Reversed* (Cambridge: Cambridge University Press, 1979), 21.

14. There have been, on average, less than 10 fatal shark attacks per year worldwide, compared to hundreds of accidental swimming pool deaths; https://en.wikipedia.org/wiki/Shark_attack; https://www.cdc.gov/drowning/facts/index.html.

15. J. Klayman, "Varieties of Confirmation Bias," *Psychology of Learning and Motivation* 32 (1995): 385–418.

16. The term *meme stock* refers to a fad stock that gains significant attention and popularity among retail investors due to its presence on social media and the internet forums, often accompanied by humorous or irreverent memes and commentary.

17. A *short squeeze* is a situation that can occur when a stock has been heavily sold short by investors and starts to rise in price. Selling short involves borrowing shares of stock and selling them, hoping to buy them back later at a lower price—it is a strategy that profits from falling prices. As the price rises, those who have bet against the stock (i.e., taken a "short" position) are forced to buy shares to cover their positions and limit their losses. This buying activity can drive the stock price up even further, potentially creating a feedback loop that pushes the price even higher.

18. Hannah Knowles, "Billionaire Blasts 'Robinhood Market' as Jon Stewart, Others Herald GameStop Stock Rebellion," *Washington Post*, January 29, 2021, https://www.washingtonpost.com/business/2021/01/29/leon-cooperman-gamestop/.

19. See, e.g., J. J. Han, "Reddit Dataset on Meme Stock: GameStop," *Journal of Open Humanities Data* 8 (2022); see also A. Aloosh, S. Ouzan, and S. J. H. Shahzad, "Bubbles across Meme Stocks and Cryptocurrencies," *Finance Research Letters* 49 (2022): 103155.

20. "Last Gasp of the Meme-Stock Era," *The Economist*, February 2, 2023; https://www.economist.com/finance-and-economics/2023/02/02/the-last-gasp-of-the-meme-stock-era.

21. G. Le Bon, *The Crowd: A Study of the Popular Mind* (London: T. F. Unwin, 1897); C. Mackay, *Extraordinary Popular Delusions and the Madness of Crowds* (New York: Simon and Schuster, 1841).

22. R. Cook, G. Bird, C. Catmur, C. Press, and C. Heyes, "Mirror Neurons: From Origin to Function," *Behavioral and Brain Sciences* 37, no. 2 (2014): 177–92.

23. D. D. Franks and V. Gecas, "Autonomy and Conformity in Cooley's Self-Theory: The Looking-Glass Self and Beyond," *Symbolic Interaction* 15, no. 1 (1992): 49–68.

24. R. Girard, *Evolution and Conversion: Dialogues on the Origins of Culture* (London: Bloomsbury Publishing, 2017).

25. C. Bellet, "The McMansion Effect: Top House Size and Positional Externalities in US Suburbs" (2019), available at SSRN 3378131;https://papers.ssrn.com/sol3/Papers.cfm?abstract_id=3378131.

26. A. R. Rottinghaus, *Upgrade Culture and Technological Change: The Business of the Future* (New York: Routledge, 2021).

27. R. Girard, *The Scapegoat* (Baltimore: Johns Hopkins University Press, 1989).

28. P. R. Haunschild, "Interorganizational Imitation: The Impact of Interlocks on Corporate Acquisition Activity," *Administrative Science Quarterly* (1993): 564–92.

29. M. Childers and S. T. McAbee, "Practitioner and Applicant Reactions to Brainteaser Interview Questions," *Journal of Personnel Psychology* 22, no. 4 (2023): 226.

30. R. Perlin, *Intern Nation: How to Earn Nothing and Learn Little in the Brave New Economy* (New York: Verso Books, 2012).

31. H. Zuckerman, "Nobel Laureates in Science: Patterns of Productivity, Collaboration, and Authorship," *American Sociological Review* (1967): 391–403.

32. P. J. DiMaggio and W. W. Powell, "The Iron Cage Revisited: Institutional Isomorphism and Collective Rationality in Organizational Fields," *American Sociological Review* (1983): 147–60.

33. C. Bicchieri, *The Grammar of Society: The Nature and Dynamics of Social Norms* (Cambridge: Cambridge University Press, 2005).

34. R. B. Cialdini and M. R. Trost, "Social Influence: Social Norms, Conformity and Compliance," in *The Handbook of Social Psychology*, ed. D. T. Gilbert, S. T. Fiske, and G. Lindzey (New York: McGraw-Hill, 1998), 151–92.

35. The economic view tends to emphasize the instrumental functions and consequences of norms. Economists are interested in how norms emerge to solve coordination problems, reduce transaction costs, and produce (or prevent) efficient outcomes. See E. Ostrom, *Governing the Commons: The Evolution of Institutions for Collective Action* (Cambridge: Cambridge University Press, 1990).

36. J. Elster, "Social Norms and Economic Theory," *Journal of Economic Perspectives* 3, no. 4 (1989), 99–117. Elster critiques economists' attempts to rationalize social norms through utility-optimizing cost-benefit analysis, arguing that it oversimplifies human behavior. Social norms cannot always be explained by individual self-interest or rational decision-making, as people often follow norms for reasons beyond economic considerations. The cost-benefit approach fails to capture the broader social consequences of adhering to or breaking norms, such as increased cooperation or trust. Moreover, some norms persist despite having no clear benefits or even causing harm, suggesting that factors like tradition or inertia play a significant role in the persistence of certain behaviors.

37. P. C. Stern, "New Environmental Theories: Toward a Coherent Theory of Environmentally Significant Behavior," *Journal of Social Issues* 56, no. 3 (2000): 407–24.

38. A. W. Gouldner, "The Norm of Reciprocity: A Preliminary Statement," *American Sociological Review* (1960): 161–78.

39. Paying someone to hold your place in line seems more socially acceptable than paying to cut ahead, as it doesn't actively displace others. This suggests norms see less injustice in paying for convenience through a proxy than directly jumping the queue. However, some may still view all paid line-standing as unfair "cheating." Queuing reveals the complex social dynamics that underlie even seemingly trivial behaviors.

40. B. Ertimur, C. Muñoz, and J. G. Hutton, "Regifting: A Multi-perspective Processual Overview," *Journal of Business Research* 68, no. 9 (2015): 1997–2004.

41. D. Cohen, R. E. Nisbett, B. F. Bowdle, and N. Schwarz, "Insult, Aggression, and the Southern Culture of Honor: An 'Experimental Ethnography,'" *Journal of Personality and Social Psychology* 70, no. 5 (1996): 945.

42. G. M. Arciniega, T. C. Anderson, Z. G. Tovar-Blank, and T. J. Tracey, "Toward a Fuller Conception of Machismo: Development of a Traditional Machismo and Caballerismo Scale," *Journal of Counseling Psychology* 55, no. 1 (2008): 19.

43. J. R. Mahalik, S. M. Burns, and M. Syzdek, "Masculinity and Perceived Normative Health Behaviors as Predictors of Men's Health Behaviors," *Social Science and Medicine* 64, no. 11 (2007): 2201–9.

44. R. Costa, M. Fávero, D. Moreira, A. Del Campo, and V. Sousa-Gomes, "Is the Link between the Dark Tetrad and the Acceptance of Sexual Violence Mediated by Sexual Machismo?," *Aggressive Behavior* 50, no. 1 (2024): e22116.

45. E. Fehr and U. Fischbacher, "Social Norms and Human Cooperation," *Trends in Cognitive Sciences* 8, no. 4 (2004): 185–90.

46. A. Etzioni, "Social Norms: Internalization, Persuasion, and History," *Law and Society Review* (2000): 157–78.

47. J. S. Coleman, *Foundations of Social Theory* (Cambridge, MA: Harvard University Press, 1994), chap. 12.

48. There are different types of social capital, including "bonding" and "bridging" social capital. Bonding social capital refers to the resources that individuals can access through close relationships with people who are similar to them (e.g., strong ties), while bridging social capital refers to the resources that individuals can access through relationships with people who are different from them (e.g., weak ties).

49. Coleman, *Foundations of Social Theory*, 306.

50. E.g., A. Mayer and S. L. Puller, "The Old Boy (and Girl) Network: Social Network Formation on University Campuses," *Journal of Public Economics* 92, no. 1–2 (2008): 329–47.

51. S. Bornschier, S. Häusermann, D. Zollinger, and C. Colombo, "How 'Us' and 'Them' Relates to Voting Behavior—Social Structure, Social Identities, and Electoral Choice," *Comparative Political Studies* 54, no. 12 (2021): 2087–122.

52. A. Toder-Alon, T. Icekson, and A. Shuv-Ami, "Team Identification and Sports Fandom as Predictors of Fan Aggression: The Moderating Role of Ageing," *Sport Management Review* 22, no. 2 (2019): 194–208.

53. V. Grimm, V. Utikal, and L. Valmasoni, "In-Group Favoritism and Discrimination among Multiple Out-Groups," *Journal of Economic Behavior and Organization* 143, C (2017): 254–71.

54. A. Ben-Ner, B. P. McCall, M. Stephane, and H. Wang, "Identity and In-Group/Out-Group Differentiation in Work and Giving Behaviors:

Experimental Evidence," *Journal of Economic Behavior and Organization* 72, no. 1 (2009): 153–70.

55. M. M. Kumar, L. Tsoi, M. S. Lee, J. Cone, and K. McAuliffe, "Nationality Dominates Gender in Decision-Making in the Dictator and Prisoner's Dilemma Games," *Plos One* 16, no. 1 (2021): e0244568.

56. S. R. Sommers and P. C. Ellsworth, "'Race Salience' in Juror Decision-Making: Misconceptions, Clarifications, and Unanswered Questions," *Behavioral Sciences and the Law* 27, no. 4 (2009): 599–609.

57. Z. Whysall, "Cognitive Biases in Recruitment, Selection, and Promotion: The Risk of Subconscious Discrimination," in *Hidden Inequalities in the Workplace: A Guide to the Current Challenges, Issues and Business Solutions*, ed. Valerie Caven, Stefanos Nachmias (New York: Springer, 2018), 215–43.

58. A. Bass, C. Wu, J. P. Schaefer, B. Wright, and K. Mclaughlin, "In-Group Bias in Residency Selection," *Medical Teacher* 35, no. 9 (2013): 747–51.

59. N. Franke, M. Gruber, D. Harhoff, and J. Henkel, "What You Are Is What You Like—Similarity Biases in Venture Capitalists' Evaluations of Start-up Teams," *Journal of Business Venturing* 21, no. 6 (2006): 802–26.

60. R. Fisman, D. Paravisini, and V. Vig, "Cultural Proximity and Loan Outcomes," *American Economic Review* 107, no. 2 (2017): 457–92.

61. J. J. Louviere, *Analyzing Decision Making: Metric Conjoint Analysis*, Quantitative Applications in the Social Sciences, no. 67 (New York: Sage, 1988).

62. Vincent Buskens and Jeroen Weesie, "An Experiment on the Effects of Embeddedness in Trust Situations: Buying a Used Car," *Rationality and Society* 12 (2000): 227–53.

63. For sofa buyers, N = 435 (48% female; 83% white; median age 43; median income $50,000; 68% w/4-yr degree or higher; 58% married); for sofa sellers, N = 446 (49% female; 85% white; median age 43; median income $50,000; 70% w/4-yr degree or higher; 60% married). Respondents were sourced from mTurk.

64. In particular, I analyzed the attribute importance and preference share in each study. These are robust, applicable, and scientific approaches to summarize conjoint analyses. This pair of measures is based on the average marginal component effect (AMCE), which is a key metric that helps quantify the causal effect of changing one attribute from one level to another while keeping all other attributes constant, averaging over the joint distribution of the other attributes. Preference share is recovered from the AMCE by multiplying it by the marginal distribution of each attribute level and summing over all possible profiles. Attribute importance is recovered by calculating the min-max range of preference shares across all levels of an attribute and then normalizing these ranges across all attributes to sum to 100%. I report attribute importance and preference share scores as stylized facts rather than raw AMCEs because the former are easier to interpret and communicate, as both reflect the relative importance of each attribute or level in terms of percentage points. See J. Hainmueller, D. J. Hopkins,

and T. Yamamoto, “Causal Inference in Conjoint Analysis: Understanding Multidimensional Choices via Stated Preference Experiments,” *Political Analysis* 22, no. 1 (2014): 1–30.

65. For car buyers, N = 458 (49% female; 83% white; median age 41; median income $50,000; 71% w/4-yr degree or higher; 60% married); for car sellers, N = 420 (53% female; 80% white; median age 44; median income $50,000; 68% w/4-yr degree or higher; 55% married). Respondents were sourced from mTurk.

66. Note that in a classic study, researchers did find discrimination in car negotiations based on a buyer’s race and gender. Specifically, they found that car dealers offered significantly lower starting prices to white males than to black or female test buyers. My findings, using a different methodology, show negligible effects for race or gender. This discrepancy could owe to changes in social attitudes over the past several decades or to biases manifesting more strongly in face-to-face interactions versus hypothetical scenarios. It could also reflect differences in the perception of discrimination versus revealed preferences under trade-off conditions. See I. Ayres and P. Siegelman, “Race and Gender Discrimination in Bargaining for a New Car,” *American Economic Review* (1995): 304–21.

67. For borrowers, N = 474 (51% female; 84% white; 67% Christian; median age 42; median income $50,000; 72% w/4-yr degree or higher; 62% married); for lenders, N = 457 (53% female; 81% white; median age 44; median income $50,000; 66% w/4-yr degree or higher; 56% married). Respondents were sourced from mTurk.

68. The preference for borrowing or lending with close ties and prioritizing the quality of the relationship is consistent with previous research on social embeddedness and relational work in informal financial transactions. See A. Portes and W. Haller, “The Informal Economy,” in *Handbook of Economic Sociology*, ed. Richard Swedberg and Neil Smelser (Princeton, NJ: Princeton University Press, 2010), 403–25.

Chapter Four

1. While it is true that certain qualified college savings accounts, such as 529 plans, do have potential tax implications or penalties if used for noneducational expenses, contributions (but not earnings) can generally be withdrawn penalty-free at any time, if contributions were made with after-tax dollars.

2. Aristotle, *The Nicomachean Ethics of Aristotle*, trans. F. H. Peters (London: K. Paul, Trench, 1886). For the Rockefeller quote, see “David Rockefeller Quotes,” BrainyQuote.com, BrainyMedia Inc., 2024, https://www.brainyquote.com/quotes/david_rockefeller_253678, accessed November 13, 2024.

3. D. Kahneman, J. L. Knetsch, and R. H. Thaler, “Experimental Tests of the Endowment Effect and the Coase Theorem,” *Journal of Political Economy* 98, no. 6 (1990): 1325–48.

4. G. R. Woirol, *Demystifying Economic Markets and Prices: Understanding Patterns and Practices in Everyday Life* (Santa Barbara, CA: Praeger [ABC-CLIO], 2019), 10.

5. S. Huck, G. Kirchsteiger, and J. Oechssler, "Learning to Like What You Have—Explaining the Endowment Effect," *Economic Journal* 115, no. 505 (2005): 689–702.

6. M. A. Ervolini, *Managing Equity Portfolios: A Behavioral Approach to Improving Skills and Investment Processes* (Cambridge, MA: MIT Press, 2014), 216–17.

7. G. Loewenstein and S. Issacharoff, "Source Dependence in the Valuation of Objects," *Journal of Behavioral Decision Making* 7, no. 3 (1994): 157–68.

8. A. P. McGraw, P. E. Tetlock, and O. V. Kristel, "The Limits of Fungibility: Relational Schemata and the Value of Things," *Journal of Consumer Research* 30, no. 2 (2003): 219–29.

9. A. P. Fiske, *Structures of Social Life: The Four Elementary Forms of Human Relations: Communal Sharing, Authority Ranking, Equality Matching, Market Pricing* (New York: Free Press, 1991). Fiske and others suggested that people use just four basic relational schemata (relational models) to generate, interpret, and coordinate aspects of most social interaction across societies. These models are termed: Communal Sharing (CS), Authority Ranking (AR), Equality Matching (EM), and Market Pricing (MP).

10. V. A. Zelizer, "How I Became a Relational Economic Sociologist and What Does That Mean?," *Politics and Society* 40, no. 2 (2012): 146.

11. N. Bandelj, F. F. Wherry, and V. A. Zelizer, eds., *Money Talks: Explaining How Money Really Works* (Princeton, NJ: Princeton University Press, 2017).

12. Here, N = 552 (57% female; 76% white; 66% w/4-yr degree or higher; 48% married; median age 40; median income $45,000). Of the respondents, 116 were randomly assigned to the willingness-to-pay (WTP) group and 106 to the baseline willingness-to-accept (WTA) group. In the scenarios,108 saw a friend who had helped in the past; 111 a deceased friend; and 109 a cheating friend. Respondents sourced from mTurk.

13. See, e.g., M. Einiö, M. Kaustia, and V. Puttonen, "Price Setting and the Reluctance to Realize Losses in Apartment Markets," *Journal of Economic Psychology* 29, no. 1 (2008): 19–34; D. Genesove and C. Mayer, "Loss Aversion and Seller Behavior: Evidence from the Housing Market," *Quarterly Journal of Economics* 116, no. 4 (2001): 1233–60; R. H. Thaler, "Anomalies: Saving, Fungibility, and Mental Accounts," *Journal of Economic Perspectives* 4, no. 1 (1990): 193–205.

14. A. S. Hayes and M. Besbris, "Earmarking Space: Relationality, Economic Judgments and Housing Wealth," *Socio-Economic Review* 21, no. 3 (2023): 1445–72. For this experiment, N = 1,593 (56% female; median age 38; 62% w/4-year degree or higher; 77% white; median income $45,000; 56% home owners). Respondents were randomly assigned to one of three

earmark conditions: a good relational match (n = 505); a relational mismatch (n = 509); or to a null control (n = 579). Respondents sourced from mTurk.

The gender of the friend in the vignette was randomized so that some respondents saw male pronouns and some female pronouns. This variation did not have any effect on the outcome of interest. We used a "grandparent" as the relational earmark because it is common for grandparents to leave homes to their grandchildren, and it is more plausible that the grandchild-grandparent relationship be distant or troubled than child-parent, generally speaking. See O. Druta and R. Ronald, "Young Adults' Pathways into Homeownership and the Negotiation of Intra-Family Support: A Home, the Ideal Gift," *Sociology* 51, no. 4 (2017): 783–99; R. Dunifon and A. Bajracharya, "The Role of Grandparents in the Lives of Youth," *Journal of Family Issues* 33, no. 9 (2012): 1168–94.

15. All reported differences are statistically significant at $p < 0.05$ or smaller. Logistic regression analysis with covariates indicated no significant effect on the outcome of interest based on home ownership, respondent gender, income, education, race, marital status, or having children. Respondent age was found to be positively associated with recommending selling the house, all else equal; perhaps as older respondents tend to prefer cash savings in preparation for retirement.

16. For this scenario, N = 1.549 (55% female; median age 38; 66% w/4-yr degree or higher; 76% white; median income $45,000; 55% home owners). Respondents were randomly assigned to one of three conditions: a good relational match (n = 503); a relational mismatch (n = 502); or a null control (n = 544). Respondents sourced from mTurk.

17. We used a mother-in-law as the relation in this vignette since in-laws are generally granted greater ambivalence than other close kinship ties. See A. S. Rossi and P. H. Rossi, "Normative Obligations and Parent-Child Help Exchange across the Life Course," in *Parent-Child Relations throughout Life*, ed. Alice S. Rossi and Peter H. Rossi (1991), 201–23 ; A. E. Willson, K. M. Shuey, G. H. Elder Jr., and K. A. S. Wickrama, "Ambivalence in Mother-Adult Child Relations: A Dyadic Analysis," *Social Psychology Quarterly* 69, no. 3 (2006): 235–52.

18. All reported differences are statistically significant at $p < 0.05$ or smaller.

19. J. E. Stellar and R. Willer, "The Corruption of Value: Negative Moral Associations Diminish the Value of Money," *Social Psychological and Personality Science* 5, no. 1 (2014): 60–66.

20. Risk tolerance quiz source: J. E. Grable and R. H. Lytton, "Financial Risk Tolerance Revisited: The Development of a Risk Assessment Instrument," *Financial Services Review* 8 (1999): 163–81.

21. College Savings Plans Network, "529 Plan Data," https://www.collegesavings.org/529-plan-data/.

22. S. Himmelweit, C. Santos, A. Sevilla, and C. Sofer, "Sharing of Resources within the Family and the Economics of Household Decision Making," *Journal of Marriage and Family* 75, no. 3 (2013): 625–39; C. Coile, "Retirement Incentives and Couples' Retirement Decisions," *Topics in Economic Analysis and Policy* 4, no. 1 (2004): 1–30.

23. See https://www.ici.org/statistical-report/ret_24_q1.

24. Prize winners were Harry Markowitz, Merton Miller, and William Sharpe in 1990. Note that the Nobel Prize in economics is not an actual Nobel Prize but a separate award funded by the Swedish central bank and given by the Royal Swedish Academy of Sciences since 1969. The official name of the prize is The Sveriges Riksbank Prize in Economic Sciences in Memory of Alfred Nobel.

25. H. Markowitz, "Portfolio Selection," *Journal of Finance* 7, no. 1 (1952): 77–91.

26. E.g., G. Charness and U. Gneezy, "Portfolio Choice and Risk Attitudes: An Experiment," *Economic Inquiry* 48, no. 1 (2010): 133–46.

27. R. H. Thaler, "Mental Accounting Matters," *Journal of Behavioral Decision Making* 12, no. 3 (1999): 183–206.

28. H. Shefrin and M. Statman, "Behavioral Portfolio Theory," *Journal of Financial and Quantitative Analysis* 35, no. 2 (2000): 127–51.

29. In a recent review of this literature, business school professors Evan Polman and Kaiyang Wu agree that research falls short in terms of self-other risk-taking: "put simply, decision making for others is not incorporated in standard economic and psychology models despite the fact that, from a practical perspective these decisions are often made." E. Polman and K. Wu, "Decision Making for Others Involving Risk: A Review and Meta-analysis," *Journal of Economic Psychology* 72, no. 1 (2019): 204.

30. Zelizer, "How I Became a Relational Economic Sociologist," 160.

31. D. Soman and H.-K. Ahn, "Mental Accounting and Individual Welfare," in *Perspectives on Framing*, ed. K. Gideon (Abingdon-on-Thames, UK: Taylor & Francis, 2011), 67.

32. Bandelj, Wherry, and Zelizer, *Money Talks*, 7.

33. F. F. Wherry, "Relational Accounting: A Cultural Approach," *American Journal of Cultural Sociology* 4, no. 2 (2016): 131–56; and F. F. Wherry, "How Relational Accounting Matters," in *Money Talks*, ed. Bandelj, Wherry, and Zelizer, 59.

34. C. Zaloom, *Indebted: How Families Make College Work at Any Cost* (Princeton, NJ: Princeton University Press, 2019).

35. While college funds and retirement savings are important financial goals for many American families, it should be acknowledged that these aspirations may reflect largely middle-class values and norms. Saving for college tuition or a comfortable retirement is less feasible for lower-income households struggling to afford basic necessities. The examples and findings presented in this chapter regarding earmarked investments therefore may not fully generalize across the socioeconomic spectrum.

36. Brodeur Research Partners, “Money and Investing: How We Think, Feel and Act with Respect to Our Finances” (2015), Brodeur Partners Relevance Research Series, http://www.brodeur.com/wpcontent/uploads/2015/03/Brodeur-White-Article-money-and-investing-v14.pdf.

37. While I look at retirement portfolio risk-taking here, other research on retirement savings behavior has found that many people fail to optimize decisions around when to claim Social Security benefits as well as how much to initially contribute to 401(k) plans. For example, a recent study showed that a majority claim Social Security early at age 62 despite higher total benefits available from delaying. Additionally, seminal research by Richard Thaler demonstrated how workplace retirement savings participation and contribution rates dramatically improve by automatically enrolling employees into 401(k) plans rather than requiring they opt-in. This body of work suggests retirement-related financial decisions are plagued by behavioral biases that lead to suboptimal outcomes. See J. B. Shoven and S. N. Slavov, “Does It Pay to Delay Social Security?,” *Journal of Pension Economics and Finance* 13, no. 2 (2014): 121–44; R. H. Thaler and S. Benartzi, “Save More Tomorrow™: Using Behavioral Economics to Increase Employee Saving,” *Journal of Political Economy* 112, S1 (2004): S164–87.

38. A. Hayes, “The Social Meaning of Financial Wealth: Relational Accounting in the Context of 401(K) Retirement Accounts,” *Finance and Society* 5, no. 1 (2019): 61–83.

39. A. Hayes and R. O’Brien, “Earmarking Risk: Relational Investing and Portfolio Choice,” *Social Forces* 99, no. 3 (2021): 1086–112.

40. N = 948 (57% female; 75% white; median age 39; 61% w/4-yr degree or higher). Respondents were randomly assigned to see that the $100 was earmarked for a gift for either themselves (n = 232); their child (n = 245); their nephew (n = 246); or their spouse/partner (n = 225). Respondents sourced from mTurk.

41. The rationale behind these relations is that they represent different types of social ties and emotional attachments that may influence how people perceive and manage risk. For example, a nephew is a more distant family member compared to a spouse or child, but is also a youth.

42. Here, N = 2,588 (46% female; 76% white; median age 39; 60% w/4-yr degree or higher). Respondents were randomly assigned to see a personal investment account (n = 304); personal retirement account (n = 348); on behalf of their child (n = 313); in a child’s college savings account (n = 303); on behalf of their nephew (n = 333); in their nephew’s college savings account (n = 321); on behalf of their spouse/partner (n = 336); in their spouse/partner’s retirement account (n = 330). Respondents sourced from mTurk.

43. All reported differences are statistically significant at $p < 0.05$ or smaller, except for self-retirement and spouse’s retirement (which we argue is because married couples often comingle retirement assets).

44. V. A. Zelizer, *Pricing the Priceless Child: The Changing Social Value of Children* (Princeton, NJ: Princeton University Press, 1994).

45. C. M. Zaloom, "Indebted No More: Paying for College Should Be Our Collective Responsibility," *American Educator* 45, no. 3 (2021): 38-43.

46. A. Damodaran, "Annual Returns on Stock, T. Bonds and T. Bills: 1928–Current" (2021), http://pages.stern.nyu.edu/~adamodar/New_Home_Page/datafile/histretSP.html.

47. See T. A. Rietz, "The Equity Risk Premium: A Solution," *Journal of Monetary Economics* 22, no. 1 (1988): 117–31.

48. M. Weber, *Economy and Society: An Outline of Interpretive Sociology*, vol. 1 (1922; Berkeley: University of California Press, 1978), 26.

49. Here, N = 1,527 (56% female; median age 38; 64% w/4-year degree or higher; 77%; median income $45,000; 58% home owners). Respondents were randomly assigned to one of three conditions: a good relational match (n = 506); a relational mismatch (n = 529); or a null control (n = 492). Respondents sourced from mTurk.

50. All reported differences are statistically significant at $p < 0.05$ or smaller. As a robustness check, we conducted a series of follow-up studies that ruled out potential alternative explanations from psychology, such as hostile priming, and found no association when the source of the loan was changed to a credit card advance (unattached to the home).

Chapter Five

1. Sociologists typically view gender (as opposed to biological sex) as a social construct and a fundamental organizing principle of social life, where masculinity and femininity exist on a spectrum. This chapter uses men/male and women/female interchangeably to refer to gender. Historically, masculine perspectives have often been privileged over feminine ones. Finance and economics, too, have embodied masculine priorities and interests as the dominant, "preferred" mode of operating. See, e.g., B. J. Risman and G. Davis, "From Sex Roles to Gender Structure," *Current Sociology* 61, no. 5–6 (2013): 733–55.

2. See, e.g., G. Charness and U. Gneezy, "Strong Evidence for Gender Differences in Risk Taking," *Journal of Economic Behavior and Organization* 83, no. 1 (2012): 50–58.

3. M. P. Kohler, "Risk-Taking Behavior: A Cognitive Approach," *Psychological Reports* 78, no. 2 (1996): 489–90; J. Herbert, "Testosterone, Cortisol and Financial Risk-Taking," *Frontiers in Behavioral Neuroscience* 12 (2018): 101.

4. See, e.g., C. E. Weller and M. E. Tolson, "The Retirement Savings Penalty Borne by Women," *Challenge* 63, no. 4 (2020): 201–18.

5. G. Young and J. A. Young, "Women versus Men in DC Plans" (Valley Forge, PA: Vanguard Research, 2015); J. Dominitz and C. F. Manski, "Expected Equity Returns and Portfolio Choice: Evidence from the Health and Retirement Study," *Journal of the European Economic Association* 5, no. 2–3 (2007): 369–79; J. Watson and M. McNaughton, "Gender Differences in

Risk Aversion and Expected Retirement Benefits," *Financial Analysts Journal* 63, no. 4 (2007): 52–62.

6. S. L. Bradley, "Financial Literacy Education: An Opportunity for Colleges and Sociology," *Sociology Compass* 15, no. 10 (2021); https://doi.org/10.1111/soc4.12922.

7. A. Lusardi, "Financial Literacy and the Need for Financial Education: Evidence and Implications," *Swiss Journal of Economics and Statistics* 155, no. 1 (2019): 1–8.

8. Organisation for Economic Co-operation and Development (OECD), *Guidelines on Financial Education at School and Guidance on Learning Framework* (final draft for public consultation, 2012); https://www.oecd.org/en/topics/sub-issues/financial-education.html.

9. A. Hasler and A. Lusardi, "The Gender Gap in Financial Literacy: A Global Perspective," Global Financial Literacy Excellence Center, George Washington University School of Business (2017).

10. TIAA, "Financial Literacy and Wellness among U.S. Women," https://www.tiaainstitute.org/about/news/financial-literacy-and-wellness-among-us-women.

11. U. Neelakantan and Y. Chang, "Gender Differences in Wealth at Retirement," *American Economic Review* 100, no. 2 (2010): 362–67; M. L. Halko, M. Kaustia, and E. Alanko, "The Gender Effect in Risky Asset Holdings," *Journal of Economic Behavior and Organization* 83, no. 1 (2012): 66–81; P. Goldsmith-Pinkham and K. Shue, "The Gender Gap in Housing Returns," *Journal of Finance* 78, no. 2 (2023): 1097–1145.

12. Y. Cha and K. A. Weeden, "Overwork and the Slow Convergence in the Gender Gap in Wages," *American Sociological Review* 79, no. 3 (2014): 457–84.

13. See T. Bucher-Koenen, A. Hackethal, J. Koenen, and C. Laudenbach, "Gender Differences in Financial Advice" (2021), https://papers.ssrn.com/sol3/papers.cfm?abstract_id=2572961; U. Bhattacharya, A. Kumar, S. Visaria, and J. Zhao, "Do Women Receive Worse Financial Advice?," *Journal of Finance* (2020), https://doi.org/10.1111/jofi.13366; and Y. Baeckström, I. W. Marsh, and J. Silvester, "Financial Advice and Gender: Wealthy Individual Investors in the UK," *Journal of Corporate Finance* 71 (2021): 101882, among others.

14. E. M. Sent and I. van Staveren, "A Feminist Review of Behavioral Economic Research on Gender Differences," *Feminist Economics* 25, no. 2 (2019): 1–35.

15. When Lehman Brothers filed for bankruptcy on September 15, 2008, it marked the largest bankruptcy in US history at the time. M. Gertler and S. Gilchrist, "What Happened: Financial Factors in the Great Recession," *Journal of Economic Perspectives* 32, no. 3 (2018): 3–30.

16. I. Van Staveren, "The Lehman Sisters Hypothesis," *Cambridge Journal of Economics* 38, no. 5 (2014): 995–1014.

17. J. Marinova, J. Plantenga, and C. Remery, "Gender Diversity and Firm Performance: Evidence from Dutch and Danish Boardrooms," *International Journal of Human Resource Management* 27, no. 15 (2016): 1777–90.

18. S. Zahidi and H. Ibarra, "The Corporate Gender Gap Report 2010," World Economic Forum, Geneva, 2010.

19. It has been argued that perhaps only certain women with particular personalities would tend to make it to the level of corporate management at financial firms, so there could be selection bias occurring. Additionally, critiques of the Lehman Sisters hypothesis have also appeared that rebuke some of Van Steveren's original claims. See, e.g., E. A. Sheedy and M. Lubojanski, "Diversity in Financial Risk Management: Revisiting the Lehman Sisters Hypothesis" (2017), available at SSRN 2965850; https://papers.ssrn.com/Sol3/papers.cfm?abstract_id=2965850.

It should be noted that while the Lehman Sisters hypothesis is intriguing, there are many reasons to believe that Lehman's collapse was the result of a number of both structural macro-economic and microlevel factors—rather than only the gender composition of Lehman's management. Nevertheless, the hypothesis serves as a valuable reminder of the importance of diverse perspectives and decision-making styles in promoting a more stable and equitable financial system.

20. J. Callegari, P. Liedgren, and C. Kullberg, "Gendered Debt—A Scoping Study Review of Research on Debt Acquisition and Management in Single and Couple Households," *European Journal of Social Work* 23, no. 5 (2020): 742–54.

21. C. Henry, L. Foss, and H. Ahl, "Gender and Entrepreneurship Research: A Review of Methodological Approaches," *International Small Business Journal* 34, no. 3 (2016): 217–41.

22. T. Morgenroth, C. Fine, M. K. Ryan, and A. E. Genat, "Sex, Drugs, and Reckless Driving: Are Measures Biased toward Identifying Risk-Taking in Men?," *Social Psychological and Personality Science* 9, no. 6 (2018): 744–53.

23. Sent and van Staveren, "Feminist Review."

24. J. List and U. Gneezy, *The Why Axis: Hidden Motives and the Undiscovered Economics of Everyday Life* (New York: Random House, 2014); A. L. Booth and P. Nolen, "Gender Differences in Risk Behaviour: Does Nurture Matter?," *Economic Journal* 122, no. 558 (2012): F56–78.

25. U. Gneezy, K. L. Leonard, and J. A. List, "Gender Differences in Competition: Evidence from a Matrilineal and a Patriarchal Society," *Econometrica* 77, no. 5 (2009): 1637–64.

26. C. West and D. H. Zimmerman, "Doing Gender," *Gender and Society* 1, no. 2 (1987): 125–51.

27. J. Stockard, "Gender Socialization," in *Handbook of the Sociology of Gender*, ed. Janet Saltzman Chafetz (New York: Springer, 2006), 215–27.

28. E. Ortiz-Ospina and M. Roser, "Economic Inequality by Gender," *Our World in Data* (2024); https://ourworldindata.org/

economic-inequality-by-gender?utm_source=OWID+Newsletter&utm_campaign=db95516e35-Newsletter_OurWorldInData_Dec2017&utm_medium=email&utm_term=0_2e166c1fc1-db95516e35-434065729.

29. S. Agnew, P. Maras, and A. Moon, "Gender Differences in Financial Socialization in the Home—An Exploratory Study," *International Journal of Consumer Studies* 42, no. 3 (2018): 275–82.

30. M. D. Newcomb and J. Rabow, "Gender, Socialization, and Money," *Journal of Applied Social Psychology* 29, no. 4 (1999): 852–69.

31. See C. Fine and E. Rush, "'Why Does All the Girls Have to Buy Pink Stuff?' The Ethics and Science of the Gendered Toy Marketing Debate," *Journal of Business Ethics* 149 (2018): 769–84; P. R. Owen and M. Padron, "The Language of Toys: Gendered Language in Toy Advertisements," *Journal of Research on Women and Gender* 6, no. 1 (2015): 67-80.

32. See M. Fulcher and A. R. Hayes, "Building a Pink Dinosaur: The Effects of Gendered Construction Toys on Girls' and Boys' Play," *Sex Roles* 79 (2018): 273–84.

33. Nurit Stadler, "Yeshiva Fundamentalism: Piety, Gender, and Resistance in the Ultra-Orthodox World," in *Yeshiva Fundamentalism* (New York: New York University Press, 2009).

34. More than one-third of Haredi women are employed as kindergarten or primary school teachers. See Y. Goldfarb, "Does God Want Me to Be a Teacher? Motives behind Occupational Choice of Israeli Ultraorthodox Women," *Journal of Career Development* 45, no. 4 (2018): 303–14.

35. Note, however, that a small but growing minority of Haredi women now seek out secular higher education and high-income employment in sectors like tech and accounting. While this subgroup of women is not segmented out in this chapter, a forthcoming study shows that these women differ from traditional Haredi women. See also Varda Wasserman and Michal Frenkel, "The Politics of (In)visibility Displays: Ultra-Orthodox Women Manoeuvring within and between Visibility Regimes," *Human Relations* 73, no. 12 (2020): 1609–31. For more detailed research that segments Haredi women into traditional women vs. high-income women working in secular occupations (a relatively small subgroup), see Adam S. Hayes and Yehudit Miletzky, "Rethinking Economic Socialization: The Intersection of Culture, Gender and Economic Life in a Religious Enclave," *Socio-Economic Review* (2024): mwae063. There, we find that high-income women score comparably on most of our measures with Haredi men who work.

36. The survey was administered in the Hebrew language. To ensure the success of our study, we partnered with a professional Israeli polling company experienced in engaging with the Haredi community. Due to their insular nature, it can be challenging for researchers to directly engage with community members, since outsiders can be met with suspicion. Outsourcing data collection ensured not only access to this community in a culturally sensitive and respectful manner but also the collection of reliable data.

37. G. Malach and L. Cahaner, "Statistical Report on Ultra-Orthodox Society in Israel 2022" (Jerusalem: Israel Democracy Institute, 2022), https://en.idi.org.il/media/20567/annual-statistical-report-on-Ultra-Orthodox-haredi-society-in-israel-2022-executive-summary.pdf.

38. Differences between women and men who work, and between men who study and men who work are statistically significant at $p < 0.01$. Women and men who study are statistically indistinguishable.

39. Because Ultra-Orthodox men initially refused to participate in the hypothetical coin flip due to its resemblance to gambling, which is prohibited in their community, we needed a different approach to assess their level of loss aversion. We devised a modified version of Dreidel, a culturally familiar game played during Hanukkah, to evaluate their loss aversion. In this version, participants started with 100 points and were told they had a 50% chance of losing half of their points if the Dreidel landed on two specific sides (Nun and Gimel). We asked them how many points they would need to win if the Dreidel landed favorably (on Hey or Shin) to accept playing the game. In a second scenario, participants faced a 50% chance of losing all their points on an unfavorable spin and were asked what they'd need to win to play. These amounts were averaged together to measure loss aversion. The fewer points required, the less loss averse (and more rational) the participants were.

40. Differences between women and men who study, and between men who study and men who work, are statistically significant at $p < 0.05$. Women and men who work are statistically indistinguishable.

41. These were more generic questions like, "I experience pleasure when I win," or "Games with no clear winners are pointless," and not questions related to economic or financial contexts.

42. All reported differences are statistically significant at $p < 0.05$ or smaller.

43. N. Stadler, "Is Profane Work an Obstacle to Salvation? The Case of Ultra Orthodox (Haredi) Jews in Contemporary Israel," *Sociology of Religion* 63, no. 4 (2002): 455–74.

44. R. Bouchouicha, L. Deer, A. G. Eid, P. McGee, D. Schoch, H. Stojic, et al., "Gender Effects for Loss Aversion: Yes, No, Maybe?," *Journal of Risk and Uncertainty* 59 (2019): 171–84.

45. M. Z. Rosaldo, L. Lamphere, and J. Bamberger, *Woman, Culture, and Society* (Stanford, CA: Stanford University Press, 1974).

46. E.g., E. Bihagen and T. Katz-Gerro, "Culture Consumption in Sweden: The Stability of Gender Differences," *Poetics* 27, no. 5–6 (2000): 327–49.

47. O. Lizardo, "The Puzzle of Women's 'Highbrow' Culture Consumption: Integrating Gender and Work into Bourdieu's Class Theory of Taste," *Poetics* 34, no. 1 (2006): 1–23.

48. A. Hasler and A. Lusardi, "The Gender Gap in Financial Literacy: A Global Perspective," Global Financial Literacy Excellence Center, George Washington University School of Business, 2017.

49. A. Amagir, W. Groot, H. M. van den Brink, and A. Wilschut, "Financial Literacy of High School Students in the Netherlands: Knowledge, Attitudes, Self-Efficacy, and Behavior," *International Review of Economics Education* 34 (2020): 100–185.

50. U. Rink, Y. M. Walle, and S. Klasen, "The Financial Literacy Gender Gap and the Role of Culture," *Quarterly Review of Economics and Finance* 80 (2021): 117–34.

51. Baeckström, Marsh, and Silvester, "Financial Advice and Gender,"101882.

52. CFP® Professional Demographics (https://www.cfp.net/knowledge/reports-and-statistics/professional-demographics); "Financial Conduct Authority (UK) Gender Diversity in UK Financial Services, 2019," https://www.fca.org.uk/publication/research/research-note-gender-diversity-in-uk-financial-services.pdf.

53. Financial subjectivities refer to the diverse ways individuals perceive, understand, and emotionally relate to financial matters, shaping their attitudes and behaviors toward money, investment, savings, and spending. See K. P. Lai, "Unpacking Financial Subjectivities: Intimacies, Governance and Socioeconomic Practices in Financialisation," *Environment and Planning D: Society and Space* 35, no. 5 (2017): 913–32.

54. P. Crosthwaite, P. Knight, N. Marsh, H. Paul, and J. Taylor, *Invested: How Three Centuries of Stock Market Advice Reshaped Our Money, Markets, and Minds* (Chicago: University of Chicago Press, 2022), 76, 670, 682.

55. C. Boggio, F. C. Moscarola, and A. Gallice, "What Is Good for the Goose Is Good for the Gander?: How Gender-Specific Conceptual Frames Affect Financial Participation and Decision-Making," *Economics of Education Review* 75 (2020): 101952.

56. Sent and van Staveren, "Feminist Review."

57. Hartford Funds, "Investors Want Gender-Neutral Financial Advice, Despite Perceived Differences in Financial Needs," https://www.businesswire.com/news/home/20220125005314/en/Investors-Want-GenderNeutral-Financial-Advice-Despite-Perceived-Differences-in-Financial-Needs.

58. C. Staats, "Understanding Implicit Bias: What Educators Should Know," *American Educator* 39, no. 4 (2016): 29.

59. F. L. Oswald, G. Mitchell, H. Blanton, J. Jaccard, and P. E. Tetlock, "Predicting Ethnic and Racial Discrimination: A Meta-Analysis of IAT Criterion Studies," *Journal of Personality and Social Psychology* 105, no. 2 (2013): 171.

60. L. A. Rudman and S. A. Goodwin, "Gender Differences in Automatic In-Group Bias: Why Do Women Like Women More Than Men Like Men?," *Journal of Personality and Social Psychology* 87, no. 4 (2004): 494.

61. B. A. Nosek and F. L. Smyth, "Implicit Social Cognitions Predict Sex Differences in Math Engagement and Achievement," *American Educational Research Journal* 48, no. 5 (2011): 1125–56.

62. E. Reuben, P. Sapienza, and L. Zingales, "How Stereotypes Impair Women's Careers in Science," *Proceedings of the National Academy of Sciences* 111, no. 12 (2014): 4403–8.

63. A. T. Ben-Shmuel, A. Hayes, and V. Drach. "The Gendered Language of Financial Advice: Finfluencers, Framing, and Subconscious Preferences," *Socius* (2024); https://journals.sagepub.com/doi/full/10.1177/23780231241267131.

64. National Association of Personal Financial Advisors (NAPFA), "2021 Survey on Americans' Sources for Financial Planning and Retirement Investing Advice," http://s3.napfa.cql-aws.com.s3.amazonaws.com/files/Consumer/NAPFA%20Fall%202021%20Full%20Report.pdf.

65. A. Hayes and A. T. Ben-Shmuel. "Under the Finfluence: Financial Influencers, Economic Meaning-Making and the Financialization of Digital Life," *Economy and Society* (2024); DOI: 10.1080/03085147.2024.2381980.

66. Collabstr, "2022 Influencer Marketing Report," https://collabstr.com/2022-influencer-marketing-report.

67. Net Influencer, "Top Personal Finance Influencers to Follow in 2022," https://www.netinfluencer.com/top-personal-finance-influencers/. Note that other top finfluencer lists also are more than 50% women.

68. In this study, N = 180 (55% female; 81% white; 68% w/a 4-yr+ degree; median age: 40; median income: $45,000; 57% married). Respondents recruited from mTurk.

69. We chose three still and one video post apiece, to keep the survey instrument from taking too long while preserving analytic power.

70. Here, N = 634 (50% female [purposefully seeking an equal gender balance]; 80% white; 61% w/4-yr degree or higher; median age 42; median income $45,000; 53% married). Respondents recruited from mTurk. We used five 5-point Likert items to create our favorability index: *I believe this is good advice*; *I would follow this advice*; *I trust this advice*; *I find this advice relatable to me*; *I would share this advice with my friends/family*. The 5 Likert items in our scale had a Chronbach's alpha > 0.925 for each post displayed, indicating a very high level of reliability.

71. Here, N = 296 (61% female; 76% white; 60% w/4yr-degree or higher; median age 41; median income $45,000; 49% married).

72. T. Bucher-Koenen, R. J. Alessie, A. Lusardi, and M. Van Rooij, "Fearless Woman: Financial Literacy and Stock Market Participation," NBER no. w28723, National Bureau of Economic Research, 2021.

73. Baeckström, Marsh, and Silvester, "Financial Advice and Gender," 101882.

74. See, e.g., L. K. Kaye and C. R. Pennington, "'Girls Can't Play': The Effects of Stereotype Threat on Females' Gaming Performance," *Computers in Human Behavior* 59 (2016): 202–9; K. Lucas and J. L. Sherry, "Sex Differences in Video Game Play: A Communication-Based Explanation," *Communication Research* 31, no. 5 (2004): 499–523; R. M. Vaughter, D. Sadh, and E. Vozzola, "Sex Similarities and Differences in Types of Play in Games and Sports," *Psychology of Women Quarterly* 18, no. 1 (1994): 85–104; J. S.

Eccles and R. D. Harold, "Gender Differences in Sport Involvement: Applying the Eccles' Expectancy-Value Model," *Journal of Applied Sport Psychology* 3, no. 1 (1991): 7–35.

75. See M. A. Ferber and J. A. Nelson, eds., *Feminist Economics Today: Beyond Economic Man* (Chicago: University of Chicago Press, 2020).

76. A. Lusardi, O. S. Mitchell, and V. Curto, "Financial Literacy among the Young," *Journal of Consumer Affairs* 44, no. 2 (2010): 358–80.

77. See, e.g., G. Chelwa, D. Hamilton, and J. Stewart, "Stratification Economics: Core Constructs and Policy Implications," *Journal of Economic Literature* 60, no. 2 (2022): 377–99.

Chapter Six

1. See J. Pierre, "Nudges against Pandemics: Sweden's COVID-19 Containment Strategy in Perspective," *Policy and Society* 39, no. 3 (2020): 478–93.

2. R. Thaler, "More Than Nudges Are Needed to End the Pandemic," *New York Times,* August 5, 2021; https://www.nytimes.com/2021/08/05/business/vaccine-pandemic-nudge-passport.html.

3. S. Benartzi and R. H. Thaler, "Heuristics and Biases in Retirement Savings Behavior," *Journal of Economic Perspectives* 21, no. 3 (2007): 81–104.

4. L. C. Van Gestel, F. M. Kroese, and D. T. De Ridder, "Nudging at the Checkout Counter–a Longitudinal Study of the Effect of a Food Repositioning Nudge on Healthy Food Choice," *Psychology and Health* 33, no. 6 (2018): 800–809.

5. R. H. Thaler and C. R. Sunstein, *Nudge: Improving Decisions about Health, Wealth, and Happiness* (New York: Penguin, 2009).

6. D. Halpern, *Inside the Nudge Unit: How Small Changes Can Make a Big Difference* (Random House, 2015).

7. Thaler, "More Than Nudges."

8. M. Maier, F. Bartoš, T. D. Stanley, D. R. Shanks, A. J. Harris, and E. J. Wagenmakers, "No Evidence for Nudging after Adjusting for Publication Bias," *Proceedings of the National Academy of Sciences* 119, no. 31 (2022): e2200300119.

9. D. Bowen, "Simple Models Predict Behavior at Least as Well as Behavioral Scientists," arXiv preprint (2022), arXiv:2208.01167.

10. S. Coleman, "The Minnesota Income Tax Compliance Experiment: State Tax Results," Minnesota Department of Revenue (1996), https://www.revenue.state.mn.us/sites/default/files/2011-11/research_reports_content_complnce.pdf.

11. For an expert takedown of *Nudge*, see the *If Books Could Kill* podcast hosted by Michael Hobbes and Peter Shamshiri, episodes: "Nudge," pts. 1 and 2; https://www.buzzsprout.com/2040953/12780949-nudge-part-1-a-simple-solution-for-littering-organ-donations-and-climate-change.

12. I do not mean to be overly intentionalist regarding norms. Social norms are often not the direct result of purposeful or even tacit agreements between people or groups. Many norms emerge gradually over time or unintentionally, without a formal consensus being reached. Power dynamics

also shape which groups get to define social norms, meaning certain voices and perspectives may be excluded or overridden in the process.

13. M. Blumenthal, C. Christian, and J. Slemrod, “Do Normative Appeals Affect Tax Compliance? Evidence from a Controlled Experiment in Minnesota,” *National Tax Journal* 54, no. 1 (2001): 125–38.

14. See also F. Mols, S. A. Haslam, J. Jetten, and N. K. Steffens, “Why a Nudge Is Not Enough: A Social Identity Critique of Governance by Stealth,” *European Journal of Political Research* 54, no. 1 (2015): 81–98.

15. A. L. Whitehead and S. L. Perry, “How Culture Wars Delay Herd Immunity: Christian Nationalism and Anti-Vaccine Attitudes,” *Socius* 6 (2020): https://doi.org/10.1177/2378023120977727.

16. J. Goodman and F. Carmichael, “Coronavirus: Bill Gates ‘Microchip’ Conspiracy Theory and Other Vaccine Claims Fact-Checked,” *BBC News*, May 29, 2020; https://www.bbc.com/news/52847648.

17. See J. J. V. Bavel, K. Baicker, P. S. Boggio, V. Capraro, A. Cichocka, M. Cikara, et al., “Using Social and Behavioural Science to Support COVID-19 Pandemic Response,” *Nature Human Behaviour* 4, no. 5 (2020): 460–71.

18. J. M. Turner, “‘The Specter of Environmentalism’: Wilderness, Environmental Politics, and the Evolution of the New Right,” *Journal of American History* 96, no. 1 (2009): 123–48.

19. See M. Feinberg and R. Willer, “The Moral Roots of Environmental Attitudes,” *Psychological Science* 24, no. 1 (2013): 56–62; J. Farrell, *The Battle for Yellowstone: Morality and the Sacred Roots of Environmental Conflict* (Princeton, NJ: Princeton University Press, 2015).

20. Customizing nudges for effectiveness could, however, violate principles of equal treatment under the law.

21. The 2022 Algorithmic Trading Survey, *theTRADE*: https://www.thetradenews.com/wp-content/uploads/2022/04/Algorithmic-Trading-Survey-Long-Only-2022.pdf.

22. See https://www.theroboreport.com/report-archives/; and https://www.statista.com/outlook/dmo/fintech/digital-investment/robo-advisors/worldwide#assets-under-management.

23. B. M. Barber, Y. T. Lee, Y. J. Liu, and T. Odean, “Just How Much Do Individual Investors Lose by Trading?,” *Review of Financial Studies* 22 (2009): 609–32.

24. A. Preda, *Noise: Living and Trading in Electronic Finance* (Chicago: University of Chicago Press, 2017).

25. To preserve anonymity and protect the privacy of the experts interviewed for this study, only their job titles are mentioned when quoting their responses. This discretion was promised to all participants to encourage candor in their commentary on the industry.

26. FINRA Investor Education Foundation, “Gauging the State of Financial Capability in the U.S.” (2021), http://www.usfinancialcapability.org/investor-survey.php.

27. A. S. Hayes, "The Active Construction of Passive Investors: Roboadvisors and Algorithmic 'Low-Finance,'" *Socio-Economic Review* 19, no. 1 (2021): 83–110.

28. "Investor" and "trader" are distinct terms. Investors hold assets long-term, focusing on capital gains through a buy-and-hold strategy. Traders frequently buy and sell assets short-term, profiting from price fluctuations rather than underlying value. Optimal strategies differ: MPT suits long-term investing, while trading strategies prioritize market timing and volatility.

29. This process is known as mean-variance optimization (MVO). In MPT, portfolio risk is measured by its standard deviation of returns.

30. Emphasis added. H. Markowitz, *Portfolio Selection: Efficient Diversification of Investments* (Hoboken, NJ: Wiley, 1959); H. Markowitz, "The Early History of Portfolio Theory: 1600–1960," *Financial Analysts Journal* 55, no. 4 (1999): 5–16.

31. J. Tobin, "Liquidity Preference as Behavior towards Risk," *Review of Economic Studies* 25, no. 1 (1958): 65–86.

32. Benartzi and Thaler, "Heuristics and Biases."

33. Some roboadvisors now offer "green" or socially responsible investment portfolios that screen for environmental, social, and governance criteria. This lets users employ value rationality in their initial investment choices. However, the roboadvisors' algorithms then take over, optimizing the selected portfolio based on modern portfolio theory principles to maximize returns for a given risk tolerance. So after an initial values-based choice, users ultimately defer to the same algorithmic logic that prioritizes efficiency and returns, just within their chosen ethical framework.

34. MPT offers more sophistication than simple low-cost index funds. While index funds passively track a market benchmark, MPT strategically allocates assets across different classes, including various types of stocks, bonds, real estate, and commodities. This diversification, often achieved through a mix of index funds or ETFs, is key to MPT's approach. It recognizes that the blend of asset classes in a portfolio significantly shapes its overall risk and return characteristics, going beyond merely mimicking a single market segment.

35. A. Soe and R. Poirier, *SPIVA US Scorecard 2017* (New York: S&P Dow Jones Indices, 2017).

36. Tom Anderson, "Most Investors Didn't Come Close to Beating the S&P 500," CNBC, January 5, 2017; https://www.cnbc.com/2017/01/04/most-investors-didnt-come-close-to-beating-the-sp-500.html.

37. Younger investors have a greater capacity to ride out long-term volatility and so have a higher objective risk tolerance. Therefore, the portfolios made for a thirty-five-year-old should plot more to the right (i.e., more risky) than those for a fifty-five-year-old.

38. Roboadvisors, as a new category of financial firm, had to convince users and regulators of their legitimacy and competence. To quickly establish trust, they rely on MPT as an established framework, rather than

developing proprietary models. Furthermore, to operate in the highly regulated domain of low-finance, roboadvisors must satisfy strict legal responsibilities designed to protect small investors. Touting MPT's basis in "Nobel Prize–winning research" helps them navigate this regulatory landscape. Therefore, the desire to create optimal client portfolios is in fact born out of the requirement to fulfill a fiduciary duty—as the former CEO of one roboadvisor explained, "I'd say we used MPT probably 80% from a regulatory standpoint, and then 20% because we felt it's the best kind of investment strategy" (A. S. Hayes, "The Active Construction of Passive Investors: Roboadvisors and Algorithmic 'Low-Finance,'" *Socio-Economic Review* 19, no. 1 [2021]: 102).

39. Such optimization techniques include, e.g., the Black-Litterman model; see table 6.1. The Black-Litterman model is an extension of MPT that allows investors to incorporate their expectations about future asset returns to generate more realistic asset allocations.

40. Portfolio returns are pretax annualized historical returns from January 1, 2015 through December 31, 2017. Portfolio standard deviations of returns are annualized over the same period, and the efficient frontier is also constructed from data over the same study period.

41. Since lazy portfolios are low-maintenance set-it-and-forget-it allocations, there is no meaningful annual cost associated with them.

42. See the AAII Individual Investor Asset Allocation Survey at https://www.aaii.com/files/surveys/asset.xls.

43. B. Barber and T. Odean, "Trading Is Hazardous to Your Wealth: The Common Stock Investment Performance of Individual Investors," *Journal of Finance* 55, no. 2 (2000): 773–806. The average individual investor, historically, has seen their annual return reduced by 5.5% due to transaction costs and trading fees (e.g., a 7.2 percent gross return would be reduced to 6.8 percent, although in recent years commission-free trading has lowered these costs).

44. These data for the study period were sourced from Research Affiliates, LLC's (RA) Asset Allocation Interactive Tool. RA is an investment manager and financial analytics firm that provides its services mainly to investment companies. See also S. Shepherd, A. Ko, and B. Kunz, *Alternative Risk Premia: Valuable Benefits for Traditional Portfolios* (Newport Beach, CA: Research Affiliates, LLC, 2018), https://interactive.researchaffiliates.com/asset-allocation#!/?category=Model¤cy=USD&model=ER&scale=LINEAR&selected=225&terms=REAL&type=Portfolios.

45. Unlike roboadvisors, self-directed fintech apps like Robinhood encourage frequent trading by offering commission-free stock trades. Their business model relies on a user interface that exploits human tendencies to overtrade, playing on emotions like fear, greed, and the thrill of gambling. Active users may check the app dozens of times daily, often prompted by push notifications.

46. The design thus frames the client's present to a future self to the exclusion of the past or contemporary alternatives, crafting what sociologist Jens Beckert refers to as imaginaries of profit opportunities—i.e., "fictional expectations" that help regulate the present state of being. See J. Beckert, "Imagined Futures: Fictional Expectations in the Economy," *Theory and Society* 42, no. 3 (2013): 219–40.

47. B. J. Dietvorst, J. P. Simmons, and C. Massey, "Algorithm Aversion: People Erroneously Avoid Algorithms after Seeing Them Err," *Journal of Experimental Psychology: General* 144 (2015): 114.

48. D. J. Middaugh, "Delusion of Control: Pushing Buttons," Medsurg *Nursing* 27, no. 6 (2018): 399.

49. A. N. Whitehead, *An Introduction to Mathematics* (1911; London: Williams & Norgate, 1992).

50. Model risk is the potential for inaccuracy when using models for financial decisions, predictions, or valuations. It arises when a model fails to capture underlying realities due to flawed assumptions, mathematical errors, or inherent limitations. Modern Portfolio Theory (MPT) is susceptible to model risk, as it assumes rational investors, efficient markets, and normally distributed asset returns—assumptions that often don't hold true in reality.

51. D. MacKenzie, *An Engine, Not a Camera: How Financial Models Shape Markets* (Cambridge, MA: MIT Press, 2006).

52. T. Cabannes, M. A. S. Vincentelli, A. Sundt, H. Signargout, E. Porter, V. Fighiera, and A. M. Bayen, *The Impact of GPS-Enabled Shortest Path Routing on Mobility: A Game Theoretic Approach* (Berkeley: University of California, 2017).

53. Technological innovations like APIs (application programming interfaces) and BaaS (Banking-as-a-Service) could plausibly enable automated, optimized bank shifting. APIs allow seamless data sharing between software platforms, while BaaS lets nonbank platforms directly offer banking services by connecting to regulated bank partners via APIs. These trends enable integrated fintech platforms that optimize money movement between banks behind the scenes, abstracting away technical complexities while promising consumers the "best" rates.

54. A bank run occurs when a large number of customers suddenly withdraw their deposits from a bank, usually due to fears that the bank might fail. This mass withdrawal can actually cause the bank to become insolvent, as banks typically don't hold enough liquid assets to cover all deposits at once. Measures like deposit insurance and central bank interventions are often used to prevent or mitigate bank runs.

55. The concept of optimizing technologies is not limited to investing, banking, and GPS navigation. And there are several other social systems where people can use algorithms or other tools to achieve rational outcomes, e.g., energy generation and distribution, search engine optimization, and communications bandwidth.

56. G. Hardin, "The Tragedy of the Commons: The Population Problem Has No Technical Solution; It Requires a Fundamental Extension in Morality," *Science* 162, no. 3859 (1968): 1243–48.

57. Preda, *Noise*.

58. A. Rahimi-Golkhandan, F. Khaghani, M. J. Garvin, and F. Jazizadeh, "Assessing the Relationship between Transportation Diversity and Road Network Congestion Using Participatory-Sensing Data," in *Computing in Civil Engineering 2019: Smart Cities, Sustainability, and Resilience*, ed. Yong K. Cho, Fernanda Leite, Amir Behzadan, and Chao Wang (Reston, VA: American Society of Civil Engineers, 2019), 420–27.

59. Peter Fleming, *The Death of Homo Economicus* (Chicago: University of Chicago Press, 2017).

60. The idea that acting in our own self-interest can be detrimental to others or to society is not new (e.g., consider "the tragedy of the commons" and the "free rider problem"), but it becomes more urgent in the context of automation.

61. Economic sociology challenges the neoclassical economics view of "free" markets as naturally emergent, self-regulating, and driven solely by individual self-interest—instead emphasizing that markets are deeply embedded in historical, social, cultural, and political structures that allow them to operate and which shape their functioning and outcomes. See N. Fligstein, *The Architecture of Markets: An Economic Sociology of Twenty-First-Century Capitalist Societies* (Princeton, NJ: Princeton University Press, 2001); K. Polanyi, *The Great Transformation* (Hoboken, NJ: Wiley-Blackwell, 1957).

62. James J. Angel and Douglas McCabe, "Fairness in Financial Markets: The Case of High Frequency Trading," *Journal of Business Ethics* 112 (2013): 585–95.

INDEX